D0821565

Philosophy of Religion in the 21st Century

Claremont Studies in the Philosophy of Religion

General Editors: **D. Z. Phillips**, Rush Rhees Research Professor, University of Wales, Swansea and Danforth Professor of the Philosophy of Religion, the Claremont Graduate School, California; **Timothy Tessin**

At a time when discussions of religion are becoming increasingly specialized and determined by religious affiliations, it is important to maintain a forum for philosophical discussion which transcends the allegiances of belief and unbelief. This series affords an opportunity for philosophers of widely differing persuasions to explore central issues in the philosophy of religion.

Titles include:

Stephen T. Davis (*editor*)
PHILOSOPHY AND THEOLOGICAL DISCOURSE

D. Z. Phillips (*editor*)
CAN RELIGION BE EXPLAINED AWAY?

D. Z. Phillips and Timothy Tessin (*editors*)
KANT AND KIERKEGAARD ON RELIGION
PHILOSOPHY OF RELIGION IN THE 21ST CENTURY
RELIGION WITHOUT TRANSCENDENCE?
RELIGION AND HUME'S LEGACY

Timothy Tessin and Mario von der Ruhr (*editors*)
PHILOSOPHY AND THE GRAMMAR OF RELIGIOUS BELIEF

Claremont Studies in the Philosophy of Religion
Series Standing Order ISBN 0–333–71465–2
(*outside North America only*)

You can receive future titles in this series as they are published by placing a standing order. Please contact your bookseller or, in case of difficulty, write to us at the address below with your name and address, the title of the series and the ISBN quoted above.

Customer Services Department, Macmillan Distribution Ltd, Houndmills, Basingstoke, Hampshire RG21 6XS, England

Philosophy of Religion in the 21st Century

Edited by

D.Z. Phillips
*Danforth Professor of Philosophy of Religion, Claremont Graduate University
and Rush Rhees Research Professor, University of Wales, Swansea*

and

Timothy Tessin

palgrave

First published 2001 by
PALGRAVE
Houndmills, Basingstoke, Hampshire RG21 6XS and
175 Fifth Avenue, New York, N. Y. 10010
Companies and representatives throughout the world

PALGRAVE is the new global academic imprint of
St. Martin's Press LLC Scholarly and Reference Division and
Palgrave Publishers Ltd (formerly Macmillan Press Ltd).

ISBN 0–333–80175–X hardback

This book is printed on paper suitable for recycling and
made from fully managed and sustained forest sources.

A catalogue record for this book is available
from the British Library.

Library of Congress Cataloging-in-Publication Data
Philosophy of religion in the 21st century / edited by D. Z. Phillips
and Timothy Tessin.
        p. cm.
    Includes bibliographical references and index.
    ISBN 0–333–80175–X (cloth)
        1. Religion—Philosophy. I. Phillips, D. Z. (Dewi Zephaniah)
    II. Tessin, Timothy. III. Series.

BL51.P534 2001
210—dc21
                                                      2001034500

10   9   8   7   6   5   4   3   2   1
10   09   08   07   06   05   04   03   02   01

Printed and bound in Great Britain by
Antony Rowe Ltd, Chippenham, Wiltshire

Contents

Acknowledgements

I am happy to acknowledge the financial support given to the Conference by Claremont Graduate University, Pomona College and Claremont McKenna College. I am grateful to the participants who contributed to the funding of future conferences by waiving their claim to royalties. Administratively, I am indebted to Helen Baldwin and Jackie Huntzinger, secretaries to the Department of Philosophy at the University of Wales, Swansea and to the Department of Religion at Claremont Graduate University, respectively. Graduate students helped during the conference in transporting the participants to various venues. They were organized by my able research assistant Richard Amesbury, who was also responsible for typing my introduction and the various 'voices in discussion'. I am extremely grateful to him for his help in this and other contexts. Finally, I thank my co-editor Timothy Tessin for proof-reading the collection and for seeing it through its various stages of publication.

D.Z.P.

Notes on the Contributors

John B. Cobb, Jr is Professor Emeritus of Theology at the Claremont School of Theology and of Religion at Claremont Graduate University. He continues as co-director of the Centre for Process Studies. Among his books are *A Christian Natural Theology Based on the Thought of Alfred North Whitehead, Christ in a Pluralistic Age, The Structure of Christian Existence, Process Theology: an Introductory Exposition* (with David Griffin), *The Liberation of Life* (with Charles Birch).

Maeve Cooke is Senior Lecturer in the Department of German at University College, Dublin. She is the author of *Language and Reason: a Study of Habermas's Pragmatics* and editor of a collection of Habermas's writings on language and communication: *On the Pragmatics of Communication*.

John D. Caputo is David R. Cook Professor of Philosophy at Villanova University. He is the author of *The Prayers and Tears of Jacques Derrida: Religion without Religion, Deconstruction in a Nutshell: a Conversation with Jacques Derrida, Radical Hermeneutics: Repetition, Deconstruction, and the Hermeneutic Project, Against Ethics: Contributions to a Poetics of Obligation with Constant Reference to Deconstruction, Demythologizing Heidegger.*

Walford Gealy was Senior Lecturer in the Department of Extra-Mural Studies at University of Wales, Aberystwyth. He is the author of *Wittgenstein*, written in Welsh, and co-editor of the journal *Efrydiau Athronyddol* (Philosophical Studies). He is the author of over fifty articles, most of them being in Welsh, his native language.

Matthias Lutz-Bachmann is Professor of Philosophy at Goethe-University in Frankfurt, Germany. His publications include *Kritische Theorie und Religion, Metaphysikkritik-Ethik-Religion* (editor), *Frieden durch Recht* (co-editor), and *Perpetual Peace: Essays on Kant's Cosmopolitan Ideal* (co-editor).

Anselm Kyongsuk Min is Professor of Religion and Theology at Claremont Graduate University. He is the author of *Dialectic of Salvation: Issues in Theology of Liberation*. He is currently working on a new theological paradigm, Solidarity of Others, as a theology after postmodernism.

Stephen Mulhall is a Fellow and Tutor in Philosophy at New College, Oxford. His recent publications include *Faith and Reason, Heidegger and 'Being and Time'*, and *The Cavell Reader* (editor).

Schubert M. Ogden is University Distinguished Professor of Theology Emeritus, Southern Methodist University. His most recent books include *Is There Only One True Religion or Are There Many?* And *Doing Theology Today*.

D.Z. Phillips is Danforth Professor of the Philosophy of Religion, Claremont Graduate University and Rush Rhees Research Professor, University of Wales, Swansea. He is the author of *The Concept of Prayer, Faith and Philosophical Enquiry, Death and Immortality, Moral Practices* (with H.O. Mounce), *Sense and Delusion* (with Ilham Dilman), *Athronyddu Am Grefydd, Religion without Explanation, Dramâu Gwenlyn Parry, Belief, Change and Forms of Life, Through a Darkening Glass, R.S. Thomas: Poet of the Hidden God, Faith after Foundationalism, From Fantasy to Faith, Interventions in Ethics, Wittgenstein and Religion, Writers of Wales: J.R. Jones, Introducing Philosophy, Recovering Religious Concepts, Philosophy's Cool Place*. He is editor of *Swansea Studies in Philosophy* and co-editor of *Claremont Studies in the Philosophy of Religion* published by Palgrave. He is also editor of the journal, *Philosophical Investigations*.

Richard Swinburne is Nolloth Professor of the Philosophy of the Christian Religion at the University of Oxford, and a Fellow of the British Academy. He is the author of *Space and Time, an Introduction to Confirmation Theory, The Coherence of Theism, The Existence of God, Faith and Reason, The Evolution of the Soul. Responsibility and Atonement, Revelation, The Christian God, Is There a God?, Providence and the Problem of Evil*.

Timothy Tessin is co-editor of *Philosophy and the Grammar of Religious Belief*. He is also co-editor of *Claremont Studies in the Philosophy of Religion* and associate editor of *Philosophical Investigations*.

William J. Wainwright is Distinguished Professor of Philosophy at the University of Wisconsin-Milwaukee. His publications include *Philosophy of Religion: an Annotated Bibliography, Mysticism, Philosophy of Religion, Reason and the Heart, God, Philosophy and Academic Culture*. He is a former editor of *Faith and Philosophy*.

Nicholas Wolterstorff is Noah Porter Professor of Philosophical Theology Emeritus at Yale Divinity School and was adjunct professor in the Departments of Philosophy and Religious Studies. He is the author of *Works and Worlds of Art, Art in Action, Reason within the Limits of Religion, John Locke and the Ethics of Belief, Divine Discourse* (1993 Wilde Lectures at Oxford), *Until Justice and Peace Embrace, Religion in the Public Square,* and *World, Mind and Entitlement to Believe* (1995 Gifford Lectures at St Andrews) and *Thomas Reid and the Story of Epistemology.* He has been President of the American Philosophical Association (Central Division) and of the Society of Christian Philosophers.

Stephen J. Wykstra is Professor of Philosophy at Calvin College. He has published articles in history and philosophy of science, and in the philosophy of religion.

Introduction

D.Z. Phillips

The symposia and discussions presented here represent the proceedings of the 1999 annual philosophy of religion conference which took place at Claremont Graduate University. Previous publications in the series Claremont Studies in the Philosophy of Religion are: *Philosophy and the Grammar of Religious Belief; Religion and Morality; Can Religion Be Explained Away?; Religion without Transcendence?; Religion and Hume's Legacy;* and *Kant and Kierkegaard on Religion.* It was thought appropriate in 1999 to prepare for the year 2000 by presenting a volume on the present state of philosophy of religion. It was impossible to include everything, so choice was made on the basis of movements which it was thought had to be represented. On the other hand, the conference was arranged with considerable trepidation, since there was always the danger that the six philosophical schools would pass each other by like ships in the night. The message in my Thai fortune-cookie, opened in the closing banquet of the conference, would have summed up my foreboding at its outset. It read, 'You would be wise not to seek too much from others at this time.' For once my fortune-cookie was not uncannily revelatory, since, as the discussions reveal, genuine attempts were made to probe and explore difficulties connected with each point of view. I am not going to rehearse these in this introduction. Instead, I am going to single out a feature of the conference which struck me most forcibly as its organizer.

The papers in the conference represent, not simply differences on specific topics, but differences concerning the very conception of philosophical enquiry. In one sense, it would be foolish to try to determine the nature of philosophy since, descriptively, this would be a futile exercise. Why insist that philosophy or philosophy of religion can only be done in one way, when it is obviously practised in a number of ways?

It is tempting to take a tolerant attitude and simply say, 'Let a thousand flowers bloom.' But, in another sense, that cannot be allowed without denying a considerable part of philosophy's history. This is because the nature of philosophy is itself a philosophical question and great philosophers have been critical of their predecessors' conception of the subject.

In the papers in this collection we are presented with marked differences in one's conception of the tasks which philosophy of religion can and should perform.

According to Richard Swinburne, philosophy of religion has, at its heart, the rational assessment of religious beliefs. They are to be assessed, as he would say any belief must, in terms of the probability of their being true. Swinburne holds that the truth and rationality of religious beliefs can be assessed in this way.

While William Wainwright is generally sympathetic to Swinburne, he is sceptical about the efficacy of probability arguments for most educated audiences today. This is because, he argues, we need a properly disposed heart in order to assess the evidence. The vital issue, as Wainwright recognizes, then becomes one of showing how these antecedent judgements are related to the evidence on has to consider.

Nicholas Wolterstorff condones Reformed Epistemology's rejection of the Enlightenment ideal of a rational religion. Something does not have to be grounded in order to be rational. As a result of a world-transforming experience, the Christian philosopher in this tradition offers, not a philosophy of religion, but a religious philosophy. Its aim is to see all aspects of human life, intellectual and non-intellectual, in the light of faith. It does not subject religion to the test of so-called neutral evidence.

Stephen Wykstra wonders whether this rejection of evidentialism itself comes from a too narrow conception of evidence, namely, inferential evidence. He finds the rejection unrealistic in a world in which faith is challenged in many ways. It may not be necessary for an individual believer to consider these challenges in detail, but unless someone in the community does so, he argues, it is too easy to see faith as simply burying one's head in the sand. One is robbed of the much-needed resources one has to turn to in face of these challenges.

Stephen Mulhall in expounding Wittgenstein on religion and Wittgensteinianism, emphasizes the contemplative character of philosophical enquiry. The main interest here is in giving a just account of religious belief by seeing to it that it is not confused with beliefs of another kind. This interest itself has a demanding ethic and is connected, he claims, with a certain kind of spiritual concern in the enquirer. This is because we cannot be true to ourselves unless we are true to our words. Walford Gealy emphasizes that some of Wittgenstein's early remarks on religion take the form that they do because of views of language he held at the time and which he rejected later. This should be remembered when these remarks are discussed. Like Mulhall, Gealy too argues that the charge that Wittgensteinians hold that religion is immune to criticism is absurd. Both writers give examples to counter this charge. On the other hand, he insists that whatever is meant by spirituality in philosophical enquiry, this should not be compared with religious spirituality. Philosophy's concerns come from its own problems and puzzlements.

John Caputo emphasizes postmodernism's rejection of the Enlightenment dream of universal reason. We must recognize that 'reason' means something different in different modes of thought and at different times and places. We must not seek a premature closure on questions of meaning and value. Some have seen, in Derrida, a formless, chaotic, openness to everything in these emphases. Caputo denies this and sees in Derrida's openness a concern with justice for the other, which involves listening to what we do not want to hear, the preparedness to be surprised, and to take risks in such encounters.

Anselm Min is more sceptical about these latter claims, seeing in Derrida, the constant appeal to openness as being uninformed by specific moral or political values. In emphasizing the impossibility of arriving at a final statement of justice, something Min endorses, there is the danger of the dream of the impossible turning us aside from the actions that are required of us now.

Again, in expounding critical theory, Matthias Lutz-Bachmann emphasizes its rejection of the objectifying tendency one finds in metaphysics. Reasoning knows no absolute. Yet, Horkheimer and Habermas want to invoke 'the unconditional' as a regulative ideal that calls us on to improve the world, without any conception of a final goal. Religion may assist this task at certain times, but this is a contingent fact. Religion is replaceable by secular hopes for a better world. Lately, Habermas has come to see that religious meanings may be sui generis, irreducible to any secular substitute. Lutz-Bachmann argues, however, that as long as Habermas bases human progress, not on values, but on what human interests happen to be, he cannot avail himself of any positive conception of justice.

Maeve Cooke recognizes the tensions in Habermas's thought which Lutz-Bachmann emphasizes. He wants his conception of truth to be pragmatic and yet absolute. It is difficult to see how religious truth can be accommodated in his system, she argues, because his criteria of vindication demand publicly assessable evidence and a public agreement, which is hard to imagine in the case of religious belief.

John Cobb emphasizes the way in which Process Thought calls the assumptions of classical metaphysics into question. It argues that 'becoming' is more fundamental than 'being' and that 'events' are more fundamental than 'substances'. Following Whitehead, Cobb argues that science is the most reliable guide to what we are given, as long as it is not permeated by the assumptions of classical metaphysics. Religion explores the more subjective side of human nature.

Cobb is sceptical about the possibility of neutral philosophy. For him, any Olympian height is such within a system. Thus he acknowledges that his Process system has its presuppositions and that these play a vital role not only in the assessment of data, but in the very possibility of seeing the data in a certain way.

Schubert Ogden insists that although philosophy is motivated by the existential questions concerning the meaning of existence, it is not constituted by them. Its task is to elucidate the necessary conditions of human discourse, and to reflect on the meanings which discourse actually has. This latter task includes reflection on the distinctive claims of Christianity, one in which philosophy and theology come together. Ogden thinks that the existential questions and theological reflections are furthered best in Process thought. On one central issue, however, he differs from most Process philosophers and theologians. They, Whitehead and Hartshorne included, treat the conditions for the possibility of discourse, or ultimate reality, as though these were a further super-fact. This confusion is found when myth is treated as a fact or when God, as ultimate reality, is treated as though it were a fact. 'God exists' is not a statement of fact.

It is clear from this brief survey of points of view represented in this collection that there are wide differences between them in their conception of philosophy. In some ways, the Wittgensteinian tradition of contemplative philosophy seems an odd one out, but would claim to be as old as Plato. In what sense does philosophy investigate reality? If, like the Presocratics, we try to give substantive accounts of 'the real' in terms of, for example, water or atoms, the problem arises of what account can be given of the reality of the water or atoms. Plato came to see that a philosophical account of reality cannot lead to answers of that kind. The philosophical interest is a conceptual one; the question of what it means to distinguish between the real or the unreal. Thus, on this view, philosophy is not itself a way of reaching the substantive judgements, but an enquiry into what it means to reach conclusions of this kind. Unlike Plato, Wittgenstein did not think that this question admitted of a single answer. Hence his promise to teach us differences. This perspective raises questions about Swinburne's assumption that all beliefs are matters of probability. Are all beliefs of the same kind? Is belief in generosity the expression of a conviction or a matter of probability? Further, is it a mere probability that we had a Conference at Claremont? If I could be convinced otherwise would I say that I had miscalculated probabilities, or that I was going insane? Is trusting God a probability?

William Wainwright is bothered, too, by some of these questions. He emphasizes that we make antecedent judgements in terms of which we see the data we are to assess. How are these antecedent judgements to be understood? The suggestion that we can make them when our faculties are working properly seems a lame analogy, since, normally, the notion of 'proper functioning' is normative and, in that sense, independent of the individual. Further, there is usually agreement on the notion of proper functioning, as the case of eyesight illustrates. Is it like this in the case of the clash between belief and unbelief?

There is another difficulty which relates to the contemplative conception of philosophy. If what can be seen is linked to the personal appropriation of the perspective in question, or to the 'proper functioning' of faculties, how is it possible to contemplate, and give an account of, different perspectives? Further, someone who does not embrace a perspective may give a better philosophical account of its character than one who does not embrace it.

In Reformed Epistemology a world-transforming religious experience is at the root of the religiously orientated philosophical vocation to see the world in the light of faith. Obviously, such a use can be made of philosophy, or this is what philosophy can amount to for someone, but what is its relation to the contemplative conception of philosophy? Can it admit that a non-believer can give a better philosophical account of religious belief than a believer? What sort of claim does a religious philosophy make? Is it a theoretical claim? If something is seen in the light of faith, how is that 'seeing' related to other non-religious 'seeings'? Can there be a philosophical interest in these differences which is not a further form of such 'seeing'?

In Postmodernism and in Critical Theory we have attacks on the ambitions of a universal metaphysics, and a recognition of differences. The question arises, however, whether in the ethical concerns of Derrida or Habermas, an ethical insight is appropriated which cannot be derived from their philosophical critique. Having abolished a universal meta-physics, there seems to be a desire to replace it with an attitude which is equally universal even when it calls itself 'open' and denies the possibility of closure.

Again, in Process Thought, we have a similar attack on classical metaphysics. This attack may be upheld in many respects, but questions may be asked as to whether one set of ultimates, 'becoming' and 'events' has now replaced another. Also, as Cobb admits, certain presuppositions are brought to bear on the data in interpreting them and he denies the possibility of a neutral philosophy. Does this mean that Process Thought can argue against this possibility? If so, there is at least one perspective it seems to deny when, at other times, it seems to recognize a plurality of systems of interpretation. Ogden says that Process Thought is the best theological system in answering central existential questions about the meaning of existence. How would this be argued in relation to different theological and atheistic perspectives? Are they shown to be conceptually confused in some sense?

Ogden recognizes, along with Wittgensteinians, that the investigation of the conditions of discourse is not an investigation of some super-fact. On the other hand, he speaks of the necessary conditions of discourse. Do they form a single class? He also speaks of God as 'ultimate reality', and says that this, too, does not refer to a matter of fact. How is this notion of reality related to the necessary conditions of discourse? Are they the same? If so, as in the case of Reformed Epistemology, here, too, we would have a religious conception of reality.

These questions are prompted by philosophical considerations which are familiar to students of Wittgenstein, but questions can be asked of Wittgensteinianism too. Is the analogy between language and games an adequate one? After all, all games do not make up one big game, whereas all language games occur within the same language. What account is to be given of the unity or identity of language? Does that lead back to a single account of reality? Without such an account is not the sense of life and living compartmentalized in unacceptable ways?

The questions asked of Wittgensteinianism can and have been addressed, for example, by Rush Rhees. No doubt the questions I have asked of the other points of view can and have been addressed too. I mention them here as questions with which the conference meeting left us. Thus, this introduction gives an indication, not of where we started, but of the points at which we would have liked to have gone on.

If philosophical enquiry is conceptual and contemplative, and recognizes the conceptual variety in human discourse, no single account of reality can be given. The enquiry will be motivated by wonder at the world and the desire to do justice to its variety in the account we give. For others, this is the road to relativism and they seek a religious conception of reality which, in some way, can be shown to be more rational than any secular alternative. Alternatively, there are those who argue that although the sense of things is open to a change and development to which philosophy cannot assign a closure, that development is itself to be informed by certain ethical and political values.

Perhaps one major difference which needs to be explored is this: are all perspectives on reality interpretations or expressions of interest, or is there such a thing in philosophy as disinterested enquiry? Is disinterested inquiry another interest, alongside others, religious and secular, or is it a different kind of interest, an interest in the variety of those religious and secular interests and the relation between them? Is an Olympian view always one from within some system or other?

Many of the participants expressed the view at the end of the conference that we needed to address these issues further. If we did so in another conference, perhaps its topic would be: Presuppositions.

Finally, a word is necessary concerning the 'Voices in Discussion'. These are notes I took in the course of the discussions which followed each session. They do not purport to be absolutely accurate, although I have aimed at reporting the course of arguments as closely as possible. This is why the names of speakers have not been used. Readers of previous volumes have had some fun in identifying the speakers. In the case of the participants this is not difficult because they begin each discussion. Some reviewers were puzzled by the fact that the number of speakers outnumbered the participants. This is truer than ever on this occasion. This is because those who chair the session need not be paper-readers. Also, at the end of each session discussion was opened up to the wider audience present. Reviewers have welcomed 'Voices in Discussion' as an addition to the collection, so I have decided to continue this practice. No account has been taken, of course, of any revisions made to the papers after the conference.

My major aim in the conferences I organize is to bring together representatives of widely differing views, so keeping alive an older tradition in the philosophy of religion which, sadly, has declined. I only hope that the result of their discussions proves as valuable for readers as it did for those of us who participated in them.

Part I
Philosophical Theism

1
Philosophical Theism

Richard Swinburne

1 History of the programme

I shall understand by 'philosophical theism' the programme of giving a
clear coherent account of the nature of God (broadly consonant with
what has been believed about him by Christian, Islamic and Jewish
thinkers of the past two millennia), and providing cogent arguments for
the existence of such a God.

Providing arguments – or, more loosely, reasons – for the existence of
God has been a concern of many theologians of the Christian tradition
(over the whole of this period). St Paul's comment that 'the invisible
things' of God 'are clearly seen, being perceived through the things that
are made',[1] gave Christian backing to the message of the middle chapters of the Old Testament *Wisdom of Solomon* that the existence and
order of the Universe shows it to be the work of a divine creator. This
Biblical tradition merged in the Hellenistic world with the arguments of
Plato to the idea of the good and to the Demiurge, and with the arguments of Aristotle to the existence of the First Mover. And so many
Christian theologians of the first millennium had their paragraph or two
summarizing a cosmological argument or an argument from design. But
it is normally only a paragraph or two,[2] and the reasoning is quick. My
explanation of why they directed so little energy to this issue is that they
felt no need to do more. Most of their contemporaries accepted that
there was something like a god; what the theologians needed to argue
for were the specially Christian doctrines about him.

But in the medieval west theologians began to produce arguments
for the existence of God at considerable length and with considerable
rigour; and they did their best to give a coherent account of the nature
of the God whose existence was purportedly demonstrated by these

arguments. The opening questions of St Thomas Aquinas's *Summa Theologiae* provide the paradigm of medieval philosophical theism. The pre-Kantian Protestant tradition also had a concern with this activity – more with arguments, than with clarifying the divine nature, and the arguments tended to be less rigorous. The classical Protestants thought that while there were good arguments for the existence of God, (or rather more loosely, that nature showed clearly its creator) this was of little use to humans corrupted by sin.[3] Liberal Protestants, by contrast, argued at some length 'from nature up to Nature's God' and thought their arguments important. It was only with the arrival of Hume and Kant that some major parts of the Christian tradition abandoned the project of natural theology, and they were in my view ill-advised to do so.

It needs to be emphasized that none of those thinkers in the first 1750 years of Christianity who thought that there are good arguments for the existence of God, thought that all or most believers ought to believe on the basis of those arguments, nor that conversion required accepting those arguments as cogent.[4] To be a Christian does involve believing that there is a God, but most Christians may well have taken God's existence for granted. Most converts may have believed beforehand that there is a God; their conversion involved accepting more detailed claims about him. And if they did not initially believe that there is a God, they may have come to believe on the basis of religious experience in some sense rather than as the basis of natural theology. Nevertheless, most Christian thinkers before 1750 held that there are these arguments available, and that those who do not initially believe that there is a God and are rational can be brought to see that there is a God by means of them.[5]

It is an interesting question why so much energy was put into the project of philosophical theology in the medieval west, when one might suppose that there was no more need of it than in earlier centuries – there were no more sophisticated atheists around, one supposes. But the answer, I suspect, is that there is a bit of the sophisticated atheist in most believers, and St Thomas and Duns Scotus were providing tools to deal with that. However, as we all know, atheism went public and expanded in the eighteenth century, until in our day in the West a large proportion of the population are atheists, and quite a lot of those who practise a theistic religion have serious doubts about whether there is a God. Yet the practices of the religion only have a point if there is a God – there is no point in worshipping a non-existent creator or asking him to do something on Earth or take us to Heaven if he does not exist; or trying to live our lives in accord with his will, if he has no will.

If someone is to be rational in practising the Christian, Islamic or Jewish religion, he needs to believe (to some degree) the credal claims which underlie the practice. These claims include as their central claim, one presupposed by all the other claims, the claim that there is a God. If someone does not believe or only half-believes, the faithful are required (as part of their religious practice) to help. Help may take various forms. If we can help someone to have a deep and cognitively compelling religious experience, let us do so; but religious experiences cannot be guaranteed. And the only way which requires the non-believer simply to exercise his existing faculties in the pursuit of something which he is almost bound to regard as a good thing (to discover whether or not there is a God), is to present him with arguments whose premises are things evident to the non-believer and whose principles of inference are ones he accepts, and to take him through them. And the only premises evident to all non-believers are the typical premises of rational theology – the existence of the world, its orderliness, the existence of human beings and so on. In our age, above all ages, theistic religion needs to have available natural theology. And since the reasons why people do not believe are not just the lack of positive grounds for believing, but because they believe (or suspect) that there are internal incoherences in the concept of God, or that the existence of suffering disconfirms the existence of God, the believer needs to help them to see that this is not so. There are other means which might have success in our day – the need for philosophical theism is great – if in fact there is a God.

But atheists are also interested in these questions, and they endeavour to show that there is no God; and since showing that an argument is not cogent or a concept is not coherent involves the same techniques as the contrary endeavour, we may also call their activity 'philosophical theism'. And if, in fact, there is no God, it is good that some shall help others to a right view of this matter, both for its own sake and also to save them from spending their time in pointless activity.

Such is the history and utility of philosophical theology. How is it pursued today and what are its prospects? A lot of very thorough, detailed and rigorous work has been done with the aid of all the tools of analytical philosophy in attempting to clarify what would be involved in there being a God, and attempting to show the claim that there is a God to be coherent or incoherent. As regards positive arguments for the existence of God, different philosophers of today have revived different kinds of argument from the past. Some have revived ontological arguments, either producing variants of one or more classical arguments or producing some entirely new ontological argument. Ontological arguments of course differ from all the other traditional arguments in that they start, not from something observable, but from purported logically necessary truths. It is easy enough to produce an ontological argument with the premises evident to all; and easy enough to produce a (deductively) valid ontological argument. But it is very hard indeed – in my view quite impossible – to produce an ontological argument with both characteristics. It seems to me fairly evident that the proposition 'there is no God' while perhaps false and even in some sense demonstrably false, is not incoherent. It does not contain any internal contradiction. And if that is so, there could not be a valid argument from logically necessary truths to the existence of God. For if there were such an argument the existence of God would be logically necessary and its negation self-contradictory.

Then there is the tradition of attempting to produce deductively valid arguments from premises evident to the senses. It is a not unreasonable interpretation of Aquinas's *Summa Theologiae* 1.2.3. that he sought there to give five such arguments. Those in our day who have sought to give such arguments have for the most part tried to do so with the aid of Thomist (or neo-Thomist) terminology. But the enterprise of producing such arguments is also, I think, an enterprise doomed to failure. For if it could be achieved, then a proposition which was a conjunction of the evident premises together with 'there is no God' would be incoherent, would involve self-contradiction. But again propositions such as 'there is a Universe, but there is no God', though perhaps false and even in some sense demonstrably false, seem fairly evidently coherent.

So my own preference is for the third tradition of natural theology. This begins from premises evident to the senses and claims that they make probable the existence of God. Such arguments purport to be inductively cogent, not deductively valid arguments. Arguments of scientists or historians from their data of observation to their general theories or claims about the past or the future, also do not purport to be deductively valid, merely inductively cogent. Thinkers were not very clear about the distinction between inductive and deductive arguments during the first one thousand years of the Christian era, and not much clearer until the eighteenth century. So it would be anachronistic to say that the patristic writers were seeking to give inductive, or alternatively deductive arguments. But the arguments of so many British empiricists of the eighteenth century, culminating in Paley's *Natural Theology*, do seem to me fairly clearly and intentionally inductive.

Arguments against the existence of God of all three kinds have also been produced in our day, but – for reasons of time – I shall concentrate on the positive.

2 My own version

I model my own arguments for the existence of God on those of the third tradition. Each of the various arguments from various observable phenomena does, I argue,[6] give some support to the claims that there is a God; and, taken together, they make it 'significantly more probable than not'.

I have sought to show this with the aid of confirmation theory (that is, the calculus of probability, used as a calculus for stating relations of evidential support between propositions. I represent by P(p/q) the probability of a proposition p on evidence q. I use Bayes's Theorem,

$$P(h/e \& k) = P(e/h \& k) \frac{P(h/k)}{P(e/k)},$$

to elucidate the relation between the probability of a hypothesis h on evidence of observation e and background knowledge k, and other probabilities. To use this calculus does not involve supposing that exact values can very often be given to the probabilities involved. That exact values cannot often be given is evident enough even when h is some paradigm scientific theory. It would be very odd to say that the probability of Quantum Theory on the evidence of the photoelectric effect was 0.3217. Some probabilities can be given exact values – but this usually happens only when the probability is 1, 0 or 1/2. More often, all we can say is that some probability has some rough value – more than this and less than that, and that in consequence some other probability has some other rough value – close to 1, or fairly high or less than that. My concern has been to prove that when e is a conjunction of propositions which set out the publicly available evidence which has been used in arguments for and against the existence of God, and k is tautological background evidence (viz. contains nothing relevant to h) and h is the existence of God, P(h/e·k) is 'significantly greater than 1/2'.

All that the calculus does is to set out in a rigorous formal way the factors which determine how observational evidence supports more general theory. The relevant points can be made easily enough in words, but less rigorously and with their implications less clear. What the calculus brings out is that a general theory h is rendered probable by observational evidence e (and if we put k as a tautology, we can now ignore it), insofar as (1) P(e/h & k) (the posterior probability of e) is high, (2) P(h/k) (the prior probability of h) is high, and (3) P(e/k) (the prior probability of e) is low. The first condition is satisfied to the extent to which you would expect to find e if h is true. Obviously a scientific or historical theory is rendered probable, insofar as the evidence is such as you would expect to find if the theory is true. (I can say 'the theory is rendered probable insofar as it yields true predictions' but only if it is understood that the 'predictions' may be evidence observed either before or after the theory was formulated. It seems irrelevant to whether evidence supports a theory whether it is 'new' evidence found by testing a theory, or 'old' evidence which the new theory explains.)

However, for any e you can devise an infinite number of different incompatible theories h which are such that for each P(e/h & k) is high but which make totally different predictions from each other for the future (that is, predictions additional to e). Let e be all the observations made relevant to your favourite theory of mechanics – let's say General Relativity (GTR). Then you can complicate GTR in innumerable ways such that the resulting new theories all predict e but make wildly different predictions about what will happen tomorrow. The grounds for believing that GTR is the true theory is that GTR is the simplest theory. P(h/k) means the a priori probability that h is true, or – put less challengingly – is the measure of the strength of the a priori factors relevant to the probability of h. The major such a priori factor is simplicity. The simplicity of a theory is something internal to that theory, not a matter of the relation of the theory to external evidence. Another a priori factor is content – the bigger a theory, the more and more precise claims it makes, the less likely it is to be true. But we can ignore this factor if we are comparing theories of similar content.

P(e/k) is a measure of how likely e is to occur if we do not assume any particular theory to be true. The normal effect of this term in assessing the probability of any particular theory h, is that e does not render h very probable if you would expect to find e anyway (for example, if it was also predicted by the main rivals to h which had significant prior probability).

For the purpose of applying this apparatus to assessing the theory that there is a God, the philosophical theist needs to spell out what is meant by this claim. God is supposed to be roughly a person without a body, essentially omnipotent, omniscient, perfectly free, perfectly good, creator and sustainer of any universe there may be, a source of moral obligation, eternal and necessary.[7] It needs to be spelled out what each of these properties amounts to, and to be shown that possession of each is compatible with possession of the others. Inevitably, to talk of the source of all being involves using words in somewhat stretched

senses – just as, in a humbler way, does talk about photons and protons. But it needs to be made to some extent clear just what the
stretching amounts to in each case, and to be made plausible that when
words are used in the stretched sense, the claims about God made with
their aid are coherent. It's no good saying 'all our talk about God is
metaphorical'. For if anyone is even to have a belief that there is a God,
let alone have grounds for that belief, there must be some difference
between that belief and the belief that there is no God, or the belief that
there is a Great Pumpkin, or whatever. And to explain to a non-believer
what that belief is, one must use words which she understands.
That involves making it clear when words are being used in stretched
senses and – insofar as it can be done – what are the boundaries of
these senses. The claim that there is a God may of course not be a
fully clear claim, but unless it is moderately clear, it cannot provide
backing for the practice of religion nor can arguments be given for or
against it.

I argue that any being who is essentially omnipotent, omniscient, and
perfectly free, and everlasting necessarily has the other divine properties,
and that the cited properties fit together in a very neat way so that the
claim that there is a God is a very simple claim, because it is a claim for
the existence of the simplest kind of person there could be. Persons are
beings with power to bring about effects intentionally, beliefs (true or
false) about how things are, and some degree of freedom to exercise
their power. God is postulated as a being with zero limits to his power,
to his true beliefs, and to his freedom. Scientists and others always prefer on grounds of simplicity hypotheses which postulate one entity
rather than many, and entities with zero or infinite degrees of their
properties rather than some finite degree thereof. They postulate that
photons have zero mass (rather than some very small mass, equally
compatible with observations); and they used to postulate that light
and the gravitational force travel with infinite velocity (rather than
some very large finite velocity, equally compatible with observations)
until observations forced a different theory on them. Although the existence of anything at all is perhaps enormously improbable a priori, the
existence of a very simple being has a far higher prior probability than
does the existence of anything else (except insofar as the latter is rendered probable by the former).

Yet if there is a God, it is not improbable that he should create a universe, an orderly universe, and within it embodied rational creatures such
as humans. For God being good will seek to bring about good things. It is
good that there should be a beautiful universe, Beauty arises from order
of some kind – the orderly interactions and movements of objects in

accord with natural laws is beautiful indeed; and even more beautiful are the plants and animals which evolved on Earth. It is a further good that there should be human beings who can choose between good and bad, choose whether to grow in power and knowledge, and so choose whether or not to enter into a loving relationship with God himself. Humans have limited power over their bodies and acquire naturally some knowledge of how the world works. We have to know which bodily movements will make what difference – and that involves there being regularities in the world which we can grasp. The movements of solid bodies in empty space follow (approximately) Newton's laws. Given such simple regularities, we can discern them and use them to increase our power over the universe – to develop our agriculture, to make houses and bridges, to send humans to the moon. So God has a further reason to create a universe orderly in its conformity to rational laws – in giving humans significant choices which affect themselves, each other and their relation to God.

But unless there is a God, it is most unlikely that there would be a universe at all. The universe is a big thing consisting of very many separate objects of varying finite size and mass. That it should exist on its own, uncreated, is therefore – by normal scientific criteria – very much less likely than that God should exist. And it is most unlikely that the Universe would come into existence caused by anything else than God, because any other possible cause is much less simple than God. And it is immensely unlikely that if there is a Universe, it should be governed by simple natural laws. For natural laws are not entities. To say that all objects obey Newton's laws is just to say that each object in the Universe behaves in a way that Newton's laws state, that is, has exactly the same properties of movement in reaction to the presence of other objects, as does every other object. It is immensely unlikely that every other object should behave in exactly the same way – a priori, unless there was a common cause of their having the properties they do. And any other possible cause is much less simple than God. (Even if you suppose some impersonal cause to be just as simple a postulate as God, there is no reason why it should bring about this sort of universe.)

So the hypothesis of theism satisfies the three criteria which I have drawn from Bayes's Theorem and are independently plausible, for the probability of a theory. The only evidence which I have mentioned is that of the existence of the Universe and its 'conformity to natural laws'. In my books I have also adduced much further evidence – the initial state of the Universe being such and the laws having such characteristics as to bring about somewhere in the Universe animals and humans (the 'fine-tuning' of the Universe); the existence of consciousness, various providential aspects of nature, the public evidence about the life, death and purported resurrection of Jesus of Nazareth, other reports of miracles, and the very widespread phenomenon of 'religious experiences', in the sense of experiences which seem to their subjects to be experiences of God. The case for the existence of God which I have just summarized is a cumulative one from many pieces of evidence. Arguments against the existence of God (for example, from evil) have also to be brought into the equation, and it needs to be shown that the hypothesis of theism retains its probability despite these.

3   Objections

What of objections? Ever since people have given arguments for the existence of God, others have tried to find fallacies in them. There are innumerable objections both to the general programme and to particular versions of it. I confine myself to objections to the arguments for the claim that there is God, and – for reasons of time – shall not consider objections to the coherence of that claim. I begin with objections to the general programme.

First, there is the objection that if arguments for the existence of God (and certain claims about what he has done) are cogent, then a prudent person will try to do what is good out of self-interest – for (probably) God will approve such behaviour and reward it. The total commitment demanded by religious faith would no longer be virtuous. Kierkegaard wrote that the suggestion that faith might be replaced by 'probabilities and guarantees' is for the believer 'a temptation to be resisted with all his strength'.[8] Of course religion involves commitment, that is, living by the assumption that the relevant religious system is true. But there is always risk in a commitment to an assumption which may be false – you may spend your life pursuing good things which you will never attain, and lose good things which you could have attained. Yet if the former good things are good enough – and plausibly the Beatific Vision of God in the company of the saints for yourself and your fellows (as well as many earthly good things) is good enough, it is a risk worth taking. The prudence of seeking such a good, despite risk of failure, is virtuous. And if it is probable (though not certain) that there is a God, it is probable that you have a duty to commit yourself to God. But there is nothing virtuous in living your life on an assumption which is certainly false – for that is pointless. Given that there is some risk that there is no God likely to reward you, as the third tradition of argument allows, this criticism fails.

Then there is Kierkegaard's objection from the opposite angle, directed at the third tradition of argument, that it would leave us with an uncertain belief open to revision – and that religion requires more.[9] I do not think that religion does require more – by way of belief. St Paul reminded us that 'we see in a mirror darkly; but then face to face: now I know in part; but then shall I know even as also I have been known,'[10] and that 'by hope were we saved: but hope that is seen is not hope: for who hopeth for that which he seeth?'[11] Religion requires more than tentative commitment, but there is no difficulty in giving that commitment to a system which is only probably true.

Then there is the objection that arguments for the existence of God, especially ones which involve probabilities, are sophisticated things; and only intellectuals can understand them. Even if this were true, it is no good objection to the project – intellectuals need their views on religion by which to live as much as does anyone else; and if their need alone can be satisfied, that is something. But in fact I suggest that almost all traditional arguments for the existence of God (apart from the ontological argument) codify in a more rigorous form the vague feeling of so many humans that the existence of the world with its various particular features cries out for an explanation, and that God's action in creating and sustaining it provides that explanation. That feeling is then open to various atheistic objections which can be dealt with in turn by more rigorous formulation and defence.

Then there is the Barthian objection that philosophical theism has too anthropomorphic a view of God. But the Christian view of God is in crucial respects anthropomorphic. It is central to the Christian tradition (as to the Jewish and Islamic traditions) that God 'created man in his own image',[12] and the very many theologians of the two Christian millennia who have dwelt on these words have seen the 'image' as primarily a matter of rationality and free will (and so of power and knowledge), that is, properties contingently present in humans in a small degree which are necessarily present in God in an infinite degree. God is like man because man is like God. If we are to be concerned with arguments for the existence of the God of Christianity, we must – with all the qualifications about stretched language mentioned earlier – be anthropomorphic about God.

There are many other general objections to the programme of philosophical theism – I find, for example, eight separate ones, in Hume's *Dialogues*. But my view is that most such objections derive any force that they may have from a positivism now largely rejected in philosophy generally (and, in particular, in philosophy of science). There is, for example, the view that causation concerns patterns of regularity in observable objects, and there is no sense in talking of the unobservable cause of a unique object. But while no object (even God) is unique in all respects, all objects are unique in some respects; and science is finding out rather a lot about the unobservable causes of the observable. I think that there is little force in any of these general objections to the programme of philosophical theism. What I believe to be much more important are detailed objections designed to show that some particular theistic claim is incoherent, or that all available versions of theistic arguments do not work. If I am right in my claim that the probability calculus captures the principles of inductive inference in a precise form, then if someone can find a fault in my version of the programme, that will suffice to render the whole programme worthless.

There are objections to each of my claims about the three elements on the right hand side of Bayes's Theorem, when this is applied to assessing the probability of the existence of God (h) on the evidence of observation (e) and tautological background evidence (k). First, the objector claims that $P(e/h \& k)$ is very low indeed, because of the problem of evil, including pain and other suffering, which is very – if not totally – improbable if there is a God. In my view the problem of evil constitutes the most substantial of all objections to the existence of God. But even to begin to meet it, my paper would need to deal solely with it. So all that I have space to do here is to say that some evils are necessary conditions of greater goods. It is not improbable that God will bestow on some creatures not merely the good of pleasure; but the goods of a free choice of good or evil which makes a significant difference to the world, the opportunity to show patience, courage and compassion, and the privilege of making it possible (by our suffering) for others to evince these virtues, and much else. I claim that God (logically) cannot provide us with these good things without causing or allowing suffering, and that it would not be wrong of him to cause or allow the suffering for a limited period in a limited way for the sake of the goods which it makes possible. But to show this at adequate length requires a very substantial theodicy, for which I can only put down a marker.[13]

Then, the objector claims that $P(h/k)$ is low because the hypothesis of theism is not nearly as simple as I suggest, and the hypothesis makes such big claims (its content is so large). I do think that this is a very substantial objection, although in the end mistaken. The content of any hypothesis able to explain the existence of the Universe will have to be pretty large. The hypothesis of theism postulates one God of infinite power, knowledge and so on, rather than one or many finite ones. In the course of a very interesting paper Mark Wynn has pointed out that there are very many different possible hypotheses, each postulating different numbers of gods with different powers, whereas there is only one hypothesis postulating one God of infinite power. Hence, he claims, although each of the former hypotheses might be less probable a priori than the hypothesis of theism, the disjunction of the former is plausibly more probable than the hypothesis of theism.[14] But if the order of the world is to be explained by many gods, then some explanation is required for how and why they cooperate in producing the same patterns of order throughout the Universe. This becomes a new datum requiring explanation for the same reason as the fact of order itself. The need for further explanation ends when we postulate one being who is the cause of the existence of all others, and the simplest conceivable such – I urge – is God.

Finally there is the objection that we can pass no judgement on the value of $P(e/k)$. What possible factors could lead us to a view about how likely it would be that there would be a universe, whether or not there is a God? But that is easy enough to answer. The probability of e is the sum of probabilities of the different ways in which e can come about, that is, the sum of the probabilities of e on each rival hypothesis, multiplied by the prior probability of that rival hypothesis. $P(e/k) = P(e/h \& k) \ P(h/k) + P(e/h_1 \& k) \ P(h_1/k) + P(e/h_2 \& k) \ P(h_2/k) \dots$ and so on. By earlier arguments, all hypotheses of similar content which lead us to expect e are much less simple than h. h_1 and the others are such that $P(h_1/k) \ll P(h/k)$. Hence $P(e/k)$ is not too much larger than $P(e/h \& k) \ P(h/k)$. When we pass judgement on the probability of any scientific theory for which there is no greatly relevant contingent background evidence k, we pass just this sort of judgement.

4   Rival programmes

How has the programme of philosophical theism engaged with other programmes represented at this conference? By far the closest programme is that of Reformed Epistemology. Indeed, I do not regard it as a separate programme, but rather as one end of a spectrum, of which philosophical theism is the other end of a spectrum of programmes defending the rationality of belief in a traditional Christian God (on a univocal understanding of 'rationality'). The canonical presentation of Reformed Epistemology is the volume edited by Plantinga and Wolterstorff, *Faith and Rationality*.[15] These writers, and all who have followed them, have used all the tools of modern analytic philosophy, as have I and many others who have tried to develop philosophical theism. What is central to Reformed Epistemology is the claim that the belief that there is a God can be entirely rational without being based on arguments from evidence; it may be 'properly basic', the sort of belief which, like mundane perceptual beliefs such as 'I see a desk', is rationally believed without being based on other beliefs. I agree with that – belief that there is a God can be, for some people, properly basic. And almost all philosophical theologians of the past two millennia would think that too. So long as it stares you in the face that some belief is true and you have no contrary evidence, then that belief is properly basic, and if anyone today is in that position with regard to their belief that there is a God, that belief is, for them properly basic. But one difference between myself and many Reformed Epistemologists is that in my view the number of people in the western world in this situation in 1999 is fairly small. Most people today need something by way of positive argument for their theistic belief to be rational. But this difference concerns merely the utility of the programme of Reformed Epistemology, not the truth of its doctrines. Some Reformed Epistemologists however seem to be saying that there are no good arguments for the existence of God – and there of course I disagree for reasons given earlier in this paper. Sometimes also they seem to be moving towards the claim that it is not rational to believe in God on the basis of arguments; and of course here too I disagree.

Until 1986, the main claim of Reformed Epistemology was simply the negative claim that the claim of others that 'there is no God' is not properly basic for anyone who had no good justification. Since then Plantinga has developed his theory of warrant, warrant being whatever it is that turns true belief into knowledge.[16] According to this theory a belief B is warranted if it satisfies a number of conditions, the crucial one of which is that 'the cognitive faculties involved in the production of B are functioning properly',[17] and that means functioning the way your creator intended them to function (if you have a creator), or (if you do not have a creator) functioning the way evolution in some sense 'intended' you to function. The application of Plantinga's theory of warrant to religious belief has the consequences that if there is a God, it is probable that a belief that there is a God is warranted; and if there is no God, it is probable that a belief that there is a God is not warranted. Even if this conclusion is correct, it is of little use to us, unless we have reason to believe that there is (or is not) a God, and that involves having a belief about the issue which is rational in a different sense from Plantinga's 'warranted'. In this alternative sense our beliefs are rational if they are probable on the evidence available to us (which will include the apparent deliverances of religious experience, as well as publicly available evidence). The probability involved here is the logical or epistemic kind with which I was operating earlier. The rationality of his or her beliefs in this sense is something internally accessible to the subject and (to a considerable degree) to everyone else as well. A reformed epistemologist needs to hold that theistic beliefs are rational in this sense, if he is to justify his claim (to himself and the world) that they are probably true. I hope that Reformed Epistemology, all of whose tools and many of whose results I endorse, will recognize the need for this strong internalist kind of rationality and not saddle itself with an exclusively externalist epistemology.

How does Philosophical Theism interact with Wittgenstein? Wittgenstein is of course one of the great philosophers of all time, recognized as such by both the analytic and continental traditions of philosophy. Any philosopher must take account of Wittgenstein; and I like to think that I have learnt a little from him and applied it to one or two particular issues. As we know, he wrote very little directly about religion, and his main influence on the philosophy of religion has been through the application by others (and especially D.Z. Phillips) of what he wrote about language in developing those few explicit remarks about religion. The resulting position has often been called 'Wittgensteinian fideism'. Now the way in which I, or indeed most analytical philosophers, approach some writer is to try to analyse what they have written in terms of a few philosophical claims and various supporting arguments; and then to attack or defend these claims by further arguments. To approach any Wittgensteinian in this way can be a frustrating experience. One is told that one's account of the philosophical claims is far too naive, and that to produce head-on arguments for or against such claims is a naive way to deal with them. One is finally left with the impression that one can only understand what the writer is saying if one endorses it.

My account of what D.Z. Phillips has been claiming over many years in fidelity to Wittgenstein's few explicit remarks on the subject, is that religion is a self-contained practice (of prayer, worship, public and private conduct, and the way we think about things), commitment to which involves no metaphysical or historical beliefs different from those of people who do not practise the religion. As an account of the Christian religion, as it has been practised by so many over two millennia, this seems manifestly false. Of course there have been a few sophisticated modern people who have gone through the motions of prayer and worship, and taken Christian stances on particular moral issues, without having any specifically Christian historical or metaphysical beliefs. Some have even used the traditional language – for example, 'Last Judgement' – in some ways utterly different from the ways of the normal Christian. But to understand Christianity, it's no good reading only Simone Weil – you need to read St Paul, Irenaeus, and Gregory of Nyssa and Luther and Francis de Sales and so on, and so on. Wittgensteinian philosophy of religion suffers from a very one-sided diet of examples. I know that there are differences between the writers I mention, but they are as nothing compared with the difference between them and, say, Don Cupitt. But having written this, I know that I shall be accused of failing to understand the subtleties of language and religion; and I await the accusation with due trepidation.

Then we come to Process Thought. I have always found the few writings of Process thinkers which I have read (despite the complexities of Whitehead's metaphysics), relatively clear. But they expound a metaphysic which seems to me a lot less probable than a more traditional Christian one. The attempt by Process Thought to dispense with the category of substance seems to me to fail, in particular in its account of persons. A subsequent person being me is not a matter of its causal relations or relations of similarity to earlier events. Many different series of subsequent events could have very close such relations to the earlier events which were mine. Yet – with immense plausibility – there would be a truth about which series of subsequent events were mine. Being me can, in consequence, only be analysed as being the same continuing substance (that is, soul). The category of substance is unavoidable; and one everlasting substance on which all depends is required to make sense of the world. While in this way, like all philosophical theists, I object to Process Theology's conceptual scheme; unlike some philosophical theists, I accept from Process Theology certain more particular views about God. God is not outside time; and God does not know infallibly the future free choices of creatures.

And finally what of Post-Modernism and Critical Theory? I am alas too ignorant of critical theory to have engaged with it. In philosophy generally I think of post-Modernism as the view that there is no truth, there are just sentences expressed in different circumstances to which people react in different ways and then utter more sentences; and I find this view in the little I have read of Derrida. As I have read so little of the Continental philosophy from which post-Modernism emerged, like so many other analytic philosophers, what I have just written may be a poor caricature; and, if so, I apologize – I am here to learn better.

But if post-Modernism is the view which I have stated, it seems to me manifestly false. For how could it be a view, a belief about how things are, unless either it is true or it is false? And in that case there is truth – either the truth of post-Modernism, or the truth that post-Modernism is false. If the former, then post-Modernism contradicts itself; and hence only the latter is possible. Now maybe post-Modernism is a bit subtler than I have represented it. Maybe it claims that there are some truths but not many. But it seems to me far more obvious than most things, that a lot of modern science is true, that the world is very old, that there are people beside myself and so on. These things are far more obvious than any philosophical doctrine. We have an enormous number of true beliefs. Post-Modernism may be warning us that different groups have different criteria of rationality and that there is not one true set of criteria. Although there are small differences between groups as to what they take as evidence for what, I do not myself believe that those differences there are greatly significant; humans have very similar criteria to each other. This is a contingent claim and I could be wrong. But if I am wrong, that does not damage my claim that there is one true set of criteria. They are those of my group, which – I am quite sure – are those of all who will hear or read this paper. We all have the modern scientific criteria of what is evidence for what, and to say that we have these criteria is just to say that we believe that the results which they yield about what is probable to be correct results. If we thought that there are no true criteria of what is evidence for what, we would think it just as likely that if we jump from a window we will fly, as that we will fall to the ground. Our conduct shows that we do not so think. One can however take a post-Modernist view about religion without becoming susceptible to the difficulties of a more general post-Modernism. One can claim that there are no religious truths (because religious claims are incoherent), or that – if there are – it is equally rational to hold any religious belief. The answer to this more detailed claim (itself presumably purportedly true and asserted as rational) is the detailed programme of philosophical theism sketched earlier. Detailed challenges to the coherence of traditional theism can be met; and it can be shown probable, and so more rational to believe than its negation, by correct criteria of rationality.

Notes

1. Epistle to the Romans 1.20.
2. For a slightly longer form of argument from design for the existence of God, and argument therefrom about the nature of God, *see* the opening chapters of St John of Damascus, *Exposition of the Orthodox Faith*.

3. *See* John Calvin, Institutes of the Christian Religion, Book 1, ch. 5.
4. Conversion of course involves not merely coming to believe certain propositions, but setting yourself to act on them in certain ways. But my concern here is only with the former necessary but not sufficient element in conversion. Hence I write of the person who does practise a religion as 'the believer' and the one who does not as 'the non-believer'.
5. 'Not that the same method of instruction will be suitable in the case of all who approach the Word...the method of recovery must be adapted to the form of the disease...[It] is necessary to regard the opinions which the persons have taken up, and so frame your argument in accordance with the error into which each have fallen, by advancing in each discussion certain principles and reasonable propositions, that thus, through what is agreed on both sides, the truth may conclusively be brought to light. Should [your opponents] say there is no God, then, from the consideration of the skilful and wise economy of the Universe he will be brought to acknowledge that there is a certain overmastering power manifested through these channels.' – St Gregory of Nyssa, *The Great Catechism*, Prologue (trans. W. Moore and H.A. Wilson, in *Selected Writings of Gregory of Nyssa*, Parker and Co., Oxford, 1893).
6. *See* my *Existence of God*, Clarendon Press, revised edition, 1990 (and the short simplified version, *Is There a God?*, Oxford University Press, 1996).
7. In the Christian tradition God is 'three persons in one substance' – that is, three persons each of whom has the listed divine characteristics – the Son and the Spirit being eternally and necessarily caused to exist by the Father. Arguments to the existence of God are then best construed as arguments to the existence of God the Father, from which the existence of Son and Spirit follow – in my view by logical entailment. The simplicity of God which I consider in the text is the simplicity of God the Father – that a simple theory has complicated consequences does not make it any less simple. I ignore this complication in subsequent discussion, for the sake of ease of exposition. For my own developed account of the divine nature *see The Coherence of Theism*, Clarendon Press, revised editions, 1993; and *The Christian God*, Clarendon Press, 1994.
8. S. Kierkegaard, *Concluding Unscientific Postscript* (trans. H.V. and E.H. Hong), Princeton University Press, 1992, p. 11.
9. For reference to this objection of Kierkegaard both to natural theology and to historical arguments about the life and teaching of Jesus, and for a developed response both to this objection and to the previous Kierkegaardian objection, *see* Robert M. Adams, 'Kierkegaard's Arguments against Objective Reasoning in Religion', in his *The Virtue of Faith*, Oxford University Press, 1987.
10. I Corinthians 13.12.
11. Romans 8.24.
12. Genesis 1.27.
13. I devoted two and half chapters of *The Existence of God* to theodicy (pp. 152–60 and chs. 10 and 11), but feeling the need for more extensive treatment, have now written a full-length book on this – *Providence and the Problem of Evil*, Clarendon Press, 1998.
14. Mark Wynn, 'Some Reflections on Richard Swinburne's Argument from Design', *Religious Studies 29* (1993), 325–35. Wynn points out that I need to

make this kind of move in a different connection in order to defeat an earlier objection of Mackie.

15. A. Plantinga and N. Wolterstorff, *Faith and Rationality*, University of Notre Dame Press, 1983.

16. *See* Plantinga's general theory of epistemology in *Warrant: the Current Debate* and *Warrant and Proper Function*, Oxford University Press, 1993; and its applications to Christian belief, in *Warranted Christian Belief*, Oxford University Press, 2000.

17. *Warrant and Proper Function*, p. 194.

2

Philosophical Theology at the End of the Century

William J. Wainwright

Many writers have commented on the revival of philosophical theology that began in analytic circles in the 1960s. Those of us who received our training in the 50s were reacting to two things. First, our predecessors' preoccupation with the question of religious discourse's meaningfulness. While not necessarily disagreeing with Basil Mitchell's, say, or John Hick's responses to Antony Flew's charge of 'death by a thousand qualifications', most of us lost interest in the debate. Second, a conviction that Hume's and Kant's vaunted critiques of natural theology didn't withstand careful scrutiny. On the positive side, developments in modal logic, probability theory, and so on, offered tools for introducing a new clarity and rigour to traditional disputes. Alvin Plantinga's work on the ontological argument, or Richard Swinburne's use of Bayesian techniques to formulate his cumulative argument for God's existence, are paradigmatic examples.

I have no quarrel with the main outlines of Swinburne's account of this development. Indeed, his own work is an exemplary instance of it. I do, however, believe it is incomplete in five ways.

1

Swinburne doesn't comment on the renewed interest in the scholastics, and in seventeenth- and eighteenth-century philosophical theology. Swinburne's and Plantinga's work has been less visibly affected by this current. But Norman Kretzmann's and Eleonore Stump's work on Aquinas, Alfred Freddoso's and Thomas Flint's discussions of Molina, William Rowe's use of Samuel Clarke, or my own examinations of Jonathan Edwards are examples of an important strand in contemporary analytic philosophy of religion. In each case, analytic techniques are employed to recover the insights of our predecessors and apply them to contemporary problems.

These historical inquiries were partly motivated by the discovery that issues central to the debates of the 1960s and 70s had been already examined with a depth and sophistication sorely missing from most nineteenth- and early twentieth-century discussions of the same problems. Two examples will suffice. By the end of the 60s it was clear that reports of the death of the ontological argument had been greatly exaggerated. Charles Hartshorne and Norman Malcolm were suddenly not alone. A spate of articles appeared attacking and defending modal versions of the argument. Many were quite sophisticated. Yet an examination of, say, Henry More, would have shown that the authors of these articles were often reinventing the wheel. For an insistence on the superiority of modal versions of the argument and the importance of the possibility premise (that a perfect being is logically possible), perfect devil objections, and so on, are all found in More's *Antidote against Atheism*. More, however, is still not widely known among analytic philosophers of religion, and his most important points were independently made by contemporary philosophers of religion. Another example, though, illustrates how historical studies sometimes *advanced* contemporary discussions. Modern interest in the freedom–foreknowledge debate was largely reawakened by Nelson Pike's 'Divine Omniscience and Voluntary Action' which appeared in *The Philosophical Review* in 1965. Marilyn Adams proposed a solution to Pike's puzzle which she (correctly) claimed to have found in Ockham, and Ockhamist solutions continue to constitute one major response to the problem. Alvin Plantinga offered another solution which turned out to have been anticipated by Molina. Freddoso's and Flint's refinements of Molinism are another popular resolution of the dilemma. With the exception of the problem of evil, no other puzzle has so dominated journal literature in the past thirty years. It is therefore instructive that sophisticated reconstructions of Ockham and Molina[1] have played an important role in this debate.

Yet there is another and, I think, equally important reason for the renewed interest in our predecessors. A significant number of analytic philosophers of religion are practising Christian or Jewish theists. Aquinas, Ockham, Maimonides, Clarke, or Edwards are attractive models for these theists for two reasons. First, there is a broad similarity between their approaches to philosophy and that of our contemporaries; precise definitions, nice distinctions and rigorous arguments are features both of scholasticism and of analytic philosophy of religion. But, second, the work of these predecessors was self-consciously Jewish or Christian. A conviction of the truth and splendour of Judaism or Christianity pervades their work. They are thus appealing models for contemporary philosophical theologians with similar commitments.

2

Swinburne's characterization of the thrust of contemporary philosophical theology (including his own important work) is inadvertently misleading in at least one important respect. He focuses upon its attempt to defend two theses: (1) That the concept of God is coherent, and that (2) God so defined exists. These two concerns are, indeed, the thrust of Swinburne's own early work, and dominated discussion in the first fifteen or so years of the period we are examining. Nor has interest in these theses died out, or the last important word been said. (Recent work on the evidential problem of evil by Rowe, Paul Draper, William Alston, Peter Van Inwagen, and Swinburne himself are examples.) It is nonetheless true that the interests of philosophical theologians have broadened in a number of interrelated ways.

In the first place, the array of topics is much wider than an uninformed reader of Swinburne's paper might infer. Since the 1980s Christian philosophical theologians have turned their attention to such specifically Christian doctrines as the Trinity, the Incarnation, and the Atonement. The essays collected in *Philosophy and the Christian Faith* are one example.[2] Swinburne's own work on the Trinity and the Atonement is another.

In the second place, many of these philosophers wish to do more than defend the coherence and rational plausibility of the doctrines in question. They are interested in their bearing on problems internal to the traditions that include them. Thus, Marilyn Adams has argued that Christian philosophers should explore the implications of Christian martyrdom and Christ's passion for the problem of evil. In her view, suffering can be a means of participating in Christ, thereby providing the sufferer with insight into, and communion with, God's own inner life. Or consider Robert Oakes, who contends that Isaac Lucia's doctrine of God's tzimzum (withdrawal) casts light on the existence of evil.[3]

Finally, a number of these philosophical theologians are convinced that theistic doctrines can help solve problems in *other* areas of philosophy. For example, Del Ratzch has argued that if natural laws are regarded as expressions of God's settled intentions with respect to the natural world, that is, as descriptions of His habitual manner of acting, one can account for their subjunctive character (the fact that empirical laws aren't mere constant conjunctions, as Hume thought, but support appropriate counterfactuals). Christopher Menzel has attempted to show that numbers, sets, and other mathematical objects can be interpreted as products of God's mental activity, and that doing so illuminates them. Robert Adams and others think that a suitably nuanced divine command theory can do a better job of accommodating two apparently conflicting intuitions: that moral values exist in minds, and that morality can command our allegiance only if it expresses a deep fact about objective reality.

3

Swinburne's account of philosophical theology creates the (perhaps unintended) impression that its primary role is apologetic. Theistic proofs, arguments for the necessity of the Atonement, and so on, are addressed to non-believers, or to the non-believer in us (page 2). Yet if this *is* their main purpose, their value is limited, and this for two reasons.

(1) Apologetic philosophical theology flourished in the early modern period. One thinks of the Boyle lectures, for example, or of the work of Samuel Clarke or William Paley. By the end of the eighteenth century, however, apologetic arguments had lost much of their power to persuade educated audiences. Those who (like Coleridge and Schleiermacher) wished to commend religion to its 'cultured despisers' adopted new approaches. Their repudiation of philosophical theology was no doubt partly due to bad philosophy. (Kant's critiques of the traditional theistic proofs, for instance, aren't clearly cogent.) It was also the result of a zeitgeist which extolled sentiment and feeling and denigrated 'mere ratiocination'. But whatever the causes, the fact is that the arguments of philosophical theology no longer produced widespread conviction in most university-educated audiences (that is, in the very people who, by education and training were, one would think, best qualified to evaluate them). They thereby lost a large part of their effectiveness as apologetic tools. Whether they have regained it seems doubtful. (Note that this is *not* an argument against employing philosophical theology as an apologetic tool. Rational arguments may persuade some, strengthen the conviction of others, and convince non-believers that theistic belief is not irrational.)

(2) A second reason for thinking that philosophical theology's apologetic value is limited is that it can't produce *faith*.[4] Let me approach this point by commenting on two observations of Swinburne's. He

responds to the charge that cogent theistic arguments would only persuade 'a prudent person [to] try to do what is good out of self-interest', by asserting that the good, while probable, isn't certain, and 'the prudence of seeking such a good despite risk of failure, is virtuous' (page 9). Jonathan Edwards, however, thought that prudence or enlightened self-interest, like natural pity, *isn't* itself virtuous although its absence is a symptom of vice.[5] Charity, or true benevolence, is alone truly virtuous.[6] Or consider Pascal who believed that a commitment based on prudence alone has no intrinsic *religious* value even though it *can* lead to action which produces genuine faith. Properly formed religious beliefs are expressions of a heart transformed by God's love. Prudential calculations may induce people to place themselves in positions where God will stir their affections, but they can't do more than this. I believe that this is correct, and that what is true of prudential arguments is also true of the apologetic arguments of philosophical theology. They can break down resistance to faith, and even produce belief.[7] But they *can't* produce the theological virtue of faith. Why not?

Consider a second comment of Swinburne's: 'Religion' doesn't 'require more by way of belief' than 'an uncertain belief open to revision' (page 9). Notice, though, that this is at variance with both Aquinas's and Calvin's insistence on faith's certainty. Thus, Calvin says that 'faith is not contented with a dubious and fickle opinion.... The certainty which it requires must be full and decisive.'[8] Aquinas is more careful. Even though faith is certain with respect to its object or cause, it is not fully certain with respect to its subject. 'Faith may accordingly be said to be greater in one man than another either when there is greater certainty and firmness on the part of the intellect, or when there is greater readiness, devotion, or confidence on the part of the will.'[9] But Aquinas, too, clearly thinks that either a lack of readiness, devotion, or confidence on the part of the will *or* a lack of certainty and firmness on the part of the intellect are theological vices. Merely probable opinion isn't sufficient.

Now, *pace* Aquinas, this certainty and firmness can't be produced by philosophical proofs. Calvin thought that 'without the illumination of the Spirit, the word has no effect'.[10] He would say the same, I think, of natural theology.[11] My point, again, is not that philosophical theology is useless but that its value is limited. A probabilistic conviction that God exists, has certain attributes, and has acted in certain ways, isn't what the tradition has meant by the intellectual component of faith. Faith involves a *firm assurance* of God's goodness and favour towards us, and this isn't produced by philosophical theology.[12]

4

Theistic arguments can be used apologetically but other purposes may be more important. For example, theistic proofs are sometimes used to settle disputes within a common tradition. Udayana's theistic arguments were not only addressed to fellow devotees of Siva but to Mimamsakas in his own Hindu tradition who interpreted the Vedas atheistically. Again, al-Ghazali employed a version of the Kalam cosmological argument to show that Averroes' and Avicenna's interpretation of the Quran was heretical.[13]

But philosophical theology is also employed devotionally. Thus, Udayana's Nyayakusumanjali (which can be roughly translated as a bouquet of arguments offered to God) has three purposes – to convince unbelievers, to strengthen the faithful, *but also to please Siva* 'by presenting it as an offering at his footstool'. Regardless of the success Udayana's arguments may or may not have had in achieving his first two goals, they have value as a gift offered to God; their construction and presentation is an act of worship. Nor is that fact that Anselm's *Proslogion* is cast in the form of a prayer accidental.[14] His inquiry is a divine–human collaboration in which he continually prays for assistance, and offers praise and thanksgiving for the light he receives. Anselm's project as a whole is framed by a desire to 'contemplate God' or 'see God's face'. His attempt to understand what he believes by finding reasons for it is simply a *means* to this end.

Swinburne wonders 'why so much energy was put into the project of philosophical theology in the medieval west when we might suppose that there was no more [and perhaps less] need of it than in earlier centuries'. He suggests that the answer may be that the medievals were 'providing tools to deal with' the 'bit of sophisticated atheist in most believers' (page 2). I suspect, however, that the answer is quite different, namely, that medieval philosophical theology wasn't primarily apologetic in intent[15] but was, instead, a tool for settling intramural disputes,[16] and (most importantly) furthering the project of contemplation by helping the faithful understand what they formerly only believed. The fact that philosophical theology seems to flourish best in ages of faith suggests that that project may be its primary purpose.

5

The medieval project (inquiry as a means to contemplation) has another feature that is especially prominent in Augustine and Anselm.

Emotional and volitional discipline are as necessary for its success as intellectual discipline. Anselm's inquiry, for instance, is punctuated by prayers to arouse his emotions and stir his will. And this brings me to the last way in which I think Swinburne's picture of contemporary philosophical theism is incomplete. It pays insufficient attention to the bearing on philosophical theology of the epistemological turn in the analytic philosophy of religion. Reformed epistemology's defence of the proper basicality of theistic belief isn't the whole story. Linda Zagzebski maintains that warranted beliefs are expressions of virtues. C. Stephen Evans and Jay Wood suggest that faith may be a necessary condition for appreciating certain reasons for religious belief. I have argued that a properly disposed heart may be needed to appreciate the force of the evidence for theistic belief. *Reason and the Heart* discusses Jonathan Edwards', John Henry Newman's, and William James's reasons for thinking that it is. Pascal, I think, had a similar view. Pascal believed that Christianity provides the best explanation of humanity's 'greatness' and 'littleness', its wretchedness, and the ambiguity of the theistic evidence. He also thought that there are good arguments from traces of design, saintly lives, and the (apparent) occurrence of miracles and fulfilled prophecy. This evidence is offset by instances of apparent disorder, evil or wasted lives, and reasons for distrusting miracle reports and prophetic claims, and so won't convince everyone. Nevertheless, it *is* sufficient to convince those who seek God or 'have the living faith in their hearts'.[17]

I will not repeat the arguments of my book here but simply note two relevant claims. First, what James called our 'passional nature' unavoidably inflects our assessment of complicated bodies of evidence for ethical, metaphysical, and religious propositions.[18] Since we can't escape its influence, claims to have dispassionately surveyed the evidence for propositions like these are illusory.[19] Second, views like Edwards's or Newman's or James's or Pascal's may be the only effective way of defusing relativism. If there really are ethical, metaphysical, and religious facts, and we have the ability to discern them, lack of progress and persistent disagreement between equally sophisticated and well-disposed inquirers[20] is surprising. In the absence of an explanation that is consistent with the objectivity of truth and the reliability of our epistemic faculties, relativistic conclusions seem called for. Views like Pascal's or Edwards's provide such an explanation. If certain dispositions of the heart are needed to reason rightly about religious matters, then deep disagreements are likely even if the relevant truths are objective and our epistemic faculties are reliable when functioning as they should.

For some will possess the appropriate dispositions and others will not. So in the absence of a better explanation, non-relativists have a powerful motive for thinking that some theory of this type is true. The view I have just described is both similar and dissimilar to evidentialist projects like Swinburne's and to Reformed epistemology (or, in any case, to Plantinga's version of it). It is dissimilar to the first because it denies that arguments like Swinburne's are sufficient to persuade all fair-minded inquirers who have the necessary information and intellectual equipment.[21] It is dissimilar to the second in its insistence that the properly formed religious beliefs of mature adults are typically based on evidence (albeit of an informal kind).[22] My intention here, however, is not to defend these views but to call attention to the fact that the epistemological investigations of contemporary analytic philosophers of religion have a direct bearing on the enterprise of philosophical theology. If they are right, an adequate account of its persuasiveness or lack thereof must pay due heed to the heart.

Let me conclude with the point with which I began. I have no quarrel with the vast majority of what Swinburne has said. He has accurately described the thrust of much contemporary philosophical theology, and his own work is an exemplary instance of it. I think, however, that the contemporary scene is richer than his remarks might lead the uninitiated to believe. I have attempted to explain why.

Notes

1. As well as of Aquinas and Jonathan Edwards.
2. Thomas V. Morris (ed.), *Philosophy and the Christian Faith* (Notre Dame, IN: University of Notre Dame Press, 1988).
3. 'Creation as Theodicy: a Defense of a Kabbalistic Approach to Evil', *Faith and Philosophy* 14 (October 1997); 510–21.
4. For Swinburne on faith *see* his *Faith and Reason* (Oxford: Clarendon Press, 1981).
5. Vicious passions can blind us to our true interests just as they can sometimes stifle pity.
6. Edwards more or less makes this point in *The Nature of True Virtue*, in Paul Ramsey (ed.), *Ethical Writings*, Works of Jonathan Edwards, vol. 8 (New Haven: Yale University Press, 1989), ch. 7.
7. Or, perhaps more accurately, a belief that God's existence, say, or Christian theism is more likely than not.
8. *Institutes of the Christian Religion* (Grand Rapids: Eerdman's, 1957), Book iii, ch. ii, no. 15.

9. *Summa Theologica*, 22ae, Q. 4, A. 8, and Q. 5, A. 4.
10. *Institutes*, Book iii, ch. ii, no. 33.
11. And even Aquinas's opinion on this point is more complicated than these remarks suggest. He says, for example, that miracles and other external signs aren't sufficient to induce belief 'for of those who see one and the same miracle, or hear the same prophecy, some will believe and others will not believe. We must therefore recognize that there is an inward cause which moves a man from within to assent to the things of faith,' 'God, who moves us inwardly by grace'. (ST 22ae, Q. 6, a. 1.) Aquinas thought that philosophical theology was a science whose results were demonstrably certain. Swinburne and I (and, I daresay, most contemporary philosophical theologians) think its results are only probable. We also recognize that many of our epistemic peers find our arguments unpersuasive. Shouldn't we conclude, then, that people's relation to the theistic evidence is very much like their relation to miracles and other external signs in Aquinas's view?
12. *See* Calvin, *Institutes*, Book iii, ch. ii, nos 15–16. Cf. Aquinas's claim that faith is 'an act of the intellect as directed to one object by the will' (ST 22ae, Q. 4, a. 1). The intellect assents because the will deems it good to do so. So Aquinas also thinks that faith involves a response to God as one's good.
13. The philosophers argued that the world was eternal, and that texts like Sura 10 ('Surely your Lord is God who created heavens and the earth in six days') should be interpreted in a way consistent with that fact. Given the Aristotelian framework within which the philosophers were working, however, eternity and necessity are coextensive. So if God eternally creates the world, He necessarily creates it, and hence doesn't freely choose it. A God without free will, though, isn't a personal agent and so isn't the God of theism. For my remarks on Udayana and al-Ghazali I am indebted to John Clayton, 'Religions, Reasons, and Gods', *Religious Studies* 23 (1987): 1–17 and 'Piety and the Proofs', *Religious Studies* 26 (1990): 19–42.
14. *See*, for example, Karl Barth, *Anselm: Fides Quaerens Intellectum* (Richmond, VA: John Knox Press, 1960); and Marilyn Adams, 'Praying the *Proslogion*', in Thomas Senor (ed.), *The Rationality of Belief and the Plurality of Faith* (Ithaca: Cornell University Press, 1995).
15. Although it sometimes was. Thomas's *Summa Contra Gentiles* is partly directed towards Muslims and Anselm's *Monologion* is addressed to the 'ignorant' as well as to his fellow monks.
16. Over the nature of God's foreknowledge, for example, or the Atonement. Cf. The disputes between Thomists and Ockhamists over foreknowledge, or between Abelard and other medieval theologians over the nature of the Atonement.
17. *Pensées* 242. For more on Pascal, see my *Philosophy of Religion*, 2nd ed. (Belmont, CA: Wadsworth Publishing Co., 1998), ch. 6. See also Daniel Clifford Fouke, 'Argument in Pascal's *Pensées*', *History of Philosophy Quarterly* 6 (1989): 57–68.
18. And not only for these propositions. In my view, our passional nature affects almost all cumulative case reasoning.
19. Although, of course, we *can* (and should) eliminate obvious prejudice, be open to new evidence and responsive to criticism, cultivate a sense of our own fallibility, and so on.

20. That is, between equally intelligent and well-informed inquirers who are equipped by training to deal with the relevant issues, and who display all the standard intellectual virtues (intellectual honesty, openness to criticism, even-handed treatment of the relevant evidence, and so on).

21. Unless I misunderstand him, Swinburne thinks that dispositions of the heart are, at best, only accidentally necessary to the success of the evidentialist project. Accidentally necessary because, in particular cases, they may play a causal role in eliminating prejudice, hostility to criticism, and other standard intellectual vices. In my view, dispositions of the heart are essential.

22. In my opinion, properly formed religious beliefs typically rest on inchoate arguments of some complexity (and, in particular, on inferences to the best explanation). Usually, however, these arguments aren't carefully articulated. The virtue of philosophical arguments like Paley's or Swinburne's is to make these more or less inarticulate arguments explicit, and to defend them against objections. My position on this issue has a certain similarity to Jacques Maritain's. Maritain argues that Aquinas's five ways are a 'development and unfolding' of a natural knowledge of God which consists of an intuition of being, and a 'prompt, spontaneous reasoning' that is 'more or less involved in it'. (*Approaches to God* (New York: Collier Books, 1962), ch. 1.) This view differs from Plantinga's. Plantinga concedes that there is little difference between himself and those who think that theistic belief is the product of inferences from the glories of nature, the promptings of conscience, and so on *when those inferences are spontaneous, compelling, and direct in the sense of involving few or no intermediate steps*. In my view (and I think also Maritain's), mature religious beliefs *may* be (more or less) spontaneous and compelling. But they are neither properly basic *nor* the result of simple immediate inferences of the sort Plantinga describes. On the contrary. Although the inferences may be implicit, and not fully articulate, they typically involve assessments of rather complex bodies of evidence.

3
Voices in Discussion

D.Z. Phillips

A: We need impartial criteria by which to assess evidence for the truth of the proposition 'There is a God'. This evidence needs to be spelled out. I take myself to be addressing a belief held by Christians, Jews and Muslims. We need religion to be rational.

People come to religious belief in various ways. Some come to it through a religious experience. Others believe on the authority of the wise men in their community. These are perfectly natural ways of coming to believe. But they are less available than they once were. There are conflicting authorities and many have not had religious experiences. In any case, logically prior to these is a claim that certain propositions are true. How is this claim to be defended by an appeal to impartial reason? There are three ways of doing so. The first of these is the ontological argument according to which the statement 'There is no God' is self-contradictory. Since the statement is clearly coherent, this argument makes an impossible claim. The second argument is from the world to God, but one which claims to be deductive. Aquinas argues that from the fact that the world has certain features, it follows, deductively, that it was created by God. But since it is clearly possible that the world was not created by God, I cannot see that this argument works either. I therefore prefer a third kind of argument from the world to God which is inferential in character, but which is an inductive argument. I think it is an argument which appeals to ordinary people when they are impressed by the ordinary world as a marvellous place.

The effect of the evidence is cumulative. Various kinds of evidence vary in strength. It is not an all-or-nothing affair. We will be satisfied with a probability of more than a half.

Let me take but one example – natural laws. Why is there such a conformity? We must ask questions like: Would you expect a phenomenon such as this if there were no God? If God is all-powerful wouldn't you expect to find order in the world? Order is a beautiful thing. Of course, human beings have choices. They can make bombs to destroy people, or grow plants to nourish them. But without order that very choice makes no sense. If there is no God you have no reason for thinking why the world is as it is. My suggestion is that when you consider this question then, as in science, you should go for the simplest explanation. I have made use of Bayes's theorem to show that probability is on the side of the theistic explanation. I believe this captures what ordinary people feel when they look at the heavens and feel that this is the work of a personal designer.

Some people have said that whereas I only offer probability, faith demands certainty. Such certainty would be nice, but many are not so blessed. So in practice, less than certainty is perfectly adequate. Live on the assumption that theism is true.

Others have said that what I do is too complicated, but all I am doing is giving a defence of a basic faith in face of the objections of others against it.

B: I am in substantial agreement with *A*. I think that evidentialism is a good project. Its arguments are generally persuasive and formulate, in more precise forms, arguments which ordinary believers employ. So I do not think that *A* is wrong, but incomplete. Let me note, therefore, five ways in which I diverge from *A*.

First, I am sceptical about the extent to which *A*'s kind of argument is effective with educated audiences today. Second, I do not think that these arguments produce faith. As Aquinas, Calvin, Kierkegaard and others have pointed out, certainty is a feature of faith. Jonathan Edwards and the Puritans distinguished between historical faith , simply believing certain propositions about God, and faith as a gift of grace. In this respect, I am more Augustinian and *A* is more Pelagian. Third, arguments were used to settle intra-mural religious disputes. This would be a case of trying to understand what is already believed. Fourth, *A* does not emphasize, as Edwards did, the importance of a properly disposed heart in assessing evidence which is, admittedly, public. These arguments concern antecedent probabilities which enable one to demand less evidence than one would do otherwise.

The question of how we make these antecedent judgements and of how they relate to the evidence is a complicated one, but it is not a new issue. I believe it is present in Plato's 'Seventh Letter' in the emphasis there on the importance of character and love of justice in judgements. I think it is also involved in Aristotle's account of moral reasoning. The task is to extend these insights to other fields. These issues are clearly important in historical judgements; for example, in what one thinks of the behaviour of the Commune in Paris after the Revolution.

Fifth, a point I did not mention in my paper. There is some sign of philosophers applying their analytic skills to non-theistic religions. These religions offer competing examples of the facts of human experience. I believe it is incumbent on us to give the same attention to these large competing world-views.

C: May I, at the opening of this first session, press *A* and *B* on their philosophical methods? They are both happy with philosophy of religion having an apologetic function. They are concerned with the truth of the proposition 'There is a God'. But there is a contemplative tradition in philosophy which is concerned with the sense of things. Until we know the sense of a proposition we do not know how to go about assessing its truth or falsity. But it will be concerned with the nature of 'truth' and what disagreements look like. I have difficulty with the accounts *A* and *B* have given of disagreement between believers and unbelievers. *A* tells us that it is a difference in the assessment of probabilities. For some scientists, for example, it is probable that the laws of nature testify to a designer, while for others it is not. But isn't that itself an improbable account of disagreement? Scientists, who trade in hypotheses and probabilities, who have been trained to do so, fail to agree about the probability of belief in God even when confronted by the same evidence.

Now *B* has an explanation for this or, at least, is attracted by one. The faculties of unbelievers aren't working properly. Locke said something similar to explain the limitations in our knowledge, but Berkeley responded by denying this. He said that we first throw up a dust and then complain we cannot see. The fault is in our own conceptual confusions. I think this of the analogy with faulty faculties. In the case of eyesight, it is essential that the norm of normal eyesight is agreed on. Thus, those who are colour-blind, or who have faulty eyesight acknowledge these defects themselves. But this is not so in the religious context. The circularity in *B*'s argument shows that the analogy doesn't work. It looks as though we are offered an explanation: people don't believe in God because their faculties are not functioning properly. What do we mean by 'not functioning properly'? That they don't believe. Further, *B* has to account for the fact that there have been philosophers who have seen sense in religious belief who are *not* believers. On *B*'s view, how is this possible? How do you respond to these methodological points?

A: I do want to say that the unbeliever is wrong. What stands in the way of his agreeing with the believer? First, there is an obstacle in that people do not like what religion asks of them, the way of life it demands, and so they resist the probability which the evidence shows. So they aren't fully rational when they do this.

Second, as I have said, people in some societies come to believe by deferring to wise men. This is true of our age where people defer too soon to scientific opinion deemed to be wise. But these people may be biased and so people are led astray in following them.

Third, let us not forget that disagreement about hypotheses occurs within science itself. In the case of religious belief the matter is not obvious and involves us in metaphysical speculation.

B: I think we must own up to the danger of intellectual phariseeism, and be aware of the sinfulness of our own epistemic faculties. We can blind ourselves to things and fall foul of self-deception.

We must also acknowledge that in our religious critique we are going to appeal to metaphysical considerations. We must admit that we are faced with a multitude of stories which interpret the facts – metaphysical world-views. Of course we have to pay attention to evidence, but we will always need to interpret it according to some world-view.

D: I am no friend of the ontological argument, but I think *A* is too hasty in his dismissal of it. Things can seem coherent when they are not. So although 'There is no God' may seem coherent, it may not be.

A: But I think 'There is no God' is obviously coherent.

E: Ontological arguments differ. Instead of dealing with logically necessary truths in the abstract, Anselm is trying to bring out certain features of the concept of God. He starts with that concept rather than arguing to a logically necessary truth.

A: But the concept he starts with is of a being whose existence is logically necessary.

F: So the God you arrive at by inferred probabilities is a different conception from that of Anselm?

A: Yes, he has the notion of a logically necessary being.

F: I think you are leaving out the religious significance of what Anselm is wrestling with – 'that than which none greater can be conceived'. This significance has been explored by thinkers like Levinas and J.-L. Marion. In analytic hands, the ontological argument has become a shadow of its historical self. It has been divorced from its religious framework.

A: I don't deny Anselm's religious concerns. I am objecting to the way he spelled them out.

G: *A*, what is the religious import of your project? We need to know this probability, you say, in order for belief to be rational. It is supposed to help, but what does it help?

A: Religion asks us to live in a certain way; it demands much of us. So we need reasons to think that the practice of religion is worthwhile. The more evidence we have the better. How much we need depends on circumstances, but I've suggested that over fifty per cent probability is enough.

G: Again, I ask: 'enough for what'? What were believers doing before they had your arguments to rely on?

A: I didn't give them any new arguments. I simply knocked the ones they already had into shape. I referred to Gregory of Nyssa in this respect.

H: I want to ask the same question as *G*. Anselm is explicating a faith he had already. And your last response to *G* might suggest a similar position. But your project makes a far stronger claim. It purports to start from a neutral starting-point.

A: Where you start depends on the times and the state of the people.

I: One of the differences in our time is the plurality of plausibility-structures. So people have searched for a critical and evaluative science. How is that going to come from the analytic context?

J: For example, how is *A*'s appeal to simplicity supposed to work?

K: And even if the probability of a first cause is established, what would that have to do with religion?

B: I don't think it is just an appeal to simplicity. *J* is right to question that. In large-scale metaphysical disputes criteria only work for those who hold the metaphysical view in question. I confess to not being so interested in the plausibility structures that *I* refers to, but I am interested in *F*'s point about the relation of world-views or interpretations to the facts of human existence.

L: That is an issue which can be raised in connection with all sorts of reasoning, not simply religion. Sensitivity to context is important.

M: In that connection, I don't think Aquinas was so much concerned with proofs as with a theological science where first principles can be used as principles of interpretation.

A: I certainly do not want to deny the importance of sensitivity. It is an essential factor in being led in one direction by the data and not others; for example, in being led to Christianity and not to some other religion. On the other hand, despite the importance of contexts, remember that the one I appeal to is universal – our involvement in the universe and the desire to know how it came about.

H: But could a believer be atheistic with respect to theism?

A: I don't see how he could.

C: I think he means 'atheistic' in the sense of denying the methods of philosophical theism.

A: As I have said, you can believe on the basis of authority. But in the absence of authority, or faced by conflicting authorities, we must have reasons for embracing religious belief.

The point of religion is getting right with God. But this would have no point if you did not believe that there is a God. You could have that belief without any religious practice, but, nevertheless, in answer to *K*, I do believe that that belief in God as a first cause is the same as that held by ordinary believers in their religious practice.

Part II
Reformed Epistemology

4
Reformed Epistemology

Nicholas Wolterstorff

The assigned task of Professor Wykstra and myself is to state what we regard as the most serious objections to Reformed Epistemology, and then to assess whether, in our judgement, those objections have been adequately met. It is our judgement, however, that so many objections to Reformed Epistemology have been based on misunderstandings that it is necessary, before we take up the assigned task, to explain what Reformed Epistemology is. Accordingly, our papers will not take the form of presentation and response but rather the form of joint presentation: I will deal mainly with the nature of Reformed Epistemology, although along the way I will deal with certain objections, and Professor Wykstra will deal mainly with objections, although along the way he will say something about the nature.

One might articulate the nature of Reformed Epistemology in purely systematic fashion. On this occasion I instead propose doing so within a narrative context. I have rather often been asked what led to the emergence of Reformed Epistemology. I propose interweaving an articulation of the nature of Reformed Epistemology with a narrative of its origins. Historians have a big advantage over philosophers in that, whereas they always have stories to tell, philosophers only now and then can tell stories. People love stories. Best then for philosophers to tell stories when they can. But my reason for interweaving narrative with analysis is not just that this will add spice to the discussion. I think one understands better the nature of Reformed Epistemology if one also understands its significance; and the best way to understand its significance is within the context of an account of its origins. Accordingly, I propose introducing my discussion with an account of the origins, the nature, and the significance of Reformed Epistemology.

Reformed Epistemology made its full appearance on the philosophical scene with the publication in 1983 of the collection *Faith and Rationality*, subtitled *Reason and Belief in God*, edited by Alvin Plantinga and myself.[1] For a good many years Plantinga and I had been teaching together in the philosophy department at Calvin College. We had known each other since the time when we were students together at Calvin, in the early 1950s. Around the mid-70s, Calvin began what it called The Calvin Center for Christian Scholarship. The Center continues to this day; and has by now acquired a very distinguished history in the promotion of Christian scholarship. In its early years, the principal activity of the Center consisted of adopting a topic for study each year, and then assembling a team composed of a few Calvin faculty members, along with a few faculty members from other institutions, to spend the year working on the topic, free of teaching responsibilities. Each year a few Calvin students were also part of the team.

The topic for the year 1979–80 was 'Toward a Reformed View of Faith and Reason'. Senior fellows for the year who were drawn from the Calvin faculty included Plantinga and myself (along with George Marsden from history, Robert Manweiler from physics, and David Holwerda from biblical studies). During the second semester, George Mavrodes, from the University of Michigan, joined us as a senior fellow. And throughout the year, William P. Alston, then at the University of Illinois, and Henk Hart, from the Institute of Christian Studies in Toronto, were adjunct senior fellows who rather frequently dropped in for discussions. The volume, *Faith and Rationality*, emerged from the work of the fellows during that year.

Above, I described the publication of *Faith and Rationality* as marking the 'full appearance' of Reformed Epistemology on the philosophical scene. I meant thereby to suggest that earlier there had been an appearance which was somewhat less than full. Or to put it in terms of 'stages': the publication of *Faith and Rationality* constituted the second stage in the development of Reformed Epistemology. The first stage came in two parts. One part consisted of some essays published by Plantinga in the late 1970s and early 80s – in particular, 'Is Belief in God Properly Basic?'[2] The other consisted of a small book of mine, *Reason within the Bounds of Religion*, published in 1976.[3]

Behind each of these there was, in turn, a pre-history. The pre-history of Plantinga's essay, 'Is Belief in God Properly Basic?' was his 1967 book, *God and Other Minds*, subtitled, *A Study of the Rational Justification of Belief in God*.[4] The pre-history of my own book, *Reason within the Bounds of Religion*, was an essay published in 1964, 'Faith and Philosophy'.[5]

Why do I say that these belong to the 'pre-history' of Reformed Episte-mology, rather than that they constitute the first stage in its history proper? Essential to Reformed Epistemology is the explicit rejection of classical foundationalism, and of the evidentialist objection to religious belief (realistically understood) which is implied by classical foundation-alism. But in Plantinga's book *God and Other Minds*, and in my essay 'Faith and Philosophy', there was no explicit recognition of classical foundationalism, and hence no explicit rejection of it. Neither Plantinga nor I had yet identified classical foundationalism as such; neither of us had yet formed the concept.

In that regard, we were not unusual. It was only later that meta-epistemology became a matter of serious interest to philosophers; and only when it did become a matter of serious interest, sometime in the 70s, was classical foundationalism identified as one distinct style of epistemology. Of course, classical foundationalism itself had been around for centuries; what was absent, until the 1970s, was a clear recognition of its nature, and a clear recognition of the fact that it was but one of many options for epistemological theory.

It was the emergence of meta-epistemology, and the conceptualizing of classical foundationalism which accompanied that emergence – indeed, which that emergence made possible – it was that emergence and that conceptualizing which made Reformed Epistemology possible. The explicit use of the concept of classical foundationalism (sometimes just called 'foundationalism') is what separates the first stage in the devel-opment of Reformed Epistemology from its pre-history.

To say that the first stage of Reformed Epistemology had a pre-history in some earlier writings of Plantinga and myself is of course to suggest some sort of continuity between the pre-history and the first stage. (I should state here, lest there be any misunderstanding, that there is in turn a long pre-history behind those early writings of Plantinga and myself.) What was that continuity? When a clear recognition of classical foundationalism, for what it is, appeared on the philosophical scene, by no means did everybody thinking about the epistemology of religious belief immediately become a Reformed Epistemologist. Why then did Reformed Epistemology emerge where it did?

Plantinga and I, from the time of our student days at Calvin College, had been profoundly shaped by a movement within the Reformed-Presbyterian tradition of Christianity; namely, the Dutch neo-Calvinist movement of the late nineteenth century, of which the great formative figure was the Dutch theologian, journalist, and statesman, Abraham Kuyper. Our most influential college teachers were all 'Kuyperians'.

Faith seeking understanding was the motto held up before us as guide and challenge for the Christian intellectual. The motto comes of course from Augustine, who in turn took it from Clement of Alexandria. I now know that the way we were taught to understand it was not, however, the way Augustine meant it. What Augustine meant was that the Christian intellectual seeks to understand those very things that already he or she believes. What we were taught to understand by the motto is that it is the calling of the Christian intellectual to conduct all of his or her inquiries in the light of faith. Not to move from *believing*, say, the doctrine of divine simplicity, to *understanding* that very same doctrine – that would fit the Augustinian understanding of the motto – but to develop history, sociology, philosophy, political theory, and so forth, in the light of faith.

A striking feature of this way of seeing the challenge facing the Christian scholar and intellectual is that nothing at all is said about the need to develop arguments for one's religious beliefs. The discussions concerning faith and reason which have preoccupied the church down through the centuries can pretty much all be classified as either discussions concerning the proper role of reason in faith or as discussions concerning the proper role of faith in one's reasoning. In the Dutch neo-Calvinist tradition, the attention was all on the latter. But that, of course, implied something concerning the former. To urge that faith seek understanding, while paying no attention at all to arguments for the existence of God, to arguments for the reliability of Scripture, and so forth, was to take for granted that the evidentialist challenge to religious belief (more about this shortly) does not have to be met. It was to take for granted that the fundamentals of faith do not typically need the support of reasoning, of argumentation, for faith to be acceptable. Plantinga, in his essay in *Faith and Rationality*, cites passages from the Dutch neo-Calvinist theologian Herman Bavinck which say exactly that.

In short, it would only be a slight exaggeration to say that Reformed Epistemology is a development that was destined to occur among philosophers within the neo-Calvinist tradition once the concept of classical foundationalism became clearly articulated.

So what then is Reformed Epistemology? It will be helpful to distinguish between Reformed Epistemology *narrowly understood*, and Reformed Epistemology *broadly understood*. Let me here describe the former; later I will explain what I have in mind by 'Reformed Epistemology broadly understood'. A preliminary observation is in order. Beliefs have a number of distinct truth-relevant merits: warranted, reliably formed, known, entitled, apt for inclusion in science, and so forth. Until rather recently, twentieth-century epistemology in the analytic tradition was conducted as if there were just two truth-relevant merits: justification, or rationality, plus knowledge, this latter being understood as what resulted when one added truth to a justifiably or rationally held belief (alternatively: what resulted when one added truth plus some Gettier-coping property). The main disputes were understood as being disputes concerning the correct analysis of justification, or rationality. Though I won't here take time to argue the point, the situation seems to me clearly instead to be that philosophers have implicitly been discussing a number of distinct, though related, merits. The relevance of this point concerning the multiplicity of doxastic merits for our purposes here is that, strictly speaking, we ought not to speak of Reformed Epistemology *tout court*, but of Reformed Epistemology concerning warrant, of Reformed Epistemology concerning entitlement, and so on. At the beginning, however, this point, about the plurality of doxastic merits, was not recognized; Reformed epistemologists spoke almost exclusively about rationality.

I can now explain what I take Reformed Epistemology, narrowly understood, to be. In the Enlightenment there emerged the ideal of a *rationally grounded* religion, the two great proponents of this ideal being John Locke and Immanuel Kant. Religion as it comes, so it was said, is not satisfactory; what it lacks is rational grounding. In Locke, it's clear that *the individual believer* is regarded as believing *irresponsibly* unless his religious beliefs are all rationally grounded; in Kant, it remains unclear how exactly the individual believer must be related to the ideal of rational grounding.

Reformed epistemology is the repudiation of this Enlightenment ideal of rationally grounded religion. Let it be said as emphatically as possible that Reformed epistemologists did not repudiate the demands of rationality (and now, after the recognition of the diversity of doxastic merits, do not repudiate the worth and the demands of warrant, entitlement, and so on). What they repudiated was the claim that, for a person's religious beliefs to be rational – in particular, for their beliefs about God to be rational – those beliefs must in their totality be rationally grounded. *Rationality is not to be equated with rational grounding.* The way the Reformed epistemologists made this point was to insist that some religious beliefs are rational even though they are held *immediately*. To say that a person holds some belief *immediately* is to say that the belief is not held on the basis of other propositions that the person believes, those other propositions functioning then as *reasons* for the person's beliefs.

Notice that Reformed Epistemology does not say that every immediate belief about God held by anybody whatsoever possesses the merit under consideration. The claim is the much more guarded claim that *some* of the immediate beliefs about God held by *some* persons possess that merit. In fact the Reformed Epistemologist is of the view that for every doxastic merit, there will surely be some persons who hold some immediate beliefs about God which lack that merit. In some such cases, the person will have *defeaters* for the belief – that is to say: there will be something in the person or the person's situation such that, given that factor or situation, if the person were functioning properly, he or she would not hold that belief immediately. The defeater, in some cases, will be a belief of the person which is a *reason* against the belief about God in question. Thus, contrary to what has sometimes been said, Reformed Epistemology is most certainly not a species of religious dogmatism.

Furthermore, the character or situation of many persons is no doubt such that for some proposition about God and some doxastic merit, their belief of that proposition could not possess the merit in question without being held for (good) reasons. For some doxastic merits and some propositions about God it may even be the case that no one could believe those propositions immediately and their belief possess that merit. And even when a person's immediate belief about God possesses the merit in question, the Reformed Epistemologist will normally not see anything wrong in the person *also* holding that belief for reasons. Reformed Epistemology is most definitely not opposed to offering reasons for one's religious beliefs. The Reformed Epistemologist is not even opposed to all forms of what might be called 'natural theology'. But if someone claims that natural theological arguments are *necessary* for any belief in God to possess some doxastic merit or other, then the suspicions of the Reformed epistemologist will be ineluctably aroused.

Be it noted that Reformed Epistemology, narrowly understood, is an epistemological claim – as indeed the name suggests. Reformed Epistemology has sometimes been criticized for its failure to give an account of the nature of religious belief and of the role of religious beliefs in our lives. Alternatively, it has sometimes been understood as aiming to give such an account and then been criticized for giving a woefully inadequate account. One finds this latter criticism (perhaps also the former) in D.Z. Phillips's book, *Faith after Foundationalism*.[6] How much more adequate, exclaims Phillips, is the account of the role in life of religious language and belief which is to be found in Wittgenstein and his followers. The 'elucidation of religious concepts, giving a perspicuous representation of them in their natural contexts, is neglected in favour of the stark assertion of a believer's right to place belief in God among his foundational beliefs,' says Phillips.[7]

But Reformed Epistemology – and it makes no difference now whether we understand it narrowly or broadly – Reformed Epistemology never intended to be anything other than epistemology. It never aimed at giving an account of the nature of religious language and belief; it never aimed at describing the role of religious language and belief in the life of the religious person. It is, and always intended to be, a contribution to epistemology. (Though in many places one finds Reformed epistemologists making remarks about role – for example, in my introduction to *Faith and Philosophy*.)

The mention of Phillips's *Faith after Foundationalism* leads me to mention another, connected, misunderstanding which inhabits the first part of that book. In stating the core thesis of Reformed Epistemology, narrowly understood, I spoke of a belief which a person holds *immediately*. Call such a belief, an *immediate belief*. Plantinga, by contrast, has usually used the term 'basic belief', rather than 'immediate belief'. And whereas I have said that we must distinguish between Reformed Epistemology concerning warrant, Reformed Epistemology concerning entitlement, Reformed Epistemology concerning aptness for theory, and so forth, Plantinga has typically used the catch-all word, 'properly'. Thus Plantinga has typically conducted the discussion in terms of what he calls 'properly basic' beliefs. (He has also sometimes spoken of 'taking' beliefs to be properly basic, when all he means – contrary to what a good many commentators have supposed – is that they *are* properly basic.)

By 'basic belief' Plantinga means the very same as what I mean by 'immediate belief'. The term 'basic' has certain connotations, however, which the term 'immediate' does not have; and those connotations have led to two all-too-typical misunderstandings. In the first place, the term 'basic' suggests that the religious beliefs in question serve as the basis, that is, the foundation, for one's structure of warranted religious beliefs, for one's structure of entitled religious beliefs, or whatever. And that has led a good many commentators to claim that the polemic of Reformed Epistemology against classical foundationalism is misleading. Reformed Epistemology is opposed, indeed, to *classical* foundationalism. But it's not opposed, so it is said, to *foundationalism* as such. It's just another version of foundationalism, a version somewhat more generous as to what it allows in the foundations than is classical foundationalism. All in all, then, so it is said, there is much less here than meets the eye.[8] But this is all a misunderstanding. Reformed Epistemology, narrowly understood, does not commit those who embrace this thesis to any form of foundationalism whatsoever. To acknowledge that some beliefs are held immediately, and to acknowledge that some of those which are held immediately possess the doxastic merit in question – that even some immediately held beliefs about God possess the merit in question – does not commit one to foundationalism of any sort. A coherentist could say as much. All foundationalists do in fact make the mediate/immediate distinction. But they are not foundationalists just by virtue of making the distinction; they are foundationalists by virtue of what they *do* with the distinction in articulating their epistemologies. I'll explain these somewhat dark sayings shortly, when I argue that the positive epistemologies which the Reformed epistemologists have developed in the third stage of Reformed Epistemology have in fact not been foundationalist in their basic structure. The thesis of Reformed Epistemology narrowly understood, though it did not commit the Reformed Epistemologist to foundationalism, did indeed leave open that possibility; the Reformed epistemologists have not, in fact, exploited that opening.

In the comparison by D.Z. Phillips of Reformed Epistemology to Wittgenstein's philosophy of religion, in chapter 4 of *Faith after Foundationalism*, one finds an additional misunderstanding of what the Reformed Epistemologist has in mind by 'basic beliefs'. Phillips assumes there that the Reformed epistemologist has his eye on the same thing that Wittgenstein has his eye on in *On Certainty*, when Wittgenstein talks about those beliefs that are certain for us because they are 'held fast' by all that surrounds them. Given the assumption that the same thing is under consideration, Phillips then criticizes Reformed Epistemology for thinking of religious beliefs in such an atomistic fashion.

But I submit that the topics here are just different; 'basic belief' is being used ambiguously. The phenomenon on which Wittgenstein had his eye is that which Plantinga, in his essay in *Faith and Rationality*, calls 'depth of ingression'. Certain beliefs are so deeply ingressed within one's belief-structure that to give them up would require giving up a vast number of other beliefs as well. The difficulty of doing that is, then, what holds them fast. My belief that the world began quite some time ago is one example of a deeply ingressed belief. So too, as one of Wittgenstein's examples suggests, is my belief that my name is 'Nicholas Wolterstorff'.

Not only is the distinction between deep and shallow ingression just a different distinction from that between immediate and mediate beliefs; there isn't even any coincidence between them. Some immediate beliefs are deeply ingressed; some are very shallowly ingressed. Indeed, it's even a distortion of Wittgenstein's thought to formulate it in terms of *beliefs*. What Wittgenstein was pointing to is what we all *take for granted* in so fundamental a way that, were we no longer to take it for granted, we would have to alter vast stretches of our beliefs *and practices*. Some of what we thus take for granted will be things *believed* by us; but much of it will never have been taken notice of sufficiently to be believed. To what extent these ideas can be used to illuminate religious beliefs is an interesting question; I myself think that religious beliefs are different in fundamental ways from the deeply ingressed, unshakeable beliefs to which Wittgenstein calls attention in *On Certainty*. But in any case, what Wittgenstein is discussing is simply different from what the Reformed Epistemologist is talking about when he speaks of basic, that is, immediate, beliefs.

But why, then, does the Reformed epistemologist talk about what he does talk about? Why all the flurry about immediately held beliefs about God, and whether they can possess the doxastic merit in question? Why, more generally, the preoccupation with epistemology? Why, in short, doesn't the Reformed epistemologist act like a good Wittgensteinian and talk about the role of religious language and belief in life?

The answer is that the polemical partner of Reformed Epistemology, narrowly understood, is not the same as the polemical partner of Wittgensteinian philosophy of religion; and that the character of both of these is in good measure shaped by their polemical partners and by how they have chosen to deal with those partners. In each case, absent knowledge of the polemical partner, the significance of the movement is in good measure lost on one.

The polemical partner of Wittgenstein, in his reflections on religion, was logical positivism. In his reflections on religion, Wittgenstein chose not to challenge positivism's criterion of cognitive meaningfulness head on, nor its principle of demarcation between science and 'metaphysics' which made use of that criterion. Instead, he undertook to exploit a concession which the later positivists had themselves already made, namely, the concession that meaningful speech is not confined to fact-stating speech. The challenge to which Wittgenstein addressed himself, in his reflections on religion, was then to describe the 'meaningfulness' of religious language – given that, so he assumed, it does not serve to state facts, that is, to make true–false claims. How does religious language function – given that, so he assumed, it cannot be contradicted, since nothing is said to which one can properly say, 'That's false.' Wittgenstein's way of dealing with his polemical partner *required* that he discuss the role of religious language and belief in life. There was no other way to make his polemical point.

By the time Reformed Epistemology came on the scene, logical positivism was dead and buried. It wasn't yet dead and buried at the time of the pre-history of Reformed Epistemology; Plantinga does battle with it at several points in *God and Other Minds*. But by the 1980s it was dead – at least among philosophers. What was not dead and buried was a challenge to religious belief of considerably greater antiquity than the positivist claim that religious language lacks meaning – viz., the challenge of which I spoke earlier, that religious beliefs, to be held rationally, must in their totality be rationally grounded. Reformed epistemologists have typically called it the *evidentialist challenge*. From the insistence that religious belief is lacking in rationality, warrant, entitlement, or whatever, if it is not held on good evidence, it just follows that it is lacking in those merits if it is held immediately. This evidentialist challenge has been so widely held among the intelligentsia of the modern world that it deserves to be regarded as part of the modern mind. In response to the challenge, many have offered arguments for their own full-blown religious beliefs; others have trimmed their religious beliefs until they no longer go beyond what they judge the arguments to support; yet others have contended that the arguments are so weak that religious belief ought to be trimmed to the point of disappearance. One way or the other, they have accepted the legitimacy of the challenge. The Reformed epistemologist, as I observed earlier, rejects the challenge. In so doing he is, I suppose, a 'postmodernist' of a sort. What made 'postmodernism' of his sort seem plausible to him, however, was not immersion in the writings of Heidegger, Derrida, and their ilk, but the 'postmodernism' which was implicit all along in the neo-Calvinist movement which he embraced.

What emerges from the foregoing is that Reformed Epistemology and Wittgensteinian philosophy of religion have in good measure just been doing different things; there is no reason why each cannot regard the other as having important insights which ought to be incorporated within a larger picture. It appears to me that on one absolutely central point, however, these two movements are in conflict. I understand Wittgenstein and most of his followers – O.K. Bouwsma being the signal exception – to hold that there is no such phenomenon as referring to God and predicating things of that to which one has referred. Religious language functions very much like the language of one's atheist friend when he exclaims, 'Thank God it's Friday.' The Reformed epistemologist, by contrast, holds that we can and do refer to God, and predicate things of that to which we have referred. He furthermore holds that these assertions about God are either true or false of God, and that they are true or false of God because of the facts of the matter. I judge this to be *the* decisive issue separating Reformed Epistemology from Wittgensteinian philosophy of religion (Bouwsma excepted). I shall say a bit about the issue at the close of my discussion.

I suggested that what distinguished the first stage of Reformed Epistemology from its pre-history was the explicit use of the concepts of *classical foundationalism and evidentialist challenge*. What, in turn, distinguishes the second stage from the first is, of course, the greater elaboration and articulation of ideas hinted at in the first stage. But something else as well. In the year we spent together in the Calvin Center for Christian Scholarship, Plantinga and I read Thomas Reid for the first time in our lives. For me (and for Plantinga as well, I think), it was the exhilarating experience of discovering a philosophical soul-mate. What was it that I (we) found in Reid? I've never been able fully to say – fully to articulate the grounds of the excitement I felt. Something about the experience has always eluded me. But I know some of what made me feel I had discovered a philosophical soul-mate.

Reid was not only the first articulate opponent of classical foundationalism in the history of Western philosophy; he was, at the same time, a metaphysical realist. That's part of what captivated me; for this was exactly the combination, *realism* plus *anti-classical-foundationalism*, which I had myself been trying to work out. What also captivated me was the articulate picture of the human being as having a number of distinct belief-forming faculties, or dispositions, and of these faculties as being innocent until proved guilty. In his attack on the sceptic, Reid argues powerfully that, in the nature of the case, suspicion, whatever its relevance, cannot be one's fundamental stance toward one's belief-forming faculties. But neither can one give a non-circular defence of the reliability of one's faculties. *Trust* must be one's fundamental stance. The neo-Calvinist version of the Augustinian tradition in which I had been reared, with its motto of *faith seeking understanding* and its tacit repudiation of evidentialist apologetics, had also made trust fundamental. So no doubt what also led me to sense in Reid a philosophical soul-mate was the fundamental role of trust in his thought. Admittedly the trust occurs at a somewhat different point, and has a somewhat different object; nonetheless, in both cases, human existence is seen as resting not on proof but trust.

The center of Reid's thought was his polemic against the explanation of perception offered by his predecessors, whom Reid lumped together as theorists of what he called 'The Way of Ideas', and his articulation of an alternative. The Way of Ideas theorists held that in perception we form beliefs about our sensations, and then draw rational inferences from the propositional content of those beliefs, to propositions about the external world. Reid polemicized powerfully and relentlessly against that account; what he put in its place was the claim that though sensations are indeed evoked by the impact of the external world on us in perception, those sensations *immediately* evoke in us conceptions and beliefs about the external world. The move, from sensations to perceptual beliefs, is not by virtue of some rational inference but by virtue of our 'hard wiring'. *Perception is not rationally grounded!*

What this picture of perception suggested to Plantinga and myself was a way of articulating John Calvin's suggestion that all humanity is naturally religious. Belief in God, so Calvin insisted, is not an invention; on the contrary, we are so created that, if we functioned as we were designed to function, we would all respond to one and another aspect of the 'design' of the world by immediate beliefs about God. One cannot understand Reformed Epistemology, as it has been developed, without discerning its commitment to an anthropology of religion of this Calvinistic sort: all humanity is naturally theistically religious. What accounts for the fact that not all human beings do in fact believe in God is that our indigenous proclivity for forming immediate beliefs about God has been overlaid by our fallenness. We no longer function as we were created to function.

Reformed Epistemology, through its first two stages, was above all a brush-clearing operation, designed to dispose of the evidentialist challenge to theistic belief and of the classical foundationalism which has typically motivated the evidentialist challenge. The third stage of Reformed Epistemology, represented by work done since *Faith and Rationality*, is differentiated from the second stage by the near-absence of any further ground-clearing and, in its place, the elaborate articulation of positive epistemological accounts which were only hinted at in *Faith and Rationality*. What I mean by Reformed Epistemology *broadly understood* is those developments in the epistemology of religious belief which have occupied the space cleared out by Reformed Epistemology in its earlier negative phase, this being what I have had in mind by Reformed Epistemology *narrowly understood*.

These broader developments have come in two areas which it is important to distinguish. For one thing, positive epistemologies of a Reformed-epistemological sort have been developed. Some of this was present already in the second stage, represented by *Faith and Rationality*; but that was only a foretaste of what has come forth since then. I have in mind, in particular, William Alston's account of religious experience and the justification it lends to religious beliefs in his *Perceiving God*; Plantinga's account of warrant in his three volumes, *Warrant: the Current Debate*, *Warrant as Proper Function*, and *Warranted Christian Belief*;[9] and my own account of entitlement in my *Divine Discourse*[10] and, much more elaborately, in my forthcoming, *World, Mind, and Entitlement to Believe*.

Secondly, a considerable number of writings have appeared dealing with the relevance of faith to theoretical activity. Admittedly it stretches the word 'epistemology' to call these discussions, 'examples of epistemology'; strictly, they belong to *Wissenschaftslehre*. Yet they have been so intimately connected with the more strictly epistemological developments of Reformed Epistemology that it would give a mistaken impression not to include them under the rubric of 'Reformed Epistemology'.

Not much of this Reformed *Wissenschaftslehre* found its way into *Faith and Rationality*; epistemology proper proved so fascinating during the year which gave rise to this volume that it pretty much blocked out reflections on the relevance of faith to theory. But such reflections were present already in what I called the 'first stage', in my book *Reason within the Bounds of Religion*. And they have appeared with fair regularity in the third stage; for example, in Plantinga's inaugural address at Notre Dame, 'Advice to Christian Philosophers', in George Marsden's recent, *The Outrageous Idea of Christian Scholarship*,[11] and in various essays of my own.

I mentioned earlier that the positive accounts of doxastic merits developed by Reformed epistemologists in this third stage have been non-foundationalist in their basic structure. Let me now explain this claim.

The cognitive-psychological distinction between mediate and immediate beliefs is one which, so it seems to me, everyone must acknowledge. Surely we all have beliefs which we have come to hold because we have inferred them from other beliefs of ours. But inference cannot be the sole mode of belief-formation. There must be some processes other than inference that produce beliefs in us; otherwise inference would have nothing to do its work on. Those will be processes that produce beliefs immediately.

What distinguishes the foundationalist from his fellow epistemologists is that he articulates his account of the presence and absence of whatever might be the doxastic merit on which he has his eye in the following way: first he offers an account of what brings it about that the merit attaches to those immediately held beliefs to which it does attach, and under what circumstances this is brought about. And then he offers an account of the circumstances under which inference succeeds in transferring that merit from immediately held beliefs which already possess it, to beliefs inferred from those. (Of course, some beliefs may be produced jointly by immediate-belief-formation processes and mediate-belief-formation processes.)

This description simply does not fit the basic structure of Plantinga's account of warrant, of Alston's account of those beliefs which are justified by their being evoked by religious experience, nor of my account of entitlement. Let me elaborate this claim just a bit for Plantinga's account of warrant.

A rough description of Plantinga's account is this: a belief is warranted just in case it is produced by faculties aimed at truth which are functioning properly, in situations for which those faculties were designed to work thus. Notice that nowhere here is the distinction between immediate and mediate beliefs appealed to. Plantinga's account of what brings it about that warrant accrues to a belief does not, in its basic structure, exhibit the bipartite structure definitive of foundationalist accounts. Whether or not the belief under consideration is mediate or immediate, the relevant question is always and only whether it was produced by a faculty aimed at truth functioning properly in a situation for which it was designed. The unified structure which Plantinga's theory exhibits allies it, in this regard, with coherentist accounts – though of course it's also not a coherentist theory.

It is true that something more requires to be said. Plantinga does accept the distinction between mediate and immediate modes of belief-formation. Indeed, when he applies his general account of warrant to an analysis of the proper functioning of our actual faculties of belief-formation, he finds it essential to make the distinction. At this second level, then, his account does exhibit a foundationalist character; nothing of the sort happens in a pure coherentist theory. Furthermore, the outcome of his analysis at this second level is that the scope of immediately formed beliefs which are warranted is considerably wider than the classical foundationalist would acknowledge. Nonetheless it remains true that *in its basic structure*, Plantinga's theory is not an expanded foundationalism but is not a foundationalism at all.

Let me call attention to another aspect of the significance of Reformed Epistemology by casting a somewhat different light on the basic structure of the positive epistemological theories which have been developed, in this third stage of their movement, by the Reformed epistemologists. (I have in mind here epistemology proper, not *Wissenschaftslehre*.) Ever since Plato, a certain picture of *the ideally formed belief* has haunted Western philosophy, and in particular, the philosophy of religion. Sometimes the picture has been incorporated within a theory of knowledge, at other times, within a theory of science, on yet other occasions, within a theory of entitlement – and over and over, within a theory of certitude.

Here is the picture. Fundamental in the life of the mind is *acquaintance* with entities, and *awareness* of having acquaintance with entities. What I call 'acquaintance' is what Kant called *Anschauung* – standardly, though not very happily, translated in the English versions of Kant as 'intuition'. Or to look at the same thing from the other side: fundamental in the life of the mind is *presence* – entities presenting themselves to us, putting in their appearance to us. Consider the definite description: 'the dizziness you felt when you rode that merry-go-round yesterday'. If you did in fact feel dizzy upon riding a merry-go-round yesterday, then I can use that definite description to pick out that particular dizziness – to pick it out well enough to make assertions about it, for example. Nonetheless, that particular dizziness was never part of the intuitional content of *my* mind; *I* was never acquainted with it, it was never presented to me. My contact with it is – and was – very different from my contact with the dizziness *I* felt when *I* rode that merry-go-round yesterday. *That* dizziness was present to me; I was acquainted with it.

To say it again: acquaintance, and its converse, presence, are in their various modes fundamental to the life of the mind. Perception has intuitional content, memory has intuitional content, introspection has intuitional content, intellection (reason) has intuitional content. Surely there could be no human mind devoid of all these; perhaps there could be no such mind at all. (To assure oneself that the four activities just mentioned do all have an intuitional component, contrast picking out some entity by means of a definite description, with perceiving, remembering, introspecting, or intellecting that entity, or an entity of that sort.) Whatever, if anything, may be true in the currently fashionable diatribes against presence, it cannot be that the mind is devoid of intuitional content.

Among the entities with which we have acquaintance are facts: I perceive *that the sun is rising*, I introspect *that I am feeling rather dizzy*, I remember *that the ride made me feel dizzy*, I intellect *that the proposition, green is a colour*, is necessarily true. And now for the picture of the ideally formed belief: sometimes, so it has been claimed and assumed, one's acquaintance with some fact, coupled, if necessary, with one's awareness of that acquaintance, produces in one a belief whose propositional content corresponds to the fact with which one is acquainted. My acquaintance with the fact that I am feeling rather dizzy produces in me the belief that I am feeling rather dizzy. The content of my belief is, as it were, read directly off the fact with which I have acquaintance. How could such a belief possibly be mistaken, it's been asked. It must be the case that it is certain.

That's one type of ideally formed belief, the *first grade*, as it were: the belief formed by one's acquaintance with a fact to which the propositional content of the belief corresponds. There is a second type, of a somewhat lower grade: the belief formed by one's acquaintance with the fact that the propositional content of the belief is logically entailed by propositions corresponding to facts of which one is aware. In such a case, the certainty of one's belief concerning the premises, coupled with the certainty of one's belief concerning the entailment, is transmitted to one's belief of the conclusion; it too is certain for one. What accounts for the fact that such a belief will typically be of a lower grade than the highest is that one may have acquaintance with the facts corresponding to the premises in an argument, and acquaintance with the fact that those premises deductively support the conclusion, without having acquaintance with the fact corresponding to the conclusion. Indeed, therein lies the point of such arguments. Deductive arguments, if grounded in acquaintance, carry us beyond acquaintance while yet preserving certitude.

Some writers – such as John Locke – have held that there is a third grade of ideally formed beliefs, viz., the belief formed by one's acquaintance with the fact that the propositional content of the belief is *probable* relative to facts with which one has acquaintance. It was especially inductive arguments that Locke had in mind. Locke recognized that inductive arguments are incapable of transmitting certainty to the conclusion; hence beliefs thus formed are of a lower grade than the others. Nonetheless, Locke quite clearly regarded inductive arguments as like deductive in that, if one has collected a satisfactory body of evidence as premises, and if one is acquainted with the facts corresponding to the premises and with the fact that the conclusion is more probable than not on those premises, then one's acceptance of the conclusion is entirely grounded in acquaintance.

One can see why The Doxastic Ideal has had the appeal which it has had: there is something admirable about beliefs which measure up to the Ideal – especially, about beliefs which measure up to the first stage of the Ideal. A belief evoked by acquaintance with the fact to which the propositional content of the belief corresponds: what could be better, more satisfying, than that, and more reassuring! A belief evoked by acquaintance with the fact that the propositional content of the belief is entailed by beliefs of the first sort: such a belief is only slightly less satisfying. But the point to be made here is that such beliefs are not ideal *for us human beings, in our situation*. What has been taken to be *The Doxastic Ideal* is not ideal *for us*. The failure of a belief to measure up to the Ideal does not, so far forth, point to a deficiency which *we human beings* ought to remove, or even to a deficiency which it would be *desirable* for us to remove. Our belief-forming constitution does not measure up to the supposed ideal in its indigenous workings; nor is it possible to revise its workings so that those workings do all measure up to the supposed ideal. And even if it were possible, even if we could somehow manage to reshape our belief-forming self so that it conformed in its workings to the supposed ideal, we would find ourselves with too scanty a body of beliefs for life to continue. Once again, when we look deep into human existence, we spy trust.

It was the two great eighteenth-century Scotsmen, David Hume and Thomas Reid, who first, powerfully and directly, challenged The Doxastic Ideal by arguing that, whatever philosophers might prefer, our human condition is such that vast numbers of the beliefs we have, and without which we could not live, were neither formed in accord with The Doxastic Ideal nor could be so formed, while yet being entitled, warranted, justified, or what have you.

Hume argued the case most powerfully for beliefs about the future formed by induction. I see that the car ahead of me has veered off the mountain road and is now unsupported in the air; that experience evokes in me immediately the belief that the car will descend with increasing rapidity. The propositional content of the belief does not correspond to the fact perceived. It may be, however, that what accounts for the formation of the belief that the car will descend with increasing rapidity is that I make a logically valid inference to this from another belief that I surely form, namely, that the car is now unsupported in the air – perhaps with some other beliefs tossed in which I have arrived at by the exercise of reason? Not at all, argued Hume. What accounts for the formation of the belief that the car will descend with increasing rapidity is not an exercise of reason but just the habit, or custom, which has been formed in me by my experience of many similar such events. Reid fully accepted this analysis by Hume of the formation of inductive beliefs, and went on to offer a broadly similar account of perceptual beliefs, of memorial beliefs, and of beliefs formed by testimony. All such beliefs are formed in us by virtue of our 'hard wiring', not by the employment of rational inference. *None is rationally grounded.*

One aspect of the significance of Reformed Epistemology, intimately related to its use of Reid to explicate Calvin's religious anthropology, is that it repudiates The Doxastic Ideal generally, and repudiates it, in particular, for religious beliefs. Consider one of Plantinga's examples. One looks up at night and perceives a starry sky – one perceives that there's a vast starry sky before one. That perception in turn evokes in one immediately the belief that God must have made all this. This latter belief may very well be warranted, Plantinga argues. Yet the content of the belief – namely, that God must have made all this – does not correspond to the fact one perceives – namely, that there's a starry sky before one. It goes beyond that. In declaring that the belief evoked may well have warrant, Plantinga is so far forth repudiating The Doxastic Ideal.

Or consider one of the cases I cite in my discussion of entitled religious belief in *Divine Discourse*. Augustine hears a child over the garden wall chanting 'take and read, take and read'. After some quick reflection, Augustine finds this uncanny. Perhaps he *believes* that it is uncanny; more likely he *hears* it *as uncanny*. It quickly occurs to him that maybe the chant is part of a game; but he can't think of any such game. That's really a throw away point, however; it makes no difference one way or the other. Augustine has an intimation that the words, whatever led the child to chant them, may well be appropriate to his condition; that's what makes the chanting acquire an uncanny character for him. And that experience evokes in him immediately the belief that God is speaking to him, telling him to open his copy of Paul's Epistles and read.

If this is how it went – Augustine's description is too brief for us to be sure of all the details – the resultant belief, in its mode of formation, certainly does not measure up to The Doxastic Ideal. The propositional content of the belief which gets formed in Augustine is that God is speaking to him. But the fact which he hears is the fact of a child chanting *'tolle lege,'* or rather, the fact of the uncanniness of the child's chanting *'tolle lege'* within his earshot right then. Nonetheless Augustine was, so I argue, entitled to the belief that God was speaking to him.

In conclusion, let me return to a point which I raised earlier but then reserved for later discussion. The Reformed Epistemologist regards a great deal of religious language as being *about* God; that is to say, he is of the view that in our use of religious language, we often refer to God. He is furthermore of the view that often, having referred to God, we predicate something of that to which we referred; and he regards such predications as true or false of God, depending on the facts of the matter. If I exclaim with the Psalmist, 'Bless the Lord, O my soul, and all that is within me, bless God's holy name,' I am referring to God but not predicating anything of God; by no means all language about God is assertory in character. This is a point that the Wittgensteinians are fond of making; and the Reformed epistemologist heartily agrees. Nonassertory 'God-talk' may nonetheless incorporate references to God, as the example just given illustrates. And a good deal of language about God is in fact assertory; it does predicate something of that to which one referred, viz., God.

My interpretation of the mainline Wittgensteinians is that they deny that we ever refer to God, and also deny, consequently, that we ever predicate things of God. 'God-talk' is not to be construed as incorporating references to God and as predicating something of that to which one referred. To conclude my discussion I propose to join the fray on this issue – without any expectation that my intervention will prove decisive!

Let me approach the battleground by expressing my disagreement with Phillips on what he sees as the status of the issue within Reformed Epistemology. At several points, Phillips describes the Reformed epistemologist as trying to 'justify' our 'epistemic practices' – by which he means, trying to show that our modes of belief-formation are reliable, in that the beliefs they produce correspond to objective reality.[12] I submit that the Reformed epistemologist attempts no such thing. To the contrary, Reformed epistemologists regularly cite Reid's argument against the sceptic to the effect that, in the nature of the case, such an attempt will prove either arbitrary or self-defeating.

'Epistemic practices' is an ambiguous term. It might mean, as I just now, following Phillips, took it to mean, *modes of belief formation*. But it might also mean, *modes of belief evaluation*. It is practices of belief evaluation that the Reformed epistemologist has in the centre of his attention. We human beings engage in the practice of evaluating our beliefs as warranted, as rational, as justified, as cases of knowledge, as entitled, and so forth. The Reformed epistemologist doesn't invent these practices. He finds them, and finds that he himself is a participant in them. And he accepts them. It's not his goal to criticize them in any general sort of way; witness Plantinga's 'epistemology from below'. Though he, like everybody else, thinks that people make mistakes in what they

appraise as warranted, as entitled, and so forth, he is not of the view
that everybody is almost entirely wrong about knowledge, almost
entirely wrong about entitlement and so forth. In the first and second
stages of the movement, what the Reformed epistemologist subjected
to critique was not our practices of doxastic evaluation but the analysis
and critique of those practices offered by the classical foundationalists.
In the third stage of the movement, his goal has been to give his own
positive account of these practices of evaluation. On this point, then,
there's no dispute between the Reformed epistemologist and the
Wittgensteinian philosopher of religion.

Rather often Wittgensteinian philosophers of religion have been
charged with offering an atheistic account of religious language.
'Absolutely not,' they say, bridling at the charge. It's their view that the
existence of God is taken for granted in all that the theistically religious
person believes and says. The last thing such a person will say is, 'God
does not exist.' The 'grammar' of theistic religious language requires *not*
saying that. Saying that would be tantamount to repudiating one's
(theistic) religion. Of course theistically religious people, when engaged
in their religious way of life, don't go around saying, 'God exists.'
Instead they praise God, bless God, petition God, and so forth. But if
pressed on the issue, they will say emphatically, 'God exists' – though
it falls strangely on their ears. In short, this way of getting at the fundamental issue which divides Reformed epistemologists from mainline
Wittgensteinian philosophers of religion proves a dead-end.

Other such dead-ends could be explored. But let me, on this occasion, resist entering all such dead-ends and state without further ado
what I regard as the fundamental point of dispute. That is this: is it
possible to *refer* to God; and, having referred, is it possible to *predicate*
things of God?

Let's take D.Z. Phillips as the paradigmatic Wittgensteinian philosopher of religion. In some of the passages in which Phillips discusses God
and reference, what he says, taken strictly, is not that we cannot refer to
God, but that God is not an *object* to which we can refer, with the context suggesting that by an 'object', Phillips means an entity occupying
a place in space. In one passage he says, for example, 'Talk of God's
existence or reality cannot be considered as talk about the existence of
an object. Neither can questions about whether we mean the same by
"God" be construed as whether we are referring to the same object.'[13]
Now I myself find it extremely unlikely that anybody likely to read
Phillips's writings does believe that God is an object occupying space;
accordingly, given the rules of 'conversational implication', one asks

oneself whether perhaps Phillips doesn't mean to say or suggest something more, or something else. Why bother telling us that God is not a spatial object? This query gains added force from the rhetorical structure of some of the relevant passages. Here is an example of what I have in mind:

> If, ... having heard of people praising the Creator of heaven and earth, glorifying the Father of us all, feeling answerable to the One who sees all, someone were to say, 'But these are only religious perspectives, show me what they refer to', this would be a misunderstanding of the grammar of such perspective. ... The religious pictures give one a language in which it is possible to think about human life in a certain way. The pictures ... provide the logical space within which such thoughts can have a place. When these thoughts are found in worship, the praising and the glorifying does not refer to some object called God. Rather, the expression of such praise and glory is what we call the worship of God.[14]

The imagined interlocutor asks to be shown what the religious perspectives refer to. Now if by 'show' he's asking to have the spatial object called God displayed to him, then indeed he's deeply confused – though to interpret his words thus is to interpret them with a woodenness that Phillips would rightly leap upon if exhibited in some philosopher's interpretation of religious language. But let that pass. Phillips does not respond to this imagined remark by correcting the confusion about the nature of God which the remark (on the interpretation being considered) exhibits. Instead he makes quite a different point. What he says is that 'The religious pictures give one a language in which it is possible to think about human life in a certain way' – not, notice, a language in which it is possible to think *about God and God's relation* to human life in a certain way, but a language in which it is possible to think *about human life* in a certain way. So too, after remarking, two sentences later, that 'the praising and the glorifying does not refer to some object called God,' he goes on to say that 'the expression of such praise and glory is what we call the worship of God'. If the mistake of the interlocutor was to suppose that God is a *spatial object* which can be referred to, how would this be an answer to that? In short, the rhetorical structure of the passage suggests that the worship of God has nothing at all to do with whether there's any reference to God, and whether praise is addressed to the being referred to. Worship of God only has to do with whether certain 'thoughts are found in worship'.

Finally, then, consider this passage:

> In face of what is given, the believer kneels. Talk of 'God' has its sense
> in this reaction. It is not the name of an individual; it does not refer
> to anything. ... It is all too easy to conclude that if religious expres-
> sions which involve talk of God are not referring expressions, if no
> object corresponds to such talk, such expressions cannot say any-
> thing nor can they be held to be true. In this chapter, however, we
> have seen that this argument contains unwarrantable assumptions.
> We have argued for other possibilities. When these are recognized we
> see that religious expressions of praise, glory, etc. are not referring
> expressions. These activities are expressive in character, and what
> they express is called the worship of God. Is it reductionism to say
> that what is meant by the reality of God is to be found in certain
> pictures which say themselves?[15]

Now all ambiguity has been dissipated. The word 'God' *does not refer
to anything*. Initially we had some reason to think that the mistake
of the interlocutor was to suppose that in our use of 'God talk' we refer
to a *spatial* object. Now we see that, on Phillips's view, his mistake
goes deeper; he doesn't get home free by conceding that, when using
'God talk', we refer to a being who transcends this spatial order.
The mistake of the interlocutor was in assuming that 'God talk' is refer-
ential. Such speech is purely expressive in character; praise is expressive activity. And when the one who praises uses 'God talk', such
expressive activity *just is* what constitutes the worship of God. There's
nothing more to the worship of God than that. Now we understand
why the passages quoted earlier have the rhetorical structure to which
I pointed.

Phillips is remarkably chary of telling us why, on his view, 'God talk'
is purely expressive – why the word 'God', as used by religious people,
'does not refer to anything'. Sometimes one gets the impression that
it's a doctrine of reference which is at work: we can only refer to that
which occupies a place in space. At other times one gets the impression
that what's operating is a certain theology, along the lines of Plotinus,
Kant and Tillich: God is not a one-among-others that can be picked
out. Best not to speculate, however. Phillips never lays out his reasons;
he contents himself with heaping ridicule on anyone who uses the
word 'individual' or 'object' when speaking of God, never telling us
what word he himself prefers, *if any*, and on insisting that religious discourse is in good measure not assertory in character.

Now it's possible that Phillips didn't really mean what he said in the passages to which I have pointed from *Religion without Explanation*. But just as I am not aware of any passage in which Phillips explains why he holds that the word 'God' 'does not refer to anything', so too I am not aware of any in which, to correct misinterpretations of his thought, he says flat out that of course he believes that 'God' is used by theists to refer; all he ever wanted to say was that God is not a *spatial object* – or all he ever wanted to say was that Plotinus was right in holding that God is not a one-among-others. So I think we have no option but to hold that Phillips did and does mean what he said there.

It's on this issue of reference and predication concerning God (along with the issue of whether theistic language implies existential quantifications over God) that Phillips's version of Wittgensteinianism clashes most directly with Reformed Epistemology. For the Reformed epistemologist understands himself, when using 'God talk', as referring to God. And though one can refer to God without predicating something of God – as when the psalmist enjoins himself to bless God's holy name – the Reformed epistemologist understands himself as often going on to predicate things of God, these predications then being true or false of God depending on the fact of the matter. The Reformed epistemologist understands his religious cohorts as regularly doing the same things he does – namely, refer to God and predicate things of God. Thus the Reformed epistemologist holds that a great deal of theistic religious language is used referentially and predicatively concerning God, and that a great deal of it entails propositions expressed with sentences which quantify over God. If there is no such being as God, then, on the account of theistic religious language which is taken for granted by the Reformed epistemologist, theistic religious language misfires in a most radical way. For of course one cannot refer to, and predicate things of, what there isn't.

Who's right on this issue? No doubt there's room here for a good deal of philosophical to-ing and fro-ing, each side pressing the other for reasons for his position, questioning those reasons, trying to extract 'absurd' consequences from the other's position, and so on. It's my own guess, however, that when the dust has settled, it's going to come down to what those who use theistic language in a serious religious way, and who grasp the philosophical issues at stake, understand themselves as intending to do when they use 'God talk'.

I judge myself to be such a person, and my fellow Reformed epistemologists to be such as well. And we understand ourselves, when using 'God talk', to be intending to refer to God and (often) to predicate things of God; likewise we understand ourselves, when using theistic language, to be saying things which imply that there is a being such that it is identical with God. If we were persuaded that those intentions were fundamentally misguided because there is no such being as God, then we would cease using 'God talk' – other than to join our atheist friends in exclaiming, 'Thank God it's Friday!' What's the point of talking about God saving us if there's no God to do the saving!

D.Z. Phillips is also someone who uses theistic language in a serious religious way, and who understands the philosophical issues at stake. Yet he does not understand himself to be meaning to use 'God talk' referentially and predicatively.

So what's the solution? One possibility is that one or the other of us fails to understand our own intentions in using 'God talk'. What strikes me as much more plausible is that we simply use theistic language in fundamentally different ways. Phillips offers what we can assume to be an accurate description of how he and his fellow mainline Wittgensteinians use theistic language; I gave what I take to be an accurate description of how I and my fellow Reformed epistemologists use theistic language. So we're both right – provided that we both avoid universalization. Phillips's account holds for himself and mainline Wittgensteinians, but not for me and my fellow Reformed epistemologists; my account holds for myself and my fellow Reformed epistemologists, but not for mainline Wittgensteinians.

What holds for all the others – for all the other users of theistic language? My own guess is that almost all of them, if they saw the issue, would say that they meant to be using theistic language as I and my fellow Reformed epistemologists use it, not as Phillips uses it. Almost all of them would feel profoundly disillusioned if they came to the view that God is not among that which is available for reference and predication – for the reason that it's not true that there exists a being which is God. If Phillips's religious use of theistic language conforms to his description, then his use represents a revision of how such language has traditionally been used; his religious use of such language is a revisionist use.

Phillips understands himself, in his writings, as speaking not religiously but philosophically; and over and over he says that his aim, as philosopher, is not to revise but describe. His description does not hold, however, for how Reformed epistemologists use theistic language; nor, I contend, for how most people use such language. His description holds only for a rather select group of Wittgensteinians and their allies. Yet his words regularly carry the suggestion that he is describing *all* serious religious use of theistic language. Accordingly, his description is, for most people, a *mis*description. And should his discussion succeed in getting some people to think they are using theistic language in his way, when in fact they have been using it in my way, then his discussion threatens to do what he says he wants at all cost to avoid doing; namely, it threatens to function not as description but as revision.

Notes

1. University of Notre Dame Press.
2. *Nous*, March 1981.
3. Grand Rapids: Eerdmans Publishing Co.
4. Ithaca: Cornell University Press.
5. Grand Rapids: Eerdmans Publishing Co.
6. New York: Routledge, 1988.
7. Ibid., p. 259.
8. *See*, for example, ibid., pp. 32–3.
9. Oxford: Oxford University Press, 1993, 1993 and 2000.
10. Cambridge: Cambridge University Press, 1995.
11. Oxford: Oxford University Press, 1997.
12. *See*, for example, ibid., p. 33.
13. *Religion without Explanation* (Oxford: Blackwell, 1976), p. 174.
14. Ibid., pp. 148–9.
15. Ibid., pp. 148, 150.

5
On Behalf of the Evidentialist – a Response to Wolterstorff

Stephen J. Wykstra

> Why don't you just scrap this God business, says one of my
> bitter suffering friends. It's a rotten world, you and I have been
> shafted, and that's that.
>   I'm pinned down. When I survey this gigantic intricate
> world, I cannot believe that it just came about. I do not mean
> that I have some good arguments for its being made and that I
> believe in the arguments. I mean that this conviction wells up
> irresistibly within me when I contemplate the world.
>
> Nicholas Wolterstorff, *Lament for a Son*

Reformed epistemology as religious philosophy

Nicholas Wolterstorff has given us an illuminating account of the
development and main claims of Reformed Epistemology. Reformed
Epistemology, he has stressed, seeks to provide an account of the
epistemological status of theistic belief, not an overall philosophy
of religion. In the 1980s, its project was primarily negative aiming to
overcome the evidentialist challenge, alleging that theistic belief is
lacking in warrant or entitlement if it is not supported by good reasons. So this phase was brush-clearing, seeking to clear away evidentialist bramble. In the 1990s, its project has become more positive, aiming,
we might say, to grow, in the place of the bramble, a garden of new
epistemological insights about what gives theistic belief its various
doxastic merits, and what makes it deeply relevant to the theoretical
and interpretive disciplines.

Reformed Epistemology is, Wolterstorff has stressed, not a philosophy
of religion; but his description of its roots indicate that it is a religious
philosophy. For it is rooted in the vision of neo-Calvinism, especially as

articulated by Abraham Kuyper. And that vision is itself *religious* in character. What, epistemologically speaking, is at its heart? It is, I think, that God has made each of us so that we can, through God's regenerating and sanctifying work in our lives, increasingly come to know God in a cognitively direct way. Direct does not here mean individualistic. Reformed thinkers prize the Scriptures, the community which is the priesthood of all believers, the sacraments, and the preaching of the Word. So the idea of directness is not that we need *these* things – the Word, the sacraments, the community less and less as we spiritually mature; to the contrary, we need these things more and more. Rather, the idea is that God has made us so that as we mature, our knowing God through these things rests more and more on something involving God's own testimony in our hearts, as he uses these things to bring us to Himself.

This conception of religious knowing is stressed by Calvin and later reformed theologians (though of course it can also be found within other currents within the great river of Christian tradition as well). It is itself a religious vision, part of a religious worldview. The Reformed Epistemologists (and here I mean Plantinga, Wolterstorff and William Alston, an Episcopalian who is a kind of honorary Reformed thinker) have used developments in meta-epistemology to give a philosophical elaboration and deployment of this vision, and used the vision to propel new developments in epistemology. They thus themselves exemplify the thesis that Christian theism is deeply relevant to the theoretical and interpretative disciplines.

Objections

What, then, of objections to Reformed epistemology? In addition to objections discussed by Wolterstorff, these have come from three main quarters.

First, there are objections from the quarters of analytic philosophers who think theistic religion is or may be unreasonable due to evidentialist deficiencies.

Second, there are objections from what we might call the pluralists those who find Reformed epistemology too complacent in what it says or fails to say about rival sources of insight which conflict with the deliverances of theistic practice. One group of rivals consists of other religious traditions; another source consists of secular sources of insight, like Nietzsche, Freud and Marx.

Third, there are objections from theists who think Reformed epistemology has insufficient appreciation for the value of evidential support
for various theistic beliefs. Catholic critics have faulted Reformed
thinkers for depreciating the role of natural theology. Evangelical critics
have pleaded for more recognition of the importance of Christian
apologetics, not so much in the tradition of natural theology, but in the
tradition of evidences of Christianity, reasoned defences of the reliability of the gospels, the historicity of the resurrection of Jesus, and so on.
   These three sources of objections overlap, of course, and certain common themes emerge. In particular, many (though not all) of the critics
think that there is more to be said on behalf of evidentialism than
Reformed thinkers have granted. And this is the issue I would like to
press. I shall do so in my own way, since I know it best. Wolterstorff
remarks that one characteristic of the positive phase of Reformed epistemology has been an almost total absence of further ground-clearing.
There has been little looking backward at the pile of evidentialist bramble that was cleared. I shall poke around in the bramble, to see if there
might still not be a green branch that belongs in the Reformed garden.

What is the real issue?

Let's begin by going back to the issue dividing Reformed thinkers from
their polemical partner, the evidentialists. That issue is whether theistic
belief needs evidence. Evidentialists think that it does; Reformed epistemologists think that it doesn't. They urge, instead, that theistic belief, at
its epistemic *best*, is a 'properly basic' belief, akin to our beliefs in physical objects or the past or other minds. I shall call this thesis basicalism,
and shall often refer to a Reformed Epistemologist as a basicalist. It is
perhaps an ugly term, but it provides the right contrast to evidentialist.
   Basicalists, then, say that theistic belief does not need evidence;
belief in God, as Plantinga puts it (1983, p. 17) can be 'entirely right,
proper, and rational without any evidence or argument at all'. Now it is
crucial to realize that when basicalists say this, they are using the term
evidence in a *narrow* sense. This is, as Plantinga himself fully realizes,
a somewhat artificial sense. I believe I have two hands: do I have
evidence of my senses. So the *natural* sense of the word evidence is
a broad sense, a sense that includes not only inferential arguments, *but
also* direct or immediate justifiers like sensory evidence, memory dispositions, and so on. Reformed thinkers, however, are not using the term
in this broad sense. When they speak of evidence, they mean, almost
always, inferential evidence. (Inferential evidence consists of other

propositions we believe, from which we infer the truth of the belief in question.) When basicalists want to speak of non-inferential justifiers, they use the term grounds rather than evidence. My belief that I have two hands does not rest on evidence, but on grounds.

So the Great Dividing Issue between basicalists and evidentialists is this: Does theistic belief *need evidence in the narrow inferential sense of evidence?* We might think we are now clear about what the dividing issue is. But are we? I do not think so. The notion of needing inferential evidence is far more slippery than one might think.

What is it for a belief to need inferential evidence? Our initial grasp of the notion tends to come from familiar examples. That the sun is shining outside my window is something I can just tell by looking and seeing; that 1 plus 1 is 2 is something immediately obvious to my reason. These claims do not need inferential evidence; they can properly be believed in a *basic* (that is, non-inferential) way. But I also believe things whose truth is not obvious in any such basic way – that the sun is about 93 million miles away, or that 17 times 139 equals 2363, or that atoms are made of protons, electrons and neutrons. So such claims, if they are to be properly believed, need to be secured by inference of an appropriate sort. Call them properly inferential propositions.

But what does it really *mean*, to say that these latter claims need inferential evidence? Take the claim about the sun; we all surely agree that in some sense, it does need inferential evidence. (We also presume, of course, that it *has* what it needs. The word 'needs' here is used in that sense that does *not* imply a lack. The paradigm is Humans need water, not I need a drink.) But *who* needs to know this evidence? Surely *I* do not personally need to know it. Certain astronomers who work on these things need to know it. And similarly for my belief that atoms are made of electrons, protons, and neutrons: for my belief to be okay, it is not necessary for *me* to know the evidence for this. Rather, it is certain physicists that must know this evidence (and, of course, I must be in some sort of appropriate relation to them).

'I must'? – for the sake of what? Imagine we learn, ten years from now, that scientists didn't really have this evidence for electrons, but had instead been duped by some extremely clever conmen in Copenhagen. Does that mean you and I, in 1999, were improper in believing what we did about electrons? That doesn't seem right. Perhaps we (looking back) would say our beliefs had some sort of defect, but the defect does not seem to be that we were *improper* in holding them.

So the notion of needing inferential evidence is slippery in two ways. First, it is not easy to say what *relation to the evidence* is needed. And second, it is not easy to say what, *for the sake of which* evidence is needed. This is so, I am suggesting, even when one thinks about simple scientific beliefs. Evidentialism seems like the right stance to take toward these beliefs: it does seem they are things that need evidence. But it is not easy to spell out this means.

Doxastic merits

Let me now connect this to a point made by Wolterstorff. He notes that there are a multiplicity of doxastic merits that beliefs can have. (In many twentieth-century disputes about the correct explication of what it is for a belief to be justified, he suggests that rival theorists actually have *different* doxastic merits in mind, and thus have different explicanda.) In particular, Wolterstorff distinguishes between the merits of entitlement and warrant. He then proposes that Reformed epistemology (in its negative phase) should be understood

> to be the claim, for some particular doxastic merit, that there are beliefs about God held immediately [non-inferentially] which possess that merit.

Accordingly, he says, in speaking of the negative phase of Reformed Epistemology:

> we ought not speak of Reformed Epistemology *tout court*, but of Reformed Epistemology concerning warrant, of Reformed Epistemology concerning entitlement, etc.

This is surely right systematically. But historically, it seems to me that this particular distinction emerged only in the third positive phase of Reformed epistemology. With the exception of a single footnote, I find no cognizance of this distinction in *Faith and Rationality*, the *locus classicus* of Reformed epistemology in its negative, or evidentialism-overcoming, phase. No, in that phase Reformed thinkers always had in mind the doxastic merit of *rationality*. In asserting that theistic belief does not need evidence, they were always claiming that theistic belief does not need evidence to be *rational*. The distinctions they drew were distinctions helping to clarify the term rational, not to distinguish it from warrant. This means they *always* construed evidentialism as claiming that if the believer believes without basing his or her belief on evidence, then he or she is in some sense *irrational*.

Rationality-evidentialism

Let us make this construal more explicit. Evidentialism, so construed, says theistic belief needs evidence if theists are to be rational (or to avoid being irrational) in their believing. But what is it, to be 'rational' (or 'irrational')? Reformed thinkers considered two broad possibilities. The first is that being rational is a matter of fulfilling our intellectual duties – our duties in matters of forming and regulating our beliefs. An irrational belief is one that violates these duties: irrationality, on this construal, is doxastic sin. The second possibility construes rationality as a matter of manifesting certain 'excellences' in belief-formation. Richard has a brain tumour, causing him to form paranoid beliefs that his wife is trying to kill him. Given the tumour, he cannot help but do this. We would not blame him, thinking he is violating some duty; nevertheless we might well call him irrational. ('How could Rich accuse me like that?,' his wife sobs. 'Jane', the doctor replies, 'you've got to remember the tumour is making him irrational.') Richard's believing falls short of standards, but these standards prescribe, not duties, but desirable or excellent ways of functioning, akin to standards informing our judgements about health. On this second construal, irrationality is not doxastic sin but doxastic sickness.

Both explications capture important ordinary uses of the term 'rational'. Moreover, they have an important commonality. On both, to deem a person irrational is to diagnose something as 'going wrong' in the subject holding the belief. It is something in this believing subject whether a culpable sin or a non-culpable sickness that needs changing or fixing, if things are to be brought up to snuff. Evaluations of rationality and irrationality are, we can put it, *subject-focused* evaluations. And evidentialism, on this construal, is thus claiming that theistic belief needs inferential evidence in order for the *believing subject* to be free of doxastic sin or doxastic sickness in his believing.

But in requiring that theistic belief be based on evidence, what relation to evidence would such an evidentialist then be claiming that theistic belief 'needs'? If we are taking evidence to be needed for the sake of the rationality of the subject, what is needed is, plausibly, that the believing subject herself be cognizant of the evidence and its evidential bearing on the proposition she believes, and that she hold the belief partly because of this. Putative evidence will not contribute to an individual's being *rational* in believing some proposition, unless this evidence fall within that individual's cognizance. So evidentialism, as addressed by Reformed epistemologists, was always construed as claiming something like this:

> Any individual believing that God exists must, in order to be *rational*, hold this belief on the basis of his/her *own inference* of it from evidence.

Let us call this *rationality-evidentialism*.

Is overcoming rationality-evidentialism enough?

But is rationality-evidentialism really the right way to construe the evidentialist's core intuition that theistic belief 'needs evidence'? Here consider Plantinga's counterexample against one variety of evidentialism construed in this way. Plantinga considers a 14 year old who believes in God, having been raised in a community where everyone so believes. This young man, stipulates that Plantinga (1983, p. 33):

> doesn't believe in God on the basis of evidence. He has never heard of the cosmological, teleological, or ontological arguments; in fact no one has ever presented him with any evidence at all. And although he has often been told about God, he doesn't take that testimony as evidence; he doesn't reason thus: everyone around here says that God loves us and cares for us; most of what everyone around here says is true; so probably *that's* true. Instead, he simply believes what he's taught.

Let's call this young man 'Hansel'. As Plantinga describes him, Hansel simply believes what his elders have taught him about God. In so doing, is Hansel necessarily irrational? Rationality-evidentialism entails that he is; but surely, says Plantinga, it is quite implausible to think that in so believing, this youth is irrational in the sense of being in violation of his doxastic duties. Plantinga seems to me right about this; and he remains right, I believe, when we construe rationality in any of its plausible senses. The case of Hansel, then, gives us reason to reject rationality-evidentialism.

But does it tell against evidentialism? Does rejecting rationality-evidentialism mean rejecting the core intuition of evidentialism? To answer this, let us return to the point I made earlier: we are, almost all of us, 'evidentialists' about *some* things. Almost all of us would want to say, intuitively, that a claim like 'electrons exist' needs inferential evidence. So most of us, even if we are Reformed thinkers about belief in God, are evidentialists about electrons (or about the distance of the sun from the earth, and so on). Now, in taking it intuitively that electron-belief 'needs evidence', are we really endorsing *rationality-evidentialism* about electrons? Are we, that is, endorsing the claim:

Any individual believing that electrons exist must, in order to be rational, hold his/her belief that electrons exist on the basis of his/her own inference of it from evidence.

Surely not. For suppose we consider some 14-year-old girl who believes that electrons exist, having been raised in a community where everyone so believes. Gretel, as we may call her, doesn't believe in electrons on the basis of evidence. She has never heard of the Millikan oil drop experiment, of electron-diffraction, or of the quantum-theoretic explanations of spectroscopic data; in fact no one has ever presented her with any evidence for electrons at all. And although she has often been told about electrons, she doesn't take that testimony as evidence; she doesn't reason thus: everyone around here says that electrons exist; most of what everyone around here says is true; so probably that's true. Instead, she simply believes what she's taught.

So Gretel, like Hansel, believes what her elders have taught her, without knowing the evidence. Now in our intuitive evidentialism about electrons, are we saying that Gretel is necessarily *irrational* in this? One hopes not. Only an epistemic Scrooge would immediately deem Gretel as doxastically sick or sinful in believing her teachers as she does. Gretel (like Hansel) need *not* be irrational in so believing; so *rationality-evidentialism* about electron belief is wrong. But does this mean that our *intuitive evidentialism* about electrons is wrong? Does admitting that Gretel might be okay entail admitting that we were wrong in our core intuition that electron theory 'needs inferential evidence'? Surely not. What the case of Gretel teaches us is *not* that our intuitive evidentialism about electrons is wrong; what it teaches us is that this evidentialism is not faithfully captured or adequately explicated by rationality-evidentialism.

But now let us suppose that what evidentialists want to say about theistic belief is what we, almost all of us, want to say (and have a hard time saying clearly) about electron-belief. Then rationality-evidentialism also does not faithfully capture what the evidentialist really wants to say about theistic belief.

Towards a more sensible evidentialism

What, then, do *we* mean, when we intuitively take electron-belief to 'need evidence'? There are two sub-questions to press here. First, what sort of *relation to* evidence do we take electron-belief (*qua* believ*ing*) to need? The case of Gretel gives a clue here. She believes in electrons on the say-so or testimony or authority of her teacher in accord with what Reid calls the Credulity Principle. And her teacher may have also acquired his belief in a similar way, so there is here a chain of testimonial grounding. But such a chain must somewhere have an anchor: Neils may believe in electrons by trusting the say-so of Ernst; and Ernst, by trusting the say-so of Wolfgang, but somewhere this chain must be anchored in someone's believing in electrons on a non-testimonial basis. And when we, as evidentialists, insist that belief in electrons needs evidence, it is this ultimate anchoring that we have in mind.

At the heart of our evidentialism regarding electrons, in other words, is the intuition that inferential evidence for electrons needs to be available to the *community* of electron-believers. We do not mean that each *individual* electron-believer needs to have sorted through this evidence or even that each believer is *able* to do so. (Hansel and Gretel may be so deficient in mathematical ability that the evidential case for electrons will forever be beyond their grasp.) No, what is needed is that they be appropriately connected to an electron-believing community, that there be an inferential case for electrons available to this community, and that some appropriate segment of that community have processed this evidence. The needed relation to evidence is a *communitarian* relation, rather than an individualistic one.

The second question is this: for the sake of what doxastic merit is evidence needed? Reformed epistemologists construe evidentialism as claiming that it is needed for the sake of avoiding irrationality. But is this why a communitarian relation to evidence is needed? Consider again Gretel, believing in electrons on the say-so of her fifth grade teacher. We presume, normally, that an evidential case for electrons is indeed available to the community to which she and her teacher belong. But is it the *rationality* of Gretel's belief that is enhanced by this presumed case? Well, imagine that we learn, ten years from now, that our presumption was mistaken – that there *is* no good evidential case for electrons, and that the entire presumed case for electrons was an elaborate hoax perpetrated by clever conmen in Copenhagen in the 1920s. Would learning this lead us to revise our judgement that Gretel was rational – would we, that is, deem that she was (and all along had been) *irrational* in believing in electrons on the say-so of her teacher? Surely not. But this means it is not for the sake of the rationality of her electron-belief that we think such evidence is needed.

Warrant

Wolterstorff refers to the distinction between entitlement and warrant; let us now ask whether we can explicate our evidentialism about electrons in terms of warrant. The term is Plantinga's; he introduces it as a covering term to refer to that special whatever-it-is which, when added to a true belief, makes that true belief a case of knowledge. Classical internalists took that Special Something to be a certain high degree of being *justified* in believing, where being justified is closely allied to being *rational* in one's believing. But externalists hold that it consists in the knowing subject and known object being in a certain type of relationship – a relationship I shall call 'successful epistemic hookup'. On 'reliabilist' theories, a belief has warrant when it is produced by a 'reliable process', a process that produces, or would produce, true beliefs a sufficiently high proportion of the time. What matters, say reliabilists, is the 'external' fact that the process is reliable – not that the subject has any awareness of or access to this reliability. Reliabilists are externalists because they reject the assumption, characteristic of classical (or pre-Gettier) internalism, that the additive that turns true belief into knowledge must be accessible within the subject's perspective.

To make the difference vivid (and determine whether your own proclivities are internalist or externalist) consider the following scenario. Cheech and Chong both wake up to the apparent sound of their alarm clock buzzing, and both form the belief that their alarm is buzzing. Now Cheech is woken by his real alarm clock actually buzzing. Chong, in contrast, has been abducted during the night by technologically advanced Alpha Centaurians, who have drugged him (needlessly), taken him to a planet orbiting Alpha Centauri, and put his brain in a vat, wiring it to a computer which is able to replicate precisely the brain's being in its old body back in the Haight. Chong's 'virtual reality' will, by their advanced technology, be as vivid and complete as Cheech's real experience. The wiring completed, the computer now sends Chong's brain the same electrical signals that it would have received waking up to the sound of his alarm clock. Chong's belief, we finally note, happens to be true, for just as Chong wakes up, a child Alpha Centaurian has wandered into the lab, carrying Chong's alarm clock, which her father had brought back as a little present. She drops the alarm, and it goes off at just the moment that Chong, groggily waking up to the computer-generated sound of an alarm clock, forms the belief 'My alarm clock is ringing.' By coincidence, Chong is thus forming a true belief.

Now though Chong's belief is true, most of us would intuitively say that in this situation he does not have *knowledge* that his alarm clock is ringing. The revealing question is what saying this will incline us to say about Cheech, waking up back on earth to the real sound of his alarm clock ringing. If we say that Chong's belief is *not* knowledge, can we still affirm that Cheech's belief *is* knowledge? Classical internalism creates an extremely strong conceptual pressure to answer 'No, we cannot affirm this.' For internalism holds that the justifiers that make true beliefs 'knowledge' must be things to which the believing subject has access. But in our scenario, Cheech has access to no more or better justifiers than does Chong. Both Cheech and Chong, after all, have the same range and quality of sensations, sensations of waking in a room to the sound and sight of their familiar alarm clocks. There is nothing in his experience to which Cheech can point that is not also available to Chong. Internalistically, the two are on epistemic par; the internalist will thus want to treat them identically. Given our initial judgement that Chong's 'justifiers' do not make his belief knowledge, it will then strongly seem, if we are classical internalists, that Cheech's justifiers cannot make his belief knowledge either.

Externalism, in contrast, allows one to treat the two cases differently. For Cheech's belief is in fact produced by the normal causal process, whereas Chong's is not. Externalists can thus say that Cheech has knowledge while Chong does not, due to some evaluatively relevant difference (say, in their *objective reliability*) between the two processes. Whether this difference was accessible within the perspective or experience of Cheech or Chong is, for externalists, not important: what matters is that the difference is actually there. If it is there, then by externalist's lights, Cheech's true belief can be knowledge though Chong's is not.

Would externalists then see Cheech as justified in his belief, but Chong as unjustified? This is a bit tricky. Sometimes philosophers simply stipulate that they will use 'justified' as the technical term for that epistemic additive, whatever it is, that turns true belief into knowledge. In that event the answer would be 'Yes'. But as Alston and Plantinga have taught us, the word 'justification', as used in ordinary English, is laden with connotations of doing as one ought. Externalists do not deny that beliefs can be evaluated with respect to this; they insist only that this is not what turns true belief into knowledge. Perspicacious externalists thus give a new name for this further thing (warrant, epistemic adequacy, positive epistemic status, Special K), allowing us to retain the old terms (rationality, reasonableness, being justified, and so on) for subject-focused dimensions. In any case, externalists are not offering an account of what is ordinarily called being justified; they are offering an account of something else, and are claiming that it is this something else that turns true belief into knowledge. As they see it, Chong's belief is just as justified (rational) as Cheech's belief: it fails to be knowledge, not because it lacks rational justification, but because it lacks *warrant*.

But will the two be entirely unrelated? Here, I think, many externalists have gone overboard. Externalism says that what soups a true belief up into knowledge is warrant – a relationship of 'positive epistemic hook-up' between the knowing subject and the known object. But a right-headed externalism, as I see it, will insist that this positive epistemic hook-up depends on things going sufficiently right at *both* the subject pole and object pole, not just at the latter. Things going right at the subject pole, especially with respect to how epistemically mature subjects can be expected to perform, given what they have access to, are matters of rationality and justification. On a right-headed account, as I see it, Chong's being sufficiently rational in his believing will remain a necessary condition for his belief's having warrant; it is just not a sufficient condition.

Sensible evidentialism

Let us now return to our question. All of us are evidentialists about some things, like belief in electrons: we intuitively regard electron-belief as needing (in a communitarian sense) evidence. But *for the sake of what* is this needed? We can now propose that it is needed for the sake of electron-beliefs having warrant (or Special K). We have just seen that a belief can lack warrant due to malfunction either at the subject pole (which typically involves irrationality) or at the object pole (which need not). If Gretel is a victim of the Copenhagen Con, the malfunction arises at the object pole. Gretel could thus be *entirely rational* in believing in electrons; nevertheless, the evidentialist (about electrons) will want to say that her belief is epistemically defective (it lacks warrant), due to a dreadful malfunction at the object pole outside her cognitive access. This, I propose, captures with some fidelity what our evidentialism about electrons comes to: about electrons, we are warrant-evidentialists, not rationality- (or entitlement-) evidentialists. Rationality-evidentialism about electrons is, as the case of Gretel helps show, a thoroughly extravagant position. (The denial of this position is, accordingly, rather uninteresting.) But warrant-evidentialism about electrons is not only truer to our intuitions, it is also a far more sensible position. I hereby dub it sensible evidentialism.

But now let us suppose that theistic evidentialists, all along, have meant to say about belief in God the same thing that we, all along, have meant to say about belief in electrons. They have not been rationality-evidentialists; they have been warrant-evidentialists. (Of course they have often *sounded* like rationality-evidentialists; but we have sounded the same way talking about electrons. They, like us, did not after all have the distinctions we now have, between rationality and warrant; so they could express their evidentialist intuitions only through a glass darkly.) The Reformed epistemologists, in all their brush-clearing, have criticized only rationality-evidentialism. But they have never, so far as I can see, sought to clarify what evidentialism about electrons might look like, and to ask whether that might be what evidentialists about God are also trying (in their philosophically juvenile way) to say. In this respect, they have indeed treated evidentialism as a polemical partner.

What is inferential evidence?

Sensible evidentialism, I have argued, holds that beliefs which need inferential evidence need it in a communitarian way (not an individualistic way), and need it for the sake of warrant (not for the sake of rationality). I now turn to one last question: What *is* this 'inferential evidence', that we may need it? Reformed epistemologists, it seems to me, have worked with rather impoverished notions of inferential evidence; I shall propose that this is because they, like the evidentialists they criticize, have fallen under the spell of strong foundationalism. Taking Reid and externalism seriously, as they ask to do, should lead us to expand our notion of inferential evidence.

Consider again Plantinga's 14-year-old theist, brought up to believe in God in a community where everyone so believes. He believes what people tell him about God, but, says Plantinga (1981, p. 33) he 'does not take what people say as evidence'. For:

he does not reason thus: everyone around here says that God loves
us and cares for us; most of what everyone around here says is true;
so probably that's true.

Instead, he *simply believes* what he's taught. Plantinga says Hansel simply believes. He believes in a basic or non-inferential way, for, says Plantinga, he 'does not reason thus'. But what *would* have to be involved, if he *were* to reason thus, so that his belief would qualify as an inferential rather than a basic one? Reformed epistemologists, it seems to me, usually suppose that three things would need to be involved:

(C1) He must explicitly and occurrently believe the propositions that constitute his evidence;

(C2) He must have some insight or putative insight into a support-relation between these occurrently believed propositions and the belief he holds on their basis;

(C3) This insight or putative insight must play a significant causal role in generating or sustaining S's belief that God exists.

Reformed epistemologists, I believe, tend to regard inferential beliefs as requiring these conditions. On C1, consider Plantinga's recent discussion of two sixth-graders, both believing that the earth is round. One of them, we might as well keep her as Gretel, believes this on the basis of evidence. (Perhaps she has, like Aristotle, noticed how sailing ships drop over the visual horizon on a clear day: judging that this is best explained by supposing that the earth is round, she concludes that probably, the earth *is* round.) The other one, let's keep him as Hansel, also believes that the earth is round, but he, in his usual credulous way, just trustingly believes what his teacher tells him. Now the beliefs of both children, Plantinga says, may have warrant, but they get this warrant in quite different ways. Gretel's belief B gets warrant by way 'of being believed on the (evidential) basis' of some other belief, A, and to get warrant in this *evidential* way, she '*must* believe A as well as B'. Hansel's belief, in contrast, gets warrant in a different *testimonial* way, a way for which, Plantinga avers (1993b, p. 138), Hansel 'need *not* explicitly believe that the testifier testifies to what he does'. That thought, Plantinga explains, 'may never cross his mind; he may be paying attention only to the testimony'. Plantinga's point is that the teacher's testimony may *occasion* Hansel's forming a warranted *basic* belief that the earth is round, without Hansel ever forming the belief that his teacher has told him this. And in exactly this respect, as I read him, Plantinga means to contrast Hansel's warranted basic belief with Gretel's warranted *inferential* belief. (An inferential or non-basic belief is one that is held on the evidential basis of other beliefs.) Hansel's belief is *triggered by* (or *grounded in*) testimony, not *inferred* from it: it can thus get warrant from the testimony 'without any explicit belief' on Hansel's part that the teacher has given this testimony. In contrast, Gretel's belief gets its warrant *evidentially* (or inferentially) from B; for this to be so, Gretel, unlike Hansel, 'must believe B'.

C2 says that for S's belief to be inferential, S must have insight or putative insight into a support-relation between the belief and its evidential basis. But what is it to take some belief to support (or be good evidence for) some other belief? Basicalists typically construe this as a matter of having some *argument* that derives the one from the other. Consider here a striking passage by Wolterstorff (1987, p. 76):

> When I survey this gigantic intricate world, I cannot believe that it just came about. I do not mean that I have some good arguments for its being made and that I believe in the arguments. I mean that this conviction wells up irresistibly within me when I contemplate the world.

Now of course, Wolterstorff sees his conviction as due to his apprehending certain features of the world; he even specifies, and so has explicit beliefs about, what these features are. It is, he says, a 'gigantic intricate world'; it is (he says a few lines later) 'full of beauty and splendor', and so on. His belief in God thus satisfies C1. Still, he does not see it as inferential, for he does not 'have good arguments' that get him from these features of the world to theism. Wolterstorff, for this reason, tends to think that his theistic conviction is not evidentially or inferentially based on his beliefs or apprehendings regarding the world's intricacy, splendour, and the like: it is triggered by them, but not inferentially based on them. To be inferentially based on them would require him to have arguments, argument involving some rational insight into support-relations between the world's being intricate, full of beauty and splendour and so on, and its being made by God.

Finally, C3. C3 can be illustrated by an example I heard some years ago from Plantinga concerning his calculator. Plantinga believes that his calculator is reliable; he also perceives that his calculator indicates (under appropriate digital manipulation) that $1+2=3$. And he takes these two things to support, by a good argument, that 1 plus 2 does indeed equal 3. C1 and C2 are thus met for his belief that $1+2=3$. Nevertheless, this belief is basic, not inferential. For his 'calculator argument' is, in Robert Audi's terminology, a reason *for what* he believes (that $1+2=3$) without being a reason *for which* he believes that $1+2=3$.

Calvinians as strong foundationalists

Now there is, no doubt, a non-null set of beliefs that have the three features just adumbrated. But are these what make a belief 'inferential'? That is to say: if we are going to carve our beliefs into those that are basic and those that are inferential, are these the features that should guide our carving? Well, what determines whether a certain way of carving the turkey is a good way or not? Classically, what made 'inferentiality' of interest is that it is one of those things that can confer, or help to confer, epistemic adequacy on a belief. Suppose we go along with this a moment, and refer to a belief as 'properly inferential' when it gets its knowledge-status by virtue of being held in some appropriate *inferential* way. (Being 'properly inferential' will then be the counterpart to being 'properly basic', with the proviso that it is warrant rather than entitlement that we have in mind by the catch-all term 'proper'.) In asking what it takes for a belief to be 'inferential', then, we will have one eye on our conception of what this Special K is; for our question is really: what must inference be, in order to confer on a belief this merit?

Now the Reformed Epistemologists have been tireless in asserting that behind evidentialism lies the bankrupt Zeitgeist of strong foundationalism, leading to impoverished conceptions of what beliefs can be properly basic. When you lift an evidentialist, writes Wolterstorff (1981, p. 142), you almost always find a strong foundationalist. I suggest, in the same spirit, that internalistic strong foundationalism lies behind these overly stringent constraints on what can count as properly inferential beliefs.

In its strongest forms, internalism holds that a belief-forming process can turn a true belief into knowledge only if it meets two requirements:

(R1) It must be something to which the subject has privileged access – something the presence of which is evident from within the subject's perspective.

(R2) It must be something whose relevance to truth is evident to the subject, so the subject can see that the presence of this feature makes a claim worthy of assent.

These requirements say that positive epistemic status is conferred only by things to whose presence and truth-relevance (respectively) we have privileged access. (Here we could also bring in the ideal of acquaintance that Wolterstorff has described.) But these requirements are clearly going to generate strictures on what can be believed in a properly inferential way, just as they do on what can be believed in a properly basic way: a process can give rise to properly (that is, warrant-conferring) inferential beliefs only if it meets requirements R1 and R2. And of course, having a good argument (conceived along Cartesian–Lockean lines) meets both requirements nicely. For such arguments rest on rational insight into 'relations of ideas' (that is, into support-relations), and this is both something one can tell from the inside that one has (meeting R1), and something whose relevance to truth is also evident (meeting R2). So the same internalism that generates strong-foundationalist strictures on the criteria of proper basicality, will also generate these strictures (C1, C2 and C3) on criteria of proper inferentiality. If a process does not meet these conditions, a strong foundationalist will regard it as non-inferential (since it is the essence of inferentiality that it be something that can confer epistemic adequacy on its products).

So let's return to the Wolterstorff passage with which I began this chapter. Wolterstorff's bitter friend asks him 'Why don't you just scrap this God business?' Wolterstorff finds that his conviction, the conviction that God made all this, wells up irresistibly in him as he surveys the world. Reflecting on this conviction, he categorizes it as a basic or non-inferential one; he can specify various features of the world giving rise to his conviction, but he does not have good arguments from them, to its being so made. But does this establish non-inferentiality? It does, if you suppose that good arguments must involve, and provide, rational insight into support-relations – a very natural supposition from the internalistic perspective of strong foundationalism. On what it takes for something to be properly inferential, I thus suggest, when you lift a Calvinian, you almost always find a strong foundationalist.

How externalism loosens the strictures

But what if one is an externalist instead? Here one holds that what generates warrant is, at least in part, something like Goldman's 'being produced by a reliable process', or like Plantinga's 'working in accord with a design plan in appropriate circumstances'. Being externalist, we drop the requirement that something can confer warrant only if the believing subject has privileged reflective access to its presence or truth-relevance. Can we not, in this event, drop some of the old strictures (C1–C3) on proper inferentiality as well?

To make this suggestion more plausible, consider, after all, how we evaluate scientific theories. It is widely agreed that given two incompatible theories, T1 and T2, which both fit the empirical data, T1 can be more rational to accept on account of its being more simple than T2.

When someone does accept T1 over T2, it seems clearly to be as a result of an inferential process. But at the same time, it usually rests on a simplicity-disposition that is barely conscious. Give science students a set of pressure-volume data, and ask them to select between several proposals about how the pressure of a gas varies as a function of its volume. Almost always, they will judge that the simpler function is more likely to be true. But in a philosophy of science class, these same students will initially often dismiss a proposed simplicity criterion with disdain: theories, they will say, must be based on observed facts, not on some wish for simplicity. So in practice, they choose, instinctively as it were, in accord with a norm of simplicity; but they do not, initially at least, feel comfortable preaching what they practise. It is only after considerable reflection that they come to articulate awareness and endorsement of this simplicity instinct in their inferential practices.

Can the inferential include such 'instinctive' dispositions? I believe it can. Copernicus's theory-preference was certainly not a matter of mere perception or memory or introspection; it was a conclusion, based in a broadly inferential way upon apprehended considerations. As Copernicus came to apprehend the simplicity of how heliocentrism explained various data, he found the conviction that the earth orbits the sun welling up irresistibly within him. He could specify the simple-making features, calling the attention of fellow astronomers to them. But he did not have good arguments from them that would persuade sceptical friends like Osiander–arguments, that is, providing rational insight – into the bearing of simplicity considerations on truth. His conviction was inferential; it rested on inferential evidence; but proper inferentiality (like proper basicality) can involve other dispositions besides the ones privileged by strong foundationalism. Internalism makes this difficult to swallow, because Copernicus's inference does not rest on 'rational insight' into a support-relation between the simplicity and the verisimilitude of a theory. Externalism, however, enables us to loosen these strictures on inferentiality without compromising the capacity of inference to contribute to warrant.

Conclusion

We thus must broaden our notion of inferential evidence. Reformed Epistemologists have rightly urged that humans possess a rich array of dispositions producing properly basic beliefs. These dispositions do not need to be justified in terms of that disposition providing rational insight of a Cartesian sort, in order to be worthy of trust, and to confer warrant. Sensible Evidentialists here ask that the processes producing inferential beliefs get parity of treatment. The rich complex of inferential dispositions, every bit as much as the complex of non-inferential ones that interacts with it, ultimately requires an epistemology of trust. And this calls us to broaden our criteria of proper inferentiality, just as we broaden our criteria of proper basicality.

And when we have appropriately broadened it, I think it will turn out that there is more to theistic evidentialism than Calvinians have seen. By this, I do not just mean that when we better understand what is inferential, we will be able to *develop* better inferential arguments for theistic beliefs. I mean that we will be able to discern inferential considerations which have *all along been playing* key roles in forming, sustaining, and shaping the convictions of the theistic community. (This would fit what my colleague Stephen Evans (Evans, 1990), appealing to Newman's account of the 'natural inferences' that play a role in ordinary but mature theistic conviction, calls a 'natural theology in a new key'.) Paul, in his Letter to the Romans, says that God has made his power and deity evident to us through the things He has made. But how does God do this? It seems to me as, incidentally, it seemed to Thomas Reid, that God does so by designing us so that our epistemic access to essential theistic truths involves reliance on *broadly* inferential considerations. This does not rule out important roles for immediate justifiers. Jesus came, Paul says in Ephesians 2:18, that through him we might 'have access in one Spirit to the Father': this access in the Spirit may well have a non-inferential dimension that contributes much to the warrant of our beliefs. Sensible evidentialists are grateful to Reformed Epistemologists for providing a rightful place for these. But sensible theistic evidentialists will urge that this experiential component contributes best, when there is available to the community, broadly inferential evidence for other larger theistic claims. For it is these larger claims that provide the framework within which we interpret the Spirit's experiential work in our lives.

Bibliography

Alston, William: 1983, 'Christian Experience and Christian Belief', in Alvin Plantinga and Nicholas Wolterstorff (eds), *Faith and Rationality: Reason and Belief in God*, University of Notre Dame Press, Notre Dame, IN, 103–34.

Alston, William: 1988a, 'Religious Diversity and Perceptual Knowledge of God', *Faith and Philosophy 5*, 433–48.

Alston, William: 1988b, 'The Perception of God', in Michael Beatty and Richard Lee (eds), *Philosophical Topics 16*, Fall 1988, 23–52.

Alston, William: 1991, *Perceiving God: the Epistemology of Religious Experience*, Cornell University Press, Ithaca, New York.

Alston, William: 1993a, 'On Knowing That We Know: the Application to Religious Knowledge', in C. Stephen Evans and Merold Westfall (eds), *Christian Perspectives on Religious Knowledge*, Eerdmans, Grand Rapids, MI, 15–39.

Alston, William: 1993b, 'Epistemic Disiderata', *Philosophy and Phenomenological Research LIII*, 527–51.

Audi, Robert: 1986, 'Direct Justification, Evidential Dependence, and Theistic Belief', in Robert Audi and William J. Wainwright (eds), *Rationality, Religious Belief, and Moral Commitment*, Cornell University Press, Ithaca, New York, 139–66.

Clark, Kelly James: 1990, *Return to Reason: a Critique of Enlightenment Evidentialism and a Defense of Reason and Belief in God*, Eerdmans, Grand Rapids, MI.

Clark, Kelly James (ed.): 1992, *Our Knowledge of God*, Kluwer, Dordrecht.

Engel, Mylan Jr.: 1992, 'Personal and Doxastic Justification in Epistemology', *Philosophical Studies 67*, 133–50.

Evans, C. Stephen: 1990, 'Apologetics in a New Key: Relieving Protestant Anxieties over Natural Theology', in William L. Craig and Mark S. McLeod (eds), *The Logic of Rational Theism*, Edwin Mellen Press, Lewiston, NY, 66–75.

Evans, C. Stephen and Merold Westphal (eds): 1993, *Christian Perspectives on Religious Knowledge*, Eerdmans, Grand Rapids, MI.

Hasker, William: 1986, 'On Justifying the Christian Practice', *The New Scholasticism 60*, 139–55.

Hoitenga, Dewey: 1991, *Faith and Reason from Plato to Plantinga: an Introduction to Reformed Epistemology*, SUNY Press, Albany, NY.

Konyndyk, Kenneth: 1986, 'Faith and Evidentialism', in Robert Audi and William J. Wainwright (eds), *Rationality, Religious Belief, and Moral Commitment*, Cornell University Press, Ithaca, NY, 82–108.

Kretzmann, Norman: 1992, 'Evidence against Evidentialism', in Kelly James Clark (ed.), *Our Knowledge of God*, Kluwer, Dordrecht.

Mavrodes, George: 1983, 'Jerusalem and Athens Revisited', in Alvin Plantinga and Nicholas Wolterstorff (eds), *Faith and Rationality: Reason and Belief in God*, University of Notre Dame Press, Notre Dame, IN, 192–218.

Mitchell, Basil: 1973, *The Justification of Religious Belief*, Seabury, NY.

Pappas, George S.: 1979, 'Basing Relations', in George Pappas (ed.), *Justification and Knowledge*, D. Reidel, Dordrecht, 51–63.

Phillips, D.Z.: 1988, *Faith after Foundationalism*, Routledge, New York.

Plantinga, Alvin: 1983, 'Reason and Belief in God', in Alvin Plantinga and Nicholas Wolterstorff (eds), *Faith and Rationality*, University of Notre Dame Press, Notre Dame, IN, 16–93.

Plantinga, Alvin: 1986, 'Coherentism and the Evidentialist Objection to Belief in God', in Robert Audi and William J. Wainwright (eds), *Rationality, Religious Belief, and Moral Commitment*, Cornell University Press, Ithaca, NY, 109–29.

Plantinga, Alvin: 1991, 'The Prospects for Natural Theology', in James E. Tomberlin (ed.), *Philosophical Perspectives 5: Philosophy of Religion, 1991*, Ridgeview Publishing, Atascadera, CA, 287–316.

Plantinga, Alvin: 1993a, *Warrant: the Current Debate*, Oxford University Press, Oxford.

Plantinga, Alvin: 1993b, *Warrant and Proper Function*, Oxford University Press, Oxford.

Plantinga, Alvin: 2000, *Warranted Christian Belief*, Oxford University Press, Oxford.

Pojman, Louis: 1987, 'Can Religious Belief Be Rational?', in Louis P. Pojman (ed.), *Philosophy of Religion: an Anthology*, Wadsworth, Belmont, CA, 480–90.

Quinn, Philip L.: 1991, 'Epistemic Parity and Religious Argument', in James E. Tomberlin (ed.), *Philosophical Perspectives 5: Philosophy of Religion, 1991*, Ridgeview Publishing, Atascadera, CA, 317–41.

Radcliffe, Elizabeth S. and Carol J. White (eds): 1993, *Faith and Practice: Essays on Justifying Religious Belief*, Open Court, Chicago, 196–207.

Reid, Thomas: 1970, *An Inquiry into the Human Mind*, ed. Timothy J. Duggan, University of Chicago Press, Chicago.

Reiter, David: 1994, 'Engel on Internalism and Externalism in Epistemology'.

Sennet, James: 1993, 'Reformed Epistemology and Epistemic Duty', in Elizabeth S. Radcliffe and Carol J. White (eds), *Faith and Practice: Essays on Justifying Religious Belief*, Open Court, Chicago, 196–207.

Swinburne, Richard: 1979, *The Existence of God*, Oxford University Press, Oxford.

Williams, Clifford: 1994, 'Kierkegaardian Suspicion and Properly Basic Beliefs', *Religious Studies 30*, 261–7.

Wolterstorff, Nicholas: 1983, 'Can Belief in God Be Rational If It Has No Foundations?', in Alvin Plantinga and Nicholas Wolterstorff (eds), *Faith and Rationality: Reason and Belief in God*, University of Notre Dame Press, Notre Dame, IN, 135–86.

Wolterstorff, Nicholas: 1986, 'The Migration of the Theistic Arguments: from Natural Theology to Evidentialist Apologetics', in Robert Audi and William J. Wainwright (eds), *Rationality, Religious Belief, and Moral Commitment*, Cornell University Press, Ithaca, 38–81.

Wolterstorff, Nicholas: 1987, *Lament for a Son*, Eerdmans, Grand Rapids, MI.

Wolterstorff, Nicholas: 1988, 'Once More: Evidentialism – This Time, Social', in Michael Beatty and Richard Lee (eds), *Philosophical Topics 16*, Fall 1988, 53–74.

Wolterstorff, Nicholas: 1992, 'What Reformed Epistemology Is Not', *Perspectives 7*, November 1992, 14–16.

Wolterstorff, Nicholas: 1999, 'Reformed Epistemology'.

Wykstra, Stephen J.: 1989, 'Toward a Sensible Evidentialism: on the Notion of "Needing Evidence"', in William L. Rowe and William J. Wainwright (eds), *Philosophy of Religion: Selected Readings*, second edition, Harcourt Brace Jovanovich, New York, pp. 426–37.

Wykstra, Stephen J.: 1990, 'Reasons, Redemptions, and Realism: the Axiological Roots of Rationality in Science and Religion', in Michael D. Beaty (ed.), *Christian Theism and the Problems of Philosophy*, University of Notre Dame Press, Notre Dame, pp. 118–61.

Zagzebski, Linda (ed.): 1993, *Rational Faith: Catholic Responses to Reformed Epistemology*, University of Notre Dame Press, Notre Dame, IN.

6
Voices in Discussion

D.Z. Phillips

G: The enlightenment ideal was that of a science of religion – a rational religion. Locke and Kant loom large in this context. Locke thought that every adult must see that belief is rationally grounded, and that rational criteria could be used as a critique of extant religion. I'm told this ideal continues to shape contemporary German philosophy of religion.

Reformed Epistemology rejects this demand. It rejects the ideal of a rationally grounded religion, but does not reject rationality. Something does not have to be grounded to be rational. This does not mean that every religious practice is to be accepted as it stands. Much in it may not be acceptable. But it doesn't need the metaphysical grounding provided by Locke and Kant. All this being so, I need to say more about rationality.

We need to distinguish between three stages of Reformed Epistemology. First, the papers which belong to the 1970s. Second, the publication of *Faith and Rationality* in 1983 where the former arguments are given a more articulate form, now influenced by Thomas Reid. The emphasis was mainly negative, showing what Reformed Epistemology denied. It is in a Dutch neo-Calvinist tradition. Its aim is not, like Augustine, to understand a faith already given, but to work out a view of all things in the light of faith. Clement of Alexandria would be an example of such an endeavour. Third, after 1983 the emphasis is more positive: on warrant and justification; application of these to particular features of human life; and the bearing of one's religious commitments on one's intellectual and non-intellectual life. It has never been the aim of Reformed Epistemology to give a general account of religion or religious practices. Critics have thought that it wanted to do more, but this is not so.

I ended my paper by trying to pinpoint the differences between Reformed Epistemology and Wittgensteinianism in the philosophy of religion. The latter seems to deny that 'God' is a referring expression, that there is a 'something' which this word picks out. Bowsma was an exception to this. I sometimes hear echoes of Kant in this view; sometimes I hear an insistence that one can only refer to what one can point to; but I really don't understand why Wittgensteinians deny that we can refer to God.

N: Reformed epistemology is to Calvin College what logical positivism is to Vienna. I feel like a country priest asked to criticize the pope. But I've been an evidentialist since the age of fourteen. I think that the evidentialist Reformed Epistemology attacks is a straw man. When I looked at the stars I thought that the question of whether God had created them could go either way. Why must rationality shun evidentialism by saying, with Plantinga, that it all depends on what you regard as 'properly basic'? Plantinga uses 'evidence' in the narrow sense of inferential evidence. Reformed epistemologists say that when you look at a daisy, or, better, a tulip, you find welling up inside you the thought that God is present. Similarly when one is told that God was reconciling the world to himself in Jesus Christ. These basic tendencies are innocent until proved guilty, so we can go along with these doxastic practices. That's Calvinism.

But I think evidence is needed if I am asked to believe that matter is composed of protons, neutrons and electrons. Other beliefs, such as 'I have two hands' are not believed on evidence. What about religious belief? Does it need evidence in Plantinga's narrow sense?

I agree that we need to get beyond the first two negative stages of Reformed Epistemology to a consideration of warrant and justification. So what is it for a belief to be rational? Rationality is a many splendoured thing, but to be irrational is to be culpable; it is not doing your duty by the evidence. Reformed epistemologists rightly reject inferential evidence, for belief in God is basic. It can be reasonable to believe that God exists. So rational belief does not entail evidence. The same is true in science where we choose to believe our teachers. We can see that the claims need evidence, but we need not have gathered it ourselves.

The notion of warrant helps us to capture these complexities. It operates at a subject pole. To be warranted at the object pole, things must be as the belief claims. But this warranting need not be something actually done at the subject pole. Yet, someone in the community must have done so. The need for evidence, then, is not that of a specific individual, but that of a community. If we think of evidence in this way, different types of evidence must be brought in.

D: Since *G* has devoted a considerable amount of space to his disagreements with *C*, I'm going to ask *C* to reply.

C: First, I want to comment on *G*'s claim that I have misunderstood Plantinga. *G* claims that when you lift an evidentialist you find a strong foundationalist. *N* responds that when you lift a Calvinian you almost always find a strong foundationalist. Was Plantinga an exception? Not on my reading of *Faith and Rationality* and the early discussions of it in *The Reformed Journal*. It is clear in them that the relation of Reformed Epistemology to foundationalism was a central issue; especially the claim that there are only two kinds of foundational propositions, the self-evident propositions of logic and mathematics, and the propositions concerning incorrigible sense experiences. Plantinga argued that since there is no adequate criterion for proper basicality, theists should not accept this restriction. The proposition that there are only two kinds of foundational propositions, he argued, is not itself a self-evident proposition. Thus, although a believer cannot demonstrate to an unbeliever why he should place belief in God in the foundations of his noetic structure, the latter has no good logical reason to prevent the believer from doing so. Reacting to this in *The Reformed Journal*, Jesse de Boer said: 'While Plantinga protests that foundationalism ought to be abandoned, what he in fact does himself is to add to the foundations our belief in God. He calls this belief 'properly basic' and so, by the sense of his own idiom, he stays inside the foundationalist camp.' *G* denies this, but de Boer's kind of point led to distinctions being made between classical foundationalism – the view that there are only two kinds of foundational propositions – and foundationalism.

G argues that the idiom of 'proper basicality' must not be used to mean 'foundations'. Plantinga did not take this advice. Here he is in the battle for foundations: 'On this view every noetic structure has a foundation; and a proposition is rational for S, or known by S, only if it stands in the appropriate relations to the foundations of S's noetic structure ... Might it not be that my belief in God is itself in the foundations of my noetic structure? Perhaps it is a member of F, in which case, of course, it will automatically be evident with respect to G.' Again, here is Plantinga responding to a classical foundationalist: 'He means to commit himself to reason and to nothing more – belief in God, for example – in its foundations. But here there is no reason for the theist to follow his example; the believer is not obliged to take his word for it. So far we have found no reason at all for excluding belief in God from the foundations.'

No doubt Reformed Epistemology has now gone in somewhat different directions. G says that by 'basic belief' Plantinga means what he means by 'immediate belief'. Perhaps – and here I speculate, G was always less enamoured with relations between 'immediate belief' and 'foundational basicality' than Plantinga, in which case his present comments could be seen as an exercise in damage limitation in this area.

G gives the impression that my criticisms depend entirely on the issue of foundations. This is not so. I spend an equal amount of time criticizing the notion of 'immediate belief' and its relation to authenticity. I criticize, on grounds of logic, the fatal slide from the fact that an individual need not, in fact, check the authenticity of an experience, to the claim that the experience is self-authenticating. Plantinga conflates psychological and logical considerations, as when he claims that the self-evidence of mathematical propositions must be relativized to persons. Whether an individual grasps a mathematical proposition does not affect its logical status as a proposition – that is determined by the arithmetical system. No matter what mathematical intuitions one may have one must still pass the examination. No matter what religious intuitions one may have, the spirits are tested to see whether they are of God in the wider religious practice. There are differences between these cases, and no doubt between them and examples discussed in *On Certainty*, but they do not affect the logical point at issue. All these points and quotations are made in *Faith after Foundationalism*, and I am disappointed that G does not address them.

Second, a word about G's conception of the issue between Reformed Epistemology and Wittgensteinianism: the question of whether 'there is any such phenomenon as *referring* to God'. He says that I deny this and hold that there is nothing we can predicate of God for the simple reason 'that there's no such being as God to refer to'. Hence the charge that I give an atheistic account of religious language. G says that he could cite passage after passage to support this view, but thinks it otiose to do so for an audience such as this, whereas, ironically, J says that I have pointed out the misunderstandings of claims like G's 'so often and so forcefully that it would seem entirely otiose even to raise the question again, if it were not for the fact that these rebuttals have been so singularly unsuccessful in achieving their aim'. Why should this be so? Because readers like G prefer to construct general theses and propositions than pay attention to the detailed grammatical analyses which have been offered by, for example, Rush Rhees, Peter Winch and myself. It is only by ignoring these analyses and examples that G can accuse me of being 'remarkably chary of telling us why there cannot be any such phenomenon as referring to God'. So let me remind him of some. Rush Rhees brings out the difference between talking about a human being and talking about God. I may know Winston Churchill without knowing that he is Prime Minister or a company director. I can point to the 'it' of which these things are true – that chap over there. But, Rhees says, 'I could not know God without knowing that he was Creator and Father of all things. That would be like saying that I might come to know Winston Churchill without knowing that he had face, hands, body, voice or any of the attributes of a human being.' There is an internal relation then between love, grace, majesty, and so forth, and God's reality. It is not that these belong to a further something, a thing, as in the case of a human being, but that these uses of 'love', 'grace' and 'majesty' are themselves the conceptual parameters of the kind of reality God has – God is divinely real. G is wrong in thinking that O.K. Bouwsma does not concur with this view. Bouwsma points out how we can be misled by the indicative form of certain sentences such as 'Great is Jehovah', 'Jehovah reigneth', into thinking that they are bits of information, descriptions of an object called 'God', whereas other sentences, such as, 'Bless Jehovah, O my soul', by their imperative form, help us to avoid that misunderstanding. He asks whether 'High is our God above all gods' is to be understood as 'High is the Empire State Building above all other buildings in New York' and, looking at the state of philosophy of religion replied sadly, 'I'm afraid so.'

G thinks that I would go to the death rather than use the word 'refer' in relation to God. On many occasions I have said that this is not so. With Rhees I have said that if not using it leads to trouble, if it leads to the view that talking about God doesn't mean anything, or if it leads G to think I hold that all religious language is metaphorical – a view I argue against in the last chapter of *Faith after Foundationalism* – or more surrealistically, if he thinks that I have reduced 'God' to an exclamation – then by all means keep the word 'refer'. Only, don't think you have achieved any clarificatory work by simply putting the word in italics. Consider: 'I have a hole in my heart', 'I have palpitations in my heart', 'I have God in my heart.' By all means say that something is referred to in all these cases, but it is not the word 'something' or 'reference' which gives sense to these expressions, but the uses of these expressions, including the uses of 'in my heart', which illuminate the grammar of 'something' and 'reference' in these contexts. Don't fight over labels – look at their use.

A final paragraph about the nature of philosophy. Wittgenstein stands in a contemplative tradition which goes back to Plato. As *N* says, *G*'s tradition offers, not a philosophy of religion, but a religious philosophy. *G* says that his task is not that of seeking to understand a faith already given, but 'to develop history, sociology, philosophy, political theory, and so forth, in the light of faith'. The nature of philosophy is itself a philosophical problem and much of its history has been spent discussing it. In Wittgenstein, we see a supreme example of an attempt to teach us differences born of philosophical wonder at the world in all its variety – the city with no main road. Thus it raises the question of what it is to see all things religiously; whether that perspective is a theoretical matter. It would want to see what other perspectives look like and what disagreement between them amounts to. It would deny that philosophy underwrites any of these perspectives. It seems that in Reformed Epistemology all subjects are the handmaid of faith which has the final say. By contrast, from a contemplative tradition Wittgenstein says: 'A philosopher is not a citizen of any community of ideas. That's what makes him a philosopher.'

F: I take *G*'s point that belief can be shaped by tradition, but can there be competing basic beliefs? Nietzsche looked at the sky and concluded that the whole is a great cosmic stupidity. The universe doesn't even know we are here. How do we solve these conflicts?

G: *F* is wary of religious authority. How do you see a person by religious authority? This is where Reid on perception came to my aid. For Descartes and Locke you begin with sensations and then infer the existence of the external world. For them, perception is reasoning by inference. Reid says that our sensations carry information about the external world. We are so 'hard-wired' that we form beliefs on the basis of these sensations, but that there is no process of reasoning which enables you to do this. We are so constructed that we trust our beliefs. There is no non-circular argument for doing so.

So Reformed Epistemology says that a religious perception of reality, if things are working properly, would form an idea of God. Whether we can find good arguments for this would be an interesting quest, as in the case of sensations and the external world, but they can't make the transition in themselves. Now *N* says, 'No. The proper analogy is not between religious belief and Reidian perception, but between religious belief and explanation in science.'

If we take the Reidian conception our beliefs will be due to our 'hard-wiring' and to which concepts are available to us. The concept of a computer may not be available to a tribe. So everything depends on which concepts get formed.

I: You say that basic beliefs are non-inferential, but how are they formed? What mediating factors make them possible? How do we choose our basic beliefs? Are basic beliefs frozen for all time?

G: There are many modes of mediation, so no general talk will do. We have to get away from the paradigmatic distinction between mediate and immediate knowledge found in Locke. The use of warrant can appeal to a variety of mediations which get us away from thinking of the foundational aspect. In response to *C*'s earlier comments I will admit that Plantinga is reluctant to come straight out and admit that this constitutes a change.

O: How does the appeal to authority get going? Is there a necessary link between Reformed Epistemology and the function of authority?

N: This depends on what claims are being made. I would never have re-entered the Christian fold if I had simply been told to accept an authority; for example, if I had simply been told, 'Read the scriptures and wait for conviction.' I needed to read F.D. Bruce and the opinion of other scholars about Biblical documents. Claims sometimes depend on their work.

O: Does that apply to 'God exists'?

N: A believer may have an inchoate sense of the evidence, in which case philosophers like Swinburne can be of help.

G: But what is being appealed to here seems to be a blend of philosophy and theology. It is essential to Reformed Epistemology that the assessment of beliefs is carried on in the context of a living faith. If you don't accept this you will be attracted to a position like *N*'s. But if *N* thinks that the Reidian view of perception is correct, why not apply it to religion?

P: But what does a child know of this inner community which recognizes the need for grace? Isn't this a dogmatic, insular view which doesn't recognize the child's situation, or the various traditions of different countries? Reformed Epistemology seems insular.

N: I think you're right. The believer needs to be convinced not only at the subject pole, but also at the object pole. He must listen to what experts say about how things are.

Q: For sophisticated people, it is claimed, it won't be enough to say 'He lives in my heart.' But doesn't a lot depend on that? What would a neutral assessment of the evidence be like?

R: Well, it's not enough for a belief to be merely in the air. A testimonial claim can be as strong as its weakest link and indefinitely long. Some claims go back to Christ. Don't we get a strong grounding for these in the community?

G: I'm not sure where N stands. At first he stresses the need for evidence. But then he says that the inference can be highly intuitive and need not be laid out by anyone. That would bring it close to unreformed canonical Reformed Epistemology. But then N adds that this highly intuitive inference must be spelled out by someone in the community. But N would not make this added requirement in the case of perception.

In conclusion, let me return to issues raised by Wittgensteinianism and respond to C's earlier comments. Take a phrase like 'Father of all things'. If C is prepared to say that this 'picks out something' to which I can relate my hopes and disappointments, there is no dispute between us.

H: But what if it said that sentences in Christian beliefs are not assertions, but performative utterances. How does that affect their truth?

G: They may be performative or relational, but they are still statements that address something. In 'Bless the Lord O my soul', the Lord is still picked out.

C: But so far we have said nothing about the grammar of either 'something' or 'pick out' in this context.

G: Agreed. That is the point at which a detailed future discussion between us would need to begin.

*   *   *

Part III

Wittgenstein and Wittgensteinianism

7
Wittgenstein and the Philosophy of Religion

Stephen Mulhall

Wittgensteinian approaches to issues in the philosophy of religion have plainly been amongst the most consequential in the discipline in the postwar period. This is not, of course, because a general consensus in their favour has been established; on the contrary, if anything unites contemporary philosophers of religion, it is their deep suspicion of both the specific claims and the general methodology of those of their colleagues who have adopted a Wittgensteinian perspective. Nevertheless, it is rare to find a philosopher of religion who does not define her own position, at least in part, by specifying the nature of and the grounds for her rejection of work carried out under the Wittgensteinian banner. In this respect, that work continues to function as an essential reference point in the discipline – something that can no longer be said of many other fields of philosophical endeavour, even in the philosophy of mind or the philosophy of language (where some of Wittgenstein's specific claims continue to attract interest, but the general methodological principles which anchor and account for them are barely mentioned, let alone specifically criticized).

Those better apprised of the radical subversion to which Wittgenstein aimed to subject the discipline of philosophy can hardly be surprised at the suspicion in which Wittgensteinian approaches to religion are held; but they are bound to be intrigued by the way in which philosophers of religion seem far less capable than their colleagues in cognate fields of simply leaving those approaches behind – of treating their own suspicions as adequate grounds for dismissing Wittgensteinian approaches rather than as endlessly renewed incentives to re-examine them. It is almost as if these approaches go with the territory – as if this perspective on the philosophy of religion resonates so intimately with some barely registered but fundamental aspect of the domain of religion itself that those fascinated by the latter naturally find themselves unable definitively to dismiss the former.

Is this sense of paradox intensified or dissipated if we further note that Wittgenstein's own remarks on the philosophy of religion are vanishingly slight in comparison with the sheer mass of his remarks on the philosophy of mind or of language? Should we conclude that philosophers somehow find it easier to get beyond the former than to dismiss the latter entirely, easier as it were to stumble over a few scattered pebbles than to vault over a mountain range? Or should we rather recognize that the very paucity of Wittgenstein's own remarks makes them difficult to construe and hence easy to misconstrue? Seen in this light, it may seem that what so many philosophers of religion stumble over is not so much Wittgenstein's few pebbles but the complex and ramified edifice that has been constructed from them; it may be that what they find objectionable is not Wittgenstein but what Wittgensteinians have made of him. These opening impressions suggest a tripartite structure for the ensuing discussion. I shall begin by examining Wittgenstein's own remarks on the philosophy of religion; then I shall look at the distinctive characteristics of Wittgensteinian approaches to this area; and I shall conclude by raising some questions about what one might call a religious interpretation of Wittgenstein's general approach to philosophy – about how one might attempt to account for the spiritual fervour that so many have sensed in his writings.

Wittgenstein's interpretation of religion

In attempting to elucidate Wittgenstein's philosophical view of religion and religious belief, we must bear in mind not only that his recorded expressions of those views are very small in number but also that few of them were recorded by him and none were originally intended for publication (our sources consist of 20 pages of his students' lecture notes[1] and a scattering of remarks in such miscellanies as *Culture and Value*[2] and *Recollections of Wittgenstein*.)[3] In other words, even these apparently direct expressions of his views are in reality multiply filtered through the memories, editorial proclivities and linguistic sensibilities of others; even here, separating Wittgenstein from the Wittgensteinians is far from simple.

The most systematically developed of these remarks (which is not to say that they are very systematically developed) are presented in the notes made of three 1938 lectures. Broadly speaking, the first lecture emphasizes important differences between religious beliefs and beliefs about matters of fact (historical and empirical matters); the second emphasizes parallel differences between a belief in God's existence and a belief in the existence of a person or object; and the third explores the significance of a belief in life after death, or in the immortality of the soul. In all three cases, Wittgenstein engages in a grammatical investigation of these topics: he attempts to clarify the nature of religious belief by clarifying the use of expressions of religious belief – the place of religious concepts and religious uses of concepts in the lives of believers and unbelievers.

What he claims to establish thereby grows from one fundamental insight – the fact that those who hold to religious doctrines do not treat those commitments in the way they would treat an empirical claim. They do not regard them as hypotheses whose credibility varies in accordance with the strength of the evidence in their favour, they do not assign them degrees of probability, and so on. Even with what appear to be historical religious propositions (for example, concerning Christ's existence and life on earth), says Wittgenstein, believers do not treat them as they do other historical propositions. His point is not just that a believer's conviction in their truth appears utterly insensitive to the kinds of ground for doubt and caution that she would apply to other propositions about the dim and distant past. It is rather that, even if propositions about Christ's life in Palestine were established beyond all reasonable doubt in just the way that (for example) some facts about Napoleon's life have been established, this kind of certainty would not have the practical consequences in our lives that a religious belief has. As Wittgenstein puts it: 'the indubitability wouldn't be enough to make me change my whole life' (LC, p. 57).

In other words, the divergence between the role played in our lives by religious beliefs and by empirical beliefs is so systematic and pervasive that they must be acknowledged to be very different kinds of belief. We would otherwise be forced to the conclusion that religious believers generally act in a manner so ludicrously irrational as to strain credibility: as blunders go, this would just be too big – certainly too big to attribute to people who don't after all treat weather forecasts in the way they treat Gospel warnings about the Last Judgement. Neither, on the other hand, would we want to say that religious beliefs are obviously rational, as if it is obviously unreasonable to reject what faith demands. Religious believers base matters of great moment on evidence that seems exceedingly flimsy by comparison with the corroboration they require before accepting claims of far less significance for their lives; and 'anyone who reads the Epistles will find it said: not only that it is not reasonable but that it is folly. Not only is it not reasonable, but it doesn't pretend to be' (LC, p. 58). It is rather that the evidence for religious beliefs, the doubts to which they may be subject and the certainty they may command are not species of empirical evidence, doubt and certainty. '[Religious] controversies look quite different from any normal controversies. Reasons look entirely different from normal reasons' (LC, p. 56). From this contention, everything else Wittgenstein says in these lectures can be derived. His claim that the religious believer and the atheist cannot be said to contradict one another in the manner of disputants over an empirical claim, and his observation that a belief in the existence of God plays a role entirely unlike that of a belief in the existence of any person or object he has ever heard of (buttressed by pointing out that, for example, our ways of employing pictures of God do not include any technique of comparing the picture to that which it depicts), simply reiterate at a more concrete level his general claim about the difference between religious beliefs and empirical ones. And his discussion of the role played by a belief in life after death proceeds on the assumption that this is not an empirical hypothesis about the relation of minds to bodies, and asks how such a claim might play a role in the lives of those who make it; he suggests that this role would be clarified if, for example, the believer connects the idea to certain notions of ethical responsibility (for example, by relating the soul's immortality to the idea of its being subject to judgement). Here Wittgenstein attempts to locate one religious concept in a grammatical network of other such concepts, and to locate that network in the context of a certain way of living – thus returning us to the opening theme of his first lecture in a manner that should surprise no-one familiar with his general methodological claim that 'to imagine a language is to imagine a form of life'.

Most of the remarks about religion scattered through the miscellanies I mentioned earlier could also be seen simply as developing this same fundamental point about the divergences between religious and empirical beliefs. This is particularly evident with respect to two remarks from *Culture and Value* that have attracted particular attention: God's essence is supposed to guarantee his existence – what this really means is that what is here at issue is not the existence of something (CV, p. 82). It strikes me that a religious belief could only be something like a passionate commitment to a system of reference (CV, p. 64).

As the sentences immediately following the former remark make clear, Wittgenstein is not denying that a belief in God's existence is a belief in the existence of something but rather that it is a belief in the existence of some thing; he is denying that God's existence is akin to the existence of a white elephant, of a physical object or entity – specifically in the sense that God (like the white elephant) might not have existed, that the grammar of the concept of 'God' is such as to allow us to talk of 'what it would be like if there were (or if there were not) such a thing as "God"'. As for the latter remark, it merely encapsulates Wittgenstein's claims in the lecture that religious believers orient their existence as a whole by reference to what he calls 'pictures' – specific, interrelated ways of interpreting and responding to the events and experiences that make up their lives, ways that can only be understood and explained in terms of religious concepts.

Strangely, however, much of the criticism directed at Wittgenstein's views on religion has been focused on these remarks rather than upon the more detailed and systematic lecture notes from which they derive; and that criticism has depended for its plausibility upon ignoring their roots in that material, as well as their more immediate contexts. For example, John Hyman, the author of the entry on 'Wittgensteinianism' (which is in fact an entry exclusively on Wittgenstein) in the recent *Blackwell Companion to the Philosophy of Religion*,[4] finds both remarks impossible to accept.[5] The former, he claims, is not supported either by the disanalogy between 'God exists' and existential propositions in science or history or geography, or by the doctrine that God cannot begin or cease to exist. 'If Democritus believed that atoms cannot begin or cease to exist, it does not follow that he did not believe that an atom is "eine Existenz" – an entity, or something which exists' (IWM, p. 261).

The difficulty with this argument is its extreme compression, or rather its apparent assumption that we can tell what exactly Democritus's beliefs about atoms amount to without far more information about their implications. In the first place, does his belief that atoms can neither begin nor cease to exist amount to a belief in their eternal existence or a belief in their endless duration (to employ a distinction of Norman Malcolm's, overlooked by Hyman despite his favourable citation of some of Malcolm's other remarks in the same essay)? A physical object or object-constituent might come into being at the beginning of the universe and remain in existence until its end; but its non-existence would remain conceivable, and hence its endless duration would be no less contingent than that of a particular white elephant. God's existence, by contrast (as a Kierkegaardian remark also quoted by Hyman asserts), is eternal: his existence is not just unending but necessary. Until we know which of these conceptions of atomic existence Democritus favours, we cannot assess its validity as a counter-example, since an endlessly enduring atom would deserve the epithet 'eine Existenz' as Wittgenstein deploys it in a way that an eternal atom would not.

Second, even if Democritus does turn out to believe that atoms have eternal existence, whilst still being inclined to call both atoms and white elephants 'existent things', this would not show that the kind of existence possessed by empirical things and that possessed by eternal beings was identical. On the contrary; the fact that Democritus conceives of atoms in such a way as to exclude certain possibilities that he leaves open with respect to elephants (and vice versa) precisely implies that the kind of existence he attributes to the former is very different from that which he attributes to the latter. Whether or not he (or we) would want to call both 'entities' or 'existent things' is entirely irrelevant; what matters is not our inclination to use the same phrase in both contexts when we give expression to our beliefs, but whether or not we put it to the same kind of use.

Hyman's objections to the second remark culled from *Culture and Value* are equally unsound. ... I see no reason to accept that coming to believe that God exists is nothing but coming to feel 'a passionate commitment to a system of reference' – that is, coming to feel committed to leading a life in which questions will be asked, obligations will be acknowledged, decisions taken and actions performed, which can only be explained or understood by the use of religious concepts. For surely, if a convert makes that commitment, perhaps because he feels compelled to, his belief that God exists will typically be part of his reason for doing so. Nothing in Wittgenstein's later philosophy, and in particular no part of his doctrine about the relation between language and forms of life, implies that a form of life cannot involve historical or metaphysical beliefs (such as that Jesus rose from the dead or that the soul is immortal) as well as concepts and attitudes: all of them – beliefs, concepts and attitudes – in a mutually supporting relation (IWM, p. 260).

Note to begin with that Wittgenstein does not claim that coming to believe that God exists is nothing but a passionate commitment to a system of reference; he claims that 'a religious belief' could only be something like such a commitment. One might legitimately question Wittgenstein's implication that there is only one possible way of understanding or living out a religious life; but to say that 'x is something like y' is plainly not equivalent to saying that 'x is nothing but y'. Furthermore, to equate a belief in God's existence with religious belief *per se* makes sense only on the assumption that a religious belief or religious faith is nothing but (either reducible to or founded upon) a belief in the existence of God – as if adopting a religious form of life is a secondary consequence of a logically prior and logically independent existential belief. And indeed, just such a model is presupposed by the objection Hyman then goes on to make to Wittgenstein's claim: he asserts that a belief in God's existence is typically one's reason for committing oneself to a religious frame of reference.

But this assertion takes it for granted that we know what such a belief amounts to or signifies – what the claim to believe that God exists (or more plausibly, the claim to believe in God) actually means. And on Wittgenstein's view, we can only establish this by determining how the concept of God functions in the practice and life of a religious believer, which means investigating the grammatical connections between this concept and the multitude of other religious concepts in terms of which a believer interprets the events and experiences of her life. But if, according to this approach, no-one can so much as understand what a belief in God's existence amounts to without grasping the location of that concept in the grammatical network of religious concepts that Wittgenstein here describes as a system of reference, it makes no sense to think that one can first establish the truth of that belief and then use it as a reason for adopting the system of reference. On the contrary, one could not acquire a belief in God's existence without both understanding and committing oneself to the broader grammatical system in which the concept of God has its life. Consequently, Hyman's objection to Wittgenstein's remark simply begs the question against Wittgenstein's whole approach – not only to the philosophy of religion but to philosophy in general.

It is worth noting that Hyman is also wrong to imply that this approach entails eliminating either the specific belief in God's existence or the very idea of religious belief more generally from our conception of what goes to make up a religious way of life. On the contrary, his claim that religious faith involves a mutually supporting relation of beliefs, concepts and attitudes is perfectly consistent with Wittgenstein's position. For first, claiming that the concept of God forms part of a system of religious concepts does not entail reducing that concept to the other concepts to which it is related, any more than noting the grammatical relations between psychological concepts and concepts of behaviour entails reducing the concept of pain to that of pain-behaviour; the concepts are internally related, not synonymous. Neither does Wittgenstein's emphasis on the system of religious concepts entail denying that religious faith involves a multitude of specific beliefs;

on the contrary, that system of concepts is what makes it possible for believers to give expression to their beliefs, and it is in part through that system and the linguistic expressions it makes possible that religious attitudes make themselves manifest. Whether we want to say with Hyman that such religious beliefs are 'historical and metaphysical' depends on precisely what these modifying adjectives imply, and whether they are meant to constitute an exhaustive classification. Wittgenstein offers us reason to doubt whether religious historical beliefs are like other kinds of historical belief; and whilst we have no reason to expect metaphysical beliefs to be any less liable to influence the religious thinking of human beings than their moral or scientific thinking, we have as yet no reason to think that they are ineliminable or dominant. This question, however, raises issues that can be more fruitfully pursued by examining the uses to which Wittgensteinians have put Wittgenstein's own insights.

Before we go on to that section of the paper, however, I would like to conclude by pointing out that the fundamental observation from which the rest of Wittgenstein's claims derive – the idea that religious beliefs are very different from empirical beliefs – is itself hardly original. For it amounts to no more than a reiteration of the core argument in Part I of Kierkegaard's pseudonymous text Concluding Unscientific Postscript,[6] which comprises chapters in which Climacus examines the objective question posed by Christianity and concludes that religious beliefs cannot be a species of historical belief because 'the greatest attainable certainty with respect to anything historical is a mere approximation'. Of course, Wittgenstein restates this claim in his own terms, and thereby eliminates from it Climacus's dubious assumption that there can be no such thing as certainty with respect to historical beliefs; but the core of his idea remains untouched, and other themes from the Postscript (passion, indirect communication, despair) pervade the long paragraph from which Wittgenstein's remark about religious belief as a commitment to a system of reference is taken.

It strikes me that a religious belief could only be something like a passionate commitment to a system of reference. Hence, although it's belief, it's really a way of living, or a way of assessing life. It's passionately seizing hold of this interpretation. Instruction in a religious faith, therefore, would have to take the form of a portrayal, a description, of that system of reference, while at the same time being an appeal to conscience. And this combination would have to result in the pupil himself, of his own accord, passionately taking hold of the system of reference. It would be as though someone were first to let me see the hopelessness of my situation and then show me the means of rescue until, of my own accord, or not at any rate led to it by my instructor, I ran to it and grasped it (CV, p. 64).

But of course, these themes will have been familiar to theologians and philosophers of religion for a number of years – they constitute a long-recognized mode of understanding Christianity and its relation to morality and philosophy, one which is certainly not universally accepted but which is equally certainly taken to be a substantial and respectable theological option, and which long pre-dates any influence Wittgenstein's writings and teaching have exerted. Why, then, when Wittgenstein restates these familiar themes, should they have elicited such an apparently undismissable intensity of interest and hostility from philosophers of religion? Perhaps an examination of the work of those influenced by Wittgenstein's remarks will help to account for this otherwise puzzling phenomenon.

Wittgensteinian interpretations of religion

Ever since the publication of Kai Neilsen's article entitled 'Wittgenstein-ian Fideism',[7] certain fundamental misunderstandings about the nature of Wittgensteinian philosophy of religion have embedded themselves seemingly beyond recovery in the collective philosophical unconscious. Writers influenced by Wittgenstein – particularly D.Z. Phillips – have identified and attempted to rebut these misconceptions so often and so forcefully that it would seem entirely otiose even to raise the question again, if it were not for the fact that these rebuttals have been so singu-larly unsuccessful in achieving their aim of clarifying the true implica-tions of the Wittgensteinian approach. What I want to do, then, is look at this issue one more time – not so much with the aim of trying to settle the dispute, but in order to try to understand a little more clearly why we seemed doomed endlessly to repeat the dance of mutual mis-understanding that this dispute now seems destined to embody.

What makes the ineradicability of the term 'Wittgensteinian Fideism' so puzzling is that its users manage thereby to imply two radically con-tradictory lines of criticism simultaneously. The first is that Wittgen-steinian approaches illegitimately render traditional religion immune to criticism; the second is that they illegitimately criticize traditional religious attempts to justify faith. Nielsen's original article focuses on the former line of argument, claiming that according to certain followers of Wittgenstein:

> [Religion] can only be understood or criticised, and then only in a piecemeal way, from within this mode by someone who has a participant's understanding of this mode of discourse. To argue ... that the very first-order discourse of this form of life is incoherent or irrational can be nothing but a confusion, for it is this very form of life, this very form of discourse itself, that sets its own criteria of coherence, intelligibility or rationality. Philosophy cannot relevantly criticise religion; it can only display for us the workings, the style of functioning, of religious discourse. (WF, p. 193)

Hyman's article includes a trenchant version of the latter line of argument.

> [S]ince evidence and argument are not the exclusive property of science, Wittgenstein cannot be right to insist that if we try to prove or support the proposition that God exists, we are treating religion as if it were science, and are therefore already trapped in confusion. It would, I think, be a mistake to maintain that because Anselm and Aquinas sought to prove the existence of God, they were peddling a variety of pseudo-science, a superstition which has nothing to do with religious faith. (IWM, p. 261)

It is certainly difficult to see how anyone could maintain both lines of argument simultaneously; but might not one or the other of them nevertheless be sound?

It must be admitted at once that the ways in which some Wittgensteinians have expressed themselves has helped to give some foundation to the first of these lines of criticism. For example, Hyman is rightly critical of D.Z. Phillips's recently expressed, incautious but revealing claim that:

> If the notion of an inner substance called 'the soul' is the philosophical chimera we have suggested it is, whatever is meant by the immortality of the soul cannot be the continued existence of such a substance. (DS,[8] p. 237)

Since, as Hyman says, there is no obvious reason why it should be impossible to espouse, sincerely and seriously, demonstrably incoherent doctrines, Phillips's inference is plainly invalid; and the fact that he failed to notice this plausibly suggests that he has a tendency to assume that religious beliefs and forms of life are essentially not illusory (if not necessarily beyond criticism). Nevertheless, such remarks can and should be dismissed as incidental slips unless it can be demonstrated that a similar tendency infects principles that are at the heart of the Wittgensteinian approach to the philosophy of religion; and we have good reason for thinking that they are not.

For example, D.Z. Phillips has repeatedly argued that Nielsen's worries are entirely unfounded, because they fail to acknowledge that Wittgensteinian analyses of religious belief work not by isolating religious discourse and practice from the rest of human experience and life but by relating them to it. The process of clarifying the meaning of a religious concept certainly involves relating that concept to other religious concepts, and to the attitudes and beliefs that go to make up a religious way of life; but it also involves relating that system of concepts, attitudes and beliefs to more general human phenomena. Praying to God, for example, makes sense only because human life includes experiences and events for which God might intelligibly be thanked, desires and purposes about which petitions might be made, and actions and thoughts which might intelligibly form the subject of a confession or request for absolution. It is precisely because religious faith can be presented as one way of responding to the ordinary problems, perplexities and joys which most people experience at some point in their lives that it has the importance it does have for so many people.

Insofar as it presents a religious system of reference in its natural setting like this, a Wittgensteinian account not only gives itself the resources to make religious concepts intelligible to non-believers as well as believers; it is also able to show that both groups have access to a number of perfectly legitimate ways of criticizing or rejecting modes of life that employ religious concepts. To begin with, religious systems of reference contain their own distinctive terms of criticism. Even setting aside the ways in which believers might discriminate orthodoxy from heresy or blasphemy, there is also the category of superstition; it is perfectly common for believers to criticize fellow-believers on the grounds that their claims and actions manifest what one might call a magical or sentimental conception of the deity, and it is perfectly possible for those outside the relevant religious tradition to comprehend and endorse such criticisms. Phillips, for example, makes much of Wittgenstein's criticisms of the scapegoat rite as described in Leviticus, in the course of which he argues that the use of an animal to shoulder the people's burden of sinfulness can plausibly be rejected as embodying a confused and crude understanding of how freedom from sin might be achieved.

However, Phillips also famously makes rather more external criticisms of certain mainstays of traditional theological and religious thinking in Christianity: I am thinking here of his critique of traditional solutions to the problem of evil, or of the standard proofs of God's existence. Plainly, such criticisms presuppose a certain grasp of the nature and significance of the religious tradition from which the beliefs and practices under criticism have emerged – how else can we ensure that those criticisms are accurately aimed? But they do not use terms of criticism that are generated or deployed exclusively by believers – importantly because they depend upon invoking certain connections between religious attitudes and the more general phenomena of human life. Phillips's critique of solutions to the problem of evil, for example, depends primarily upon certain central moral principles concerning the intrinsic and incommensurable value of human life, and upon certain ordinary human responses to the suffering of others – principles and responses that are plainly not the exlusive preserve of those within a religious tradition.

Moreover, although Phillips does not make much of this possibility in his writings, there is no reason why even more apparently external modes of criticism might not be deployed against religious belief in a manner consistent with Wittgenstein's principles. For example, Nietzsche's suspicions of Christianity as embodying sado-masochistic self-hatred, and Freud's suspicions of institutionalized religion as pandering to psychologically immature dependence on a father-figure should both provide food for thought even for believers. They identify new forms – or at least potentially illuminate new interpretations of old forms – of religious pathology, and help to alert a believer to perhaps unappreciated variants of the ills to which religious thought and practice is heir.

Wittgensteinians would, however, be less comfortable with the idea that such theories might legitimately be used to justify a wholesale rejection of religious belief as such – exactly the kind of rejection which Neilsen, for example, wishes to leave open. Here again, unfortunately, this discomfort has been formulated – by Wittgensteinians and perhaps by Wittgenstein himself – in potentially misleading ways. Phillips, for example, quotes the following remark of Wittgenstein's as support for his claim that, whilst we can legitimately criticize certain religious rituals as confused or superstitious, we cannot make the same criticism of religious practices as a whole. It is true that we can compare a picture that is firmly rooted in us to a superstition; but it is equally true that we always eventually have to reach some firm ground, either a picture or something else, so that <u>a picture which is at the root of all our thinking is to be respected and not treated as a superstition</u> (CV, p. 83).

The context of this remark makes it unclear exactly what Wittgenstein has in mind when he talks of 'a picture at the root of all our thinking', but it is surely plain that the inference he proposes is invalid if we think of it in application to religious pictures. For <u>from the fact that certain religious pictures guide an individual's life, and lie at the root of all that she says and does, it certainly does not follow that they are worthy of respect</u>. Why, after all, should the depth or pervasive influence of a picture make it incoherent to judge that it embodies a degrading or immature attitude to life? What is needed for me to make such a criticism is, as Wittgenstein says, some firm ground from which to evaluate the religious picture, a competing picture or something else of the kind that is fundamental to my life; but such pictures are precisely designed to provide a base from which to criticize opposing pictures that lie at the root of other people's lives. Indeed, <u>one of the key facts about religious pictures nowadays is that, although they lie at the root of some people's thinking, they do not lie at the root of our thinking, of everyone's thinking</u>; hence, unlike the pictures to which Wittgenstein appears to be referring, they are precisely open to criticism and rejection.

There are, however, other and better reasons for baulking at the thought of a wholesale rejection of religious belief as such; for such a rejection would fail to acknowledge even the possibility that certain versions of such ways of life might avoid the ills to which others succumb. <u>It is far from easy to see how there could be an a priori demonstration that all possible ways of deploying religious systems of reference are pathological</u>, because that would amount to establishing that it is impossible even to conceive of a way of using those concepts as part of a form of life that does not manifest the relevant attitudes (of sado-masochism or immaturity).

These qualms become even more overwhelming when the critic wishes – as does Kai Neilsen – to be able to reject a religious mode of discourse as a whole on the grounds that it is incoherent or irrational or illogical. There is, of course, no difficulty with the idea that someone might regard religious belief as imprudent (like gambling) or oppressive (like footbinding) or pointless (like motor racing); and given that the laws of logic apply to religious discourse as they do to any other, a religious statement that is on the face of it logically incoherent (such as 'God is three and one') stands in need of an explanation which reveals that this is not in fact so. But there can be no ground for assuming a priori that such an explanation cannot be forthcoming; we have to look and see how the statement functions in the relevant context before we can establish what it means. And since any attempt to demonstrate the global irrationality of religious belief as such must presuppose that the religious discourse under criticism has a particular significance, it will fail to apply to any actual or possible mode of employing that discourse which confers a different significance upon it.

What, then, of the opposing weakness attributed to 'Wittgensteinian Fideists' – their tendency not to render religious belief immune from radical criticism, but rather to subject traditional modes of defending religious belief to radical criticism? Note that the real issue here is not whether or not Wittgensteinian accounts can consistently conflict with what religious believers are inclined at first blush to say about their beliefs and practices. As Phillips has repeatedly pointed out:

> [T]he suggestion [that we should accept the believer's gloss as the last word on the issue] is baffling. These philosophers would not dream of advocating this procedure elsewhere in philosophy. I can be told any day of the week in my local pub that thinking is a state of consciousness. Does that settle the matter? (WR,[9] p. 243)

A Wittgensteinian is committed, not to the defence of common sense, but to the clarification of the grammar of the words in which common sense and any other intelligible utterances are given expression. What provides that clarification in the case of religious belief is not whatever religious believers are at first inclined to say about themselves – that is philosophical raw material, not its end-product – but rather how they in fact employ religious concepts in the practices which go to make up their lives. Any interesting version of this line of criticism must therefore make out a case for the claim that Wittgensteinian approaches are committed to subjecting traditional religious practices to radical criticism.

Hyman's way of developing this claim unfortunately begins from a mistaken reading of Wittgenstein's claims about this issue. His argument, as we saw earlier, runs as follows:

> [S]ince evidence and argument are not the exclusive property of science, Wittgenstein cannot be right to insist that if we try to prove

or support the proposition that God exists, we are treating religion as if it were science, and are therefore already trapped in confusion.

It would, I think, be a mistake to maintain that because Anselm and Aquinas sought to prove the existence of God, they were peddling a variety of pseudo-science, a superstition which has nothing to do with religious faith. (IWM, p. 261)

In effect, Hyman assumes that, because Wittgenstein in his lectures accuses one Father O'Hara of illicitly transforming religious belief into superstition, then he is committed to accusing Anselm and Aquinas of the same error. But what Wittgenstein actually objects to in O'Hara's approach is that he is 'one of those people who make [religious belief] a question of science' (LC, p. 57); in other words, he treats a belief in God's existence as a kind of empirical hypothesis, and so treats God as a kind of physical object or entity. So the criticism would only transfer to Anselm or Aquinas if their attempts to defend or support religious belief betrayed a similar tendency. Hyman thinks that they do because he thinks that Wittgenstein regards any attempt to support religious belief as tantamount to treating religion as if it were science. But this is simply not true: Wittgenstein thinks that it would be as misleading to present religious belief as reasonable as it would be to describe it as irrational, but he does not think that there is no such thing as arguing about or offering reasons for or against religious belief. On the contrary, he tells us that '[religious] controversies look quite different from any normal controversies. Reasons look entirely different from normal reasons' (LC, p. 56) – remarks which presuppose that there are such things as religious controversies, and reasons for and against religious belief.

Whether or not Anselm and Aquinas fall foul of Wittgenstein's criticism therefore depends, not on whether or not they try to defend their religious beliefs, but on how they do so – on whether or not they involve treating God as a kind of physical object, or treating a belief in God's existence as a kind of empirical hypothesis. The simple fact that these proofs tend to minimize as far as possible any reliance upon empirical premises, and aspire to establishing certainty of a kind more akin to that available in the realms of mathematics and logic than that of science, suggests that there might at least be initial grounds for distinguishing Father O'Hara's efforts from those of his illustrious predecessors. And of course, Wittgensteinian philosophers of religion have devoted much labour to the task of showing that, although traditional proofs of God's existence of the kind offered by Anselm and Aquinas can be understood as versions of Father O'Hara's kind of thinking, they need not be. Phillips's analyses of the argument from Design and the Cosmological argument are one example of this nuanced treatment; but Norman Malcolm's account of Anselm's two versions of the Ontological argument is perhaps the single most influential and impressive example of this kind of Wittgensteinian work, since it aims to establish that the whole point of the Ontological argument is to remind us that God is not 'eine Existenz'. Nevertheless, insofar as Anselm and Aquinas or their followers have understood their proofs to be proofs of an empirical hypothesis, and to have embodied such an understanding in their practices, then they will indeed count as superstitious from a Wittgensteinian perspective. And the critics take it that such a categorization of certain religious practices and perspectives amounts to a species of prescriptive revisionism, and so as antithetical to Wittgensteinian descriptive methods – as subverting their claim to be merely describing the practices and forms of life with language that are the focus of their philosophical concern. Phillips has attempted to block this inference by denying that such categorizations have any critical or revisionary implications: 'Whether a ritual is superstitious is shown in its practice. Philosophy, in making this explicit, is not prescriptive' (WR, p. 245).

This claim lacks any real plausibility, however. For of course, even if the applicability of the concept of 'superstition' to a given practice can be judged only by describing the form of that practice, the concept itself has a primarily critical force, and criticism implies the need for change: superstition is, after all, something to be avoided. So, if Phillips succeeded in demonstrating to the satisfaction of a given religious believer that some aspect of their beliefs, rituals or practices deserved to be called 'superstitious', he would have given them the best possible reason to alter it in the direction of a more genuinely religious attitude to life. Such believers might well be grateful for the intervention. After all, since all religious traditions alter over time (in part because of shifts in the theological and philosophical understandings of their concepts and practices), their adherents might actually come to embrace revisionary accounts of their traditional self-understandings as embodying a deeper understanding of the true nature of their inheritance. Any such intervention would, however, undeniably be revisionary in its consequences.

The charge of 'prescriptivism' cannot, therefore, be as easily dismissed as Phillips seems to think. But it is important to acknowledge that Wittgensteinians are not here engaging in the business of using one language game to combat another, deploying modes of criticism that are entirely external or alien to the practices criticized – for the terms of criticism deployed are ones which form a more or less intimate part of the system of reference under description. To put it in Phillips's preferred terminology: certain confusions in certain religious practices are identified by reference to other aspects of what religious believers say and do, both as part of their explicitly religious lives and as part of their common moral and intellectual inheritance. Nevertheless, this identification of confusion cannot be uncoupled from its critical or prescriptive implications; and this does suggest that Wittgensteinians must reconcile themselves to acknowledging that <u>there is at least one</u> important sense in which their philosophical practice does not 'leave everything as it is' – that it does not accept forms of life as given. And since the terms of criticism employed (ones which identify confusions as species of 'superstition', and so on) have their original home in religious or spiritual contexts, the question arises: is there a more than purely coincidental relation between a Wittgensteinian philosophical practice and religious forms of life? <u>Why is it that a prescriptive element in Wittgensteinian philosophy seems to emerge most explicitly and naturally with respect to religion?</u>

Religious interpretations of Wittgenstein

Wittgenstein himself famously remarked: 'I am not a religious man: but I cannot help seeing every problem from a religious point of view' (RW, p. 79).

This remark can only confirm the feelings of those who – in what appear to be increasing numbers in recent years – claim to detect <u>an air of spiritual fervour throughout Wittgenstein's philosophical writings, both early and late.</u> It has recently been the focus of a wonderfully illuminating discussion between two of the most highly respected members of a group of philosophers whose work was heavily influenced by Wittgenstein's own thought – Norman Malcolm and Peter Winch;[10] and I would like to conclude this essay by exploring that exchange. Even though its full elaboration was cut short by his untimely death, Malcolm's view of the matter is fairly clearly summarized at the end of his essay.

[T]here are four analogies between Wittgenstein's conception of the grammar of language, and <u>his view of what is paramount in a religious life.</u> First, in both there is an end to explanation; second, in both there is an inclination to be amazed at the existence of something [language games, in the one case, and the world, in the other]; third, into both there enters the notion of an 'illness'; fourth, in both, doing, acting, takes priority over <u>intellectual understanding and reasoning</u>. (RPV, p. 92)

I think it is fair to say that Peter Winch's tactful but relentless essay in response to Malcolm's own shows beyond doubt that both the main elements and the overall approach of Malcolm's analysis are seriously awry. In particular, the claimed analogies can appear to hold only if one fails to acknowledge not only critical differences between the significance of similar words employed in very different contexts, but also what Wittgenstein would think of as <u>critical differences between philosophical and religious approaches to phenomena in general</u>. Thus, for example, Winch points out that the first of Malcolm's four analogies runs together two distinct points of comparison – that the expression of religious belief is itself a language-game for which it makes no sense to ask for an explanation, and that for the religious believer within such a language game a reference to God's will signals 'an end to explanation'. But the former point holds of all language games, and so fails to distinguish religious practices from any other; whereas the latter precisely marks a disanalogy between philosophy and religion, since no Wittgensteinian is, as it were, professionally committed to the view that we must accept language games as they are because their existence and specific form are manifestations of God's will. On a more general level, Winch is suspicious of the particular angle from which Malcolm approaches the remark Wittgenstein is reported to have made, and which his four analogies are designed to elucidate. For, quite apart from the fact that our only evidence for its having been made is the recollection of a friend, Winch is alert to the further fact that, as reported, Wittgenstein's remark identifies the religious point of view as that from which he approaches 'every problem' – not every philosophical problem, as Malcolm presupposes. At best, therefore, it can be held to characterize Wittgenstein's relation to philosophical problems, and so his philosophical practice, only insofar as it characterizes his relation to the problems of life as a whole – and not, as Malcolm assumes, entirely independently of that general attitude. Nevertheless, Winch is inclined to see that something important about Wittgenstein's philosophical practice is captured by the reported remark, and he ends his response to Malcolm by sketching in his own interpretation of it. This sketch is more than a little difficult to render consistent in places. For example, after making a connection between Wittgenstein's views of religion and of philosophy by talking of the passion with which he practises the latter, and noting that Wittgenstein follows Kierkegaard in contrasting the passion of faith with the cold passionlessness of wisdom, Winch immediately suggests that the Philosophical Investigations can be thought of as expressing Wittgenstein's ideal of 'a certain coolness. A temple providing a setting for the passions without meddling with them' (CV, p. 2). In the end, however, the key point Winch wishes to make emerges quite clearly: it involves a sense that 'for someone to whom philosophical issues matter, a lack of clarity about them can have grave implications for his or her own relation to life' (RPV, p. 130).

Winch illustrates his point by referring to a passage by Wittgenstein on how the sensation of pain can have a relation to a human body.

> But isn't it absurd to say of a body that it has pain? – And why does one feel an absurdity in that? In what sense is it true that my hand does not feel pain, but I in my hand?
>   What sort of issue is: Is it the body that feels pain? – How is it to be decided? What makes it plausible to say that it is not the body? – Well, something like this: If someone has a pain in his hand, then the hand does not say so (unless it writes it) and one does not comfort the hand, but the sufferer: one looks into his face. (PI,[11] p. 286)

Winch's commentary on this passage deserves quotation in full.

> That last sentence gives me a wonderful sense of a fog suddenly lifting; the confused shapes that loom up and disappear again in the familiar philosophical discussions of 'mind and body' vanish and I am left with a clear view of something very familiar of which I had not noticed the importance. Its 'importance' lies in the first instance in its relation to the philosophical discussion. At the same time in attending to the minute detail that plays such an enormous role in our relations to each other, my sense of the dimensions of those relations is both transformed and enriched: when comforting someone who has been hurt, I look into the sufferer's eyes. (RPV, p. 130)

I find this passage to be just as wonderful as the passage from Wittgenstein to which it is a response; but it seems to me that two qualifications Winch imposes on the scope of its implications are difficult to justify.

First, we might ask: is it really plausible to restrict the transformation and enrichment that Wittgenstein's grammatical reminders can engender to 'our sense of the dimensions of our interpersonal relations'? Winch figures Wittgenstein's insights as removing the fog which has blocked my view of something entirely familiar; he thereby restricts the transformation those insights produce to our understanding of our lives rather than to what is thereby understood. The idea is that philosophical confusions reside exclusively in the views we take of our lives, not the lives themselves. But this seems a particularly artificial distinction with respect to grammatical reminders about psychological concepts. Take, for example, Wittgenstein's related reminders concerning the commonly expressed philosophical view that no other person can have exactly the same pain as me; Wittgenstein argues that this view depends upon incoherently treating the possessor of the pain as a property of it, and so manifests a false sense of our separateness as persons by imposing a non-existent uniqueness on our experience. But the scepticism of which this belief is the intellectual expression is also something that can and does pervade our ordinary lives, affecting not just our sense of the dimensions of interpersonal relations but the dimensions themselves. We can and do exist within this mislocated sense of our separateness and commonality; we live our scepticism.

Winch's second qualification finds expression in his claim that the spiritual implications of grammatical unclarity apply only to those for whom philosophical issues matter. This restriction is reinforced and explained in a footnote, which reads: 'I make this qualification since I am sure that Wittgenstein did not – like Socrates? – want to make philosophical clarity quite generally a sine qua non of spiritual health' (RPV, p. 135). If we question Winch's first qualification by questioning the distinction between our philosophically expressed views of life and our lives themselves, this second qualification will already look rather implausible. But there are also independent grounds for concern; for the second qualification seems to depend upon an equally artificial distinction between those for whom philosophical issues matter and those for whom they do not. First, if Winch's own line of argument is correct, there can be no-one who stands in need of philosophical clarity for whom that clarity cannot matter; if you suffer from the confusion, you need the clarity – that clarity matters to you – whether you know it or not. So the distinction which his qualification really presupposes must be one between those for whom philosophical problems arise, and those for whom they do not. But any such distinction can be at best provisional, for there is no good reason to think that there are any human beings who are constitutionally immune to philosophical confusions; <u>any creature complicated enough to be burdened</u>

by language is necessarily vulnerable to such confusions. To be sure, a given person at a given time might escape confusion, and so stand in no need of grammatical clarity at that time; after all, one might almost define a philosophical problem as one which is not always live for us, but which, once living, is undismissable. But this temporary freedom has nothing to do with whether or not one is a professional philosopher, or well-educated, or an inhabitant of complex civilizations – as Winch's qualification seems to imply. The truth of the matter is that philosophical confusions are not restricted to inhabitants of certain disciplines, or sectors of culture, or classes within societies, or societies as a whole. They are part of our inheritance as human beings; and in this important sense, philosophical issues matter to everyone. If, then, we contemplate pushing beyond Winch's conclusions by removing his two restrictions, but in the direction that those conclusions have already sketched out, we might feel the need to inquire a little more closely into the nature of the philosophical confusions against which Wittgenstein sets the resources of his philosophical practice of reminding us of what we say when, recalling us to the grammar or criteria of our ordinary words. If such recalling is necessary, that must be because our confusion has led us to go beyond those criteria – to lose control of our words, to attempt to speak outside or beyond language games. But how and why might we make such an attempt? Why and how can otherwise competent speakers suffer such a loss of control when under the pressure to philosophize?

We know that, for Wittgenstein, that over which they lose control – criteria – constitute the limits or conditions of the human capacity to know, think or speak about the world and the various things that are in it: they are that without which human knowledge of the world would not be possible. But of course, it is fatally easy to interpret limits as limitations, to experience conditions as constraints. Indeed, this is precisely how the sceptic often understands her own motives: she repudiates our ordinary reliance upon criteria because she regards what we ordinarily count as knowledge as nothing of the kind, as failing to put us into contact with the world as it really is. But it would only make sense to think of the conditions of human knowledge as limitations if we could conceive of another cognitive perspective upon the world that did not require them; and philosophers from Kant onwards have variously striven to show that there is no such perspective – that the absence of the concepts or categories in terms of which we individuate objects would not clear the way for unmediated knowledge of the world, but would rather remove the possibility of anything that might count as knowledge.

In other words, what the sceptic understands as a process of disillusionment in the name of true knowledge, Wittgenstein interprets as an inability or refusal to acknowledge the fact that human knowledge – the knowledge available to finite creatures, subjective agents in an objective world – is necessarily conditioned. But it is worth recalling that nothing is more human than the desire to deny the human, to interpret limits as limitations and to repudiate the human condition of conditionedness or finitude in the name of the unconditioned, the transcendent, the superhuman – the inhuman. On this understanding of criteria, the human desire to speak outside language games is an inflection of the prideful human craving to be God, and Wittgenstein's philosophical practice aims not so much to eradicate this ineradicable hubris but to diagnose it and track down the causes of its specific eruptions from case to case of its perennial, endlessly renewed realization.

An interpretation of Wittgenstein's method along these lines has been most famously advanced and elaborated by Stanley Cavell, who thinks of philosophy practised under such a self-understanding as a species of perfectionism.[12] In Cavell's thought, the unending sequence of specific manifestations of scepticism in modernity reveals that human beings are possessed of a nature in which the sceptical impulse is (apparently) ineradicably inscribed. What is needed if it is to be combated is a fully acknowledged relationship with a particular human other (the philosopher, whether Wittgenstein or those who would inherit his task) – one whose words have the power to identify and make us ashamed of our present confused and disoriented state, one who, by exemplifying a further, attainable state of clarity and self-possession, can attract us to it whilst respecting our autonomy and individuality. Now, measure this self-understanding against the following theological structure. In Christian thought, our unending sequence of particular sinful acts reveals that human beings are possessed of a nature which disposes them to sin and prevents them from escaping their bondage by using their own resources. What they need to attain their new nature is a fully acknowledged relationship with a particular person – one through whose words divine grace is made accessible, one who exemplifies the further, unattained but attainable human state to which God wishes to attract every individual whilst respecting her freedom to deny its attractions and spurn His grace. Against this background, it is not just a sense of the reality of our hubristic railings against our finitude that links Wittgensteinian philosophy and religion, but a surprisingly detailed conception of its precise forms and of the available ways of attempting to overcome them. The precision of the mapping here might well be what underlay the third of the analogies Malcolm wished to draw between Wittgenstein's view of philosophical problems and religious belief, and to which Winch devotes comparatively little attention in his response: that between the religious attitude of regarding oneself as radically imperfect or 'sick' and the idea that philosophical puzzlement is a symptom of a disease. It may be, in other words, that some recognizable inflection of the notion of Original Sin is more pertinent to the insight that Winch himself began to develop than he was able to see, that he and Malcolm were in this sense less far apart than may appear. Whatever the truth of this matter, it seems at least arguable that if we are to attain a deeper understanding of Wittgenstein's 'religious point of view', and attain thereby a better grasp of the uncanny, undismissable intimacy between Wittgensteinian philosophy of religion and religion itself, we would do well to take seriously Stanley Cavell's interpretation of the Philosophical Investigations.

Notes

1. In *Lectures and Conversations on Aesthetics, Psychology and Religious Belief*, edited by Cyril Barrett (University of California Press, Berkeley, 1966) – hereafter LC.
2. Edited by G.H. von Wright and H. Nyman, trans. Peter Winch (Oxford: Basil Blackwell, 1980) – hereafter CV.
3. Edited by Rush Rhees (Oxford University Press, Oxford, 1981) – hereafter RW.
4. Edited by Quinn and Taliaferro (Oxford: Blackwell, 1997) – pp. 150–8.
5. Instead of referring to his Companion entry, I shall use quotations from Dr Hyman's earlier paper 'Immortality without Metaphysics' (published in D.Z. Phillips (ed.), *Can Religion Be Explained Away?* [London: St Martin's Press, 1996] – hereafter IWM), where he advances exactly the same lines of argument. Since the original paper was presented at an earlier Claremont Conference, this choice of reference point seemed best suited to the present occasion.
6. Trans. H.V. and E.H. Hong (Princeton, NJ: Princeton University Press, 1992) – hereafter CUP.
7. Philosophy XLII, No. 161, July 1967 – hereafter WF.
8. 'Dislocating the Soul', the essay to which Hyman's own article 'Immortality without Metaphysics' is a reply, is published in the same collection.
9. D.Z. Phillips, *Wittgenstein and Religion* (London: Macmillan, 1993) – hereafter WR.
10. N. Malcolm, *Wittgenstein: a Religious Point of View?* (edited with a response by Peter Winch) (London: Routledge, 1993) – hereafter RPV.

11. L. Wittgenstein (trans. G.E.M. Anscombe), *Philosophical Investigations* (Oxford: Blackwell, 1953).
12. Many of the key Cavell texts are collected in S. Mulhall (ed.), *The Cavell Reader* (Oxford: Blackwell, 1996) – *see* especially Essay 16 and the Epilogue. Further elaboration and defence of Cavell's interpretation of Wittgenstein can be found in my *Stanley Cavell: Philosophy's Recounting of the Ordinary* (Oxford: Oxford University Press, 1994) – *see* especially ch. 12.

8
Wittgenstein and the Philosophy of Religion: a Reply to Stephen Mulhall

Walford Gealy

I want to begin by congratulating Stephen Mulhall on his beautifully written and solidly constructed paper. The title given, 'Wittgenstein and the Philosophy of Religion' allowed the possibility of a wide approach to be taken to the subject, and Mulhall has taken full advantage of this space in his tripartite response. The excellence of some sections of his paper has rendered any further comment on them wholly superfluous. I have particularly in mind those parts in which Mulhall is critical of other writers, such as his penetratingly astute arguments against John Hyman in both the first and second divisions of the paper. However, no two people would have approached this set topic in the same way, and there are some issues which I would have liked to have seen given greater emphasis, especially the assessment of Wittgenstein's contribution to the philosophy of religion. But I also think that, in some ways, Mulhall could have been more critical of Wittgenstein's own views on religion. I appreciate that these comments are, of course, essentially evaluative, and I found it difficult to discover much that is amiss with Mulhall's logic. In my reply I wish to concentrate primarily on the first part of Mulhall's paper which deals specifically with Wittgenstein's own comments on religion, including those remarks contained in the celebrated three lectures on religious belief, although what I have to say about these has some bearing on issues raised in the other two sections of Mulhall's essay.

If the general question were asked, 'What has Wittgenstein contributed to the philosophy of religion?' it would not be inappropriate, even for those who have embraced his standpoint, to answer in two apparently contradictory ways. On the one hand, it could be maintained that he contributed next to nothing to the subject, while, on the other hand, it could be claimed, with some considerable justification, that no one in this century has contributed more to the discipline. On the negative side, Mulhall refers to the 'few scattered pebbles' of Wittgenstein's remarks on religious belief – and it is indubitably the case that Wittgenstein wrote very little about religion. And, in my view, what he did write, or perhaps more accurately as a generalization, what he is reported to have *said* about religious faith, appears to me to be largely unimpressive – particularly from a religious perspective – and, in philosophical terms, it is certainly not representative of, or even comparable with, what is best in Wittgenstein. His comments on religion often appear idiosyncratic and banal, and, sometimes, plainly incorrect. On the positive side, and in sharp contrast to the 'pebbles' alluded to, Wittgenstein's work on the philosophy of logic and language appear, in Mulhall's own phrase, like 'mountainous ranges', and for most Wittgensteinian thinkers it is the implications of this logic that makes his indirect contribution to the philosophy of religion so invaluable. Let us then look briefly at these different ways of evaluating Wittgenstein's contribution to this field of philosophy, beginning with the positive aspect – the claim that, arguably, Wittgenstein's contribution to the philosophy of religion in this century is unparalleled.

Even though it is fashionable to distinguish between the various philosophies of Wittgenstein, there is, throughout his thinking, one central unifying preoccupation. From the very first he was solely concerned with the issue of the intelligibility of symbolism or of language. This concern with the nature of language or symbolism had developed from his initial interest in mathematics and from his subsequent reading of the works of Frege and Russell. As such, Wittgenstein's thinking forms part of a wider philosophical movement that became ultimately responsible for placing logical considerations at the heart of philosophical activity, and that for the greater part of the twentieth century. What this concern with logic displaced was epistemology – a discipline which, in Wittgenstein's earlier work, was relegated to the realm of psychology, while in his later work, epistemology is seen to be, as most other philosophical issues, the product of conceptual confusion. The traditional general question, 'What is the nature of knowledge?' is both misleading and ambiguous. It presupposes that there is such a thing as the essence of knowledge. But Wittgenstein showed that what knowledge amounts to depends on the context in which the claim to knowledge is made, and on how things 'hang together' within that specific context. So that to know myself, for instance, or to know what pain a person is going through, or to know that Cardiff is the capital city of

Wales, or that the chemical formula of salt is NaCl, or to know God, are different forms of knowing, in the sense that each claim is connected with different sets of concepts that go together – so that what can be said or asked about each form of knowledge differs in each case. Or, expressed in a different way, if one were challenged to defend one's claim to knowledge in any of these instances, the reply would be different – to a greater or lesser extent. Wittgenstein's exhortation that we should consider if all games have something in common is equally applicable to the concept of knowledge. And if we 'look and see' we have to arrive at the same conclusion that we 'will not see something that is common to all, but similarities, relationships and a whole series of them at that' (P.I., para 65). Hence, traditional epistemological systems are confused attempts to get at the essence of knowledge – an essence that simply does not exist.

When Mulhall refers to the 'radical subversion to which Wittgenstein aimed to subject the discipline of philosophy' I suppose he was referring, at least in part, to this fundamental reorientation of the discipline away from epistemology and towards logic. The impact of this change is immeasurable: it displaced the central philosophical tradition that had been rooted, certainly in Europe, for centuries. In Britain, for instance, since the dawn of modern philosophy, the dominant philosophical creed has been that of empiricism. From the middle of the seventeenth century to the twentieth, almost without exception, leading British philosophers (Hobbes, Locke, Berkeley, Hume, Bentham, Mill, Russell and Moore) have been empiricists. Now, although Mulhall may, sadly, be perfectly correct in stating that Wittgenstein's work may no longer 'function as an essential reference point' in many 'fields of philosophical endeavour' (p. 1), those who have espoused the changes initiated by Wittgenstein still perceive these as constituting the strongest challenge to this established British empiricist tradition and, indeed, to any other philosophical tradition that has an epistemological theory at its centre. But it may also be the case that one reason for the prominence gained by Wittgensteinian writers in the field of the philosophy of religion is that the implications of the Wittgensteinian critique of epistemological systems may be seen to be more effective in this realm than in any other branch of philosophy. And there may even be a straightforward reason for this, particularly when Wittgenstein's thinking is placed against the background of British empiricism. For, more than any other system, an empiricist epistemology has difficulty in accommodating claims to a knowledge of God. Even in its traditional mildest form, as we find it, say, in Locke, empiricist beliefs are never easily reconciled with religious belief – despite Locke's own claim that Christianity is to be embraced on account of its 'reasonableness'. The gap between the claim about what can be known with certainty through sensation and reflection on the one hand, and the claim to know a transcendent Deity 'whom no man hath seen', on the other hand, always has to be bridged within an empiricist epistemological framework. And that bridge has never been satisfactorily or consistently constructed. The recourse to some alleged experiences, such as that of a 'leap of faith' or of some 'intuitive disclosures', does not close the gap between experiences of an empirical nature and knowledge of a God that is, in some sense, 'beyond' this visible, tangible world. And neither is, in my view, what appears to be a more consistent position from an empiricist standpoint, the claim that, on the basis of evidence, the truth of the belief in God is a matter of high probability, religiously satisfactory either. Of course, empiricism in its most virulent form, leads either to a Hume-type form of scepticism or, to an equally pernicious form of scientism such as that fostered by Logical Positivism from the 1930s onwards. In the second half of this century, both forms of empiricism, the mild and the virulent, have still exercised considerable influence, and I think that it is correct to say that the English have remained true to what is, primarily, their tradition. And it is against the background of a long-standing, resistant British empiricism that one must, at least in part, assess the contribution of the later Wittgenstein to the philosophy of religion.

The emancipation of the philosophy of religion from the constraints of an empirical epistemological system was not Wittgenstein's only contribution to the philosophy of religion. Of greater importance was his insistence on the indeterminate nature of the criteria of intelligibility. In the *Tractatus*, Wittgenstein had attempted to lay down a single, absolute measure of the distinction between sense and nonsense. But in the *Philosophical Investigations*, it is maintained that it is not always that easy to distinguish between sense and nonsense – and this is partly the case because of the complexity of that distinction. In the *Philosophical Investigations*, language is inextricably connected with our living, with our day-to-day practices. The speaking of language is part of an activity, or a form of life' (P.I., para 23). Hence, understanding language means understanding what is going on – and vice versa. What it makes sense to say, or not to say, depends on what is the precise nature of the activity under consideration. And if our practices are so diverse and, in principle, without any predetermined boundaries (as, for instance, old practices cease to be and are replaced by novel ones, and so there are constantly new ways of speaking while others become obsolete), then the criteria of the intelligibility are equally indeterminate. The boundaries of intelligibility are in a constant state of flux. The expression, 'This language game is played' encapsulates, possibly most directly, the new freedom from the traditional kind of externally imposed, rigid, single criterion of meaning – the kind of criterion that had been adopted by philosophers in the past – with the inevitable consequence of artificially limiting the possibilities of language. This does not mean that, according to the *Philosophical Investigations, anything* goes – for there both are standards within activities that determine what is meaningful and what is not. But, also, of paramount importance is the fact that the activities themselves are related to each other in a variety of ways. They form a 'complicated network' and, as a consequence, they have a bearing on each other. In this sense, the intelligibility of one way of saying something is related to the intelligibility of other ways of speaking. No single activity, completely isolated from others, would be intelligible. Now there may be all sorts of aberrations or distortions of correct practices, which would be deemed false or foul or unreasonable practices, and they would be determined to be such in terms of *either* the standards internal to the practices themselves *or* by being shown to be incompatible with standards of a related practice or practices *or* both. It is important to underline that practices are not isolated from each other, for its neglect can lead to all sorts of confusion. That language games have their own identity is important too – for if it were not for such an identity it would be meaningless to speak of relationships. But all the practices form part of 'the stream of life' – a complex, but indeterminate, cultural whole. What we have, according to Wittgenstein, is 'a complicated network of similarities overlapping and criss-crossing: sometimes overall similarities, sometimes similarities of detail.' (P.I., para 66)

Those preoccupied with religious matters, and theologians in particular, who had been condemned by the Logical Positivisits as confused babblers, have felt emancipated as a result of the implications of Wittgenstein's new understanding of the conditions of intelligibility. It is for this reason that one wants to say that no one in this century, no one perhaps at any time, has done a greater service to the philosophy of religion – for, it seems that, at no other time in the history of Western philosophy, had religion been under such an acute attack as it was from those professional practitioners of philosophy, earlier in this century, who had condemned religious language as meaningless. And, by now, over fifty years after those initial pernicious attacks on religion, it is often claimed that the philosophy of religion has undergone a renaissance, particularly in the English-speaking world. If this is true, as I believe it is, it is in no small measure, a direct consequence of the new life breathed into it by the implications of Wittgenstein's later philosophy.

This was an issue that I had wished Mulhall would have said more about. But he may have taken all this for granted. Yet, the impression I have from his paper is that Wittgenstein's sole contribution to philosophy is his method for clearing up conceptual confusion. This is a view that is widely in vogue. Of course, it is an important part of Wittgenstein's legacy, and the significance of this contribution is not to be underestimated. It is also true that, in the final part of his paper, Mulhall does refer to 'the transformation and enrichment that Wittgenstein's grammatical reminders can engender' – and he is even critical of Winch's attempt to impose limitations on this enrichment! Yet, in the paper itself, there is very little development of what this enrichment might mean in the realm of religion. In most of his essay, Mulhall is content to underline the significance of the innovation that religious propositions are different from empirical propositions. But this is not to say much. It is a negative thesis. It says nothing positive, for instance, about the kind of language that religious language itself is. Not that we find much of that in Wittgenstein either. However, by emphasizing the indeterminacy of the logic of language, Wittgenstein was drawing our attention to the richness and diversity of human experiences. Having succeeded in casting off the straitjacket of a single, rigid but artificial criterion of meaning, Wittgenstein allowed language to be itself in all its diversity, richness and splendour. He wanted to show language as it is and also the possibilities of language that enable us to see things in a variety of new and different ways. Logical formalism with its rigidity is banished and in its place we have diversity, fluidity, imagination and creativity. It is in the opening up of these possibilities, in showing us how human practices may be understood in different ways, that one can claim that no one has contributed more in recent times, indirectly, to the philosophy of religion.

Now let us turn to what appear to me to be some difficulties in Wittgenstein's thinking about religious matters. Not that I wish to suggest that everything in this field that belongs to him is problematic. But I have found certain aspects of the contents of the three lectures on religious belief (as they are found in the *LC*) quite unacceptable. Some of Wittgenstein's remarks, in this specific context, appear both strange and confused – this, again, often in stark contrast to many of the numerous *ad hoc* religious remarks found scattered elsewhere in his writings. There are three basic points that I wish to make about these *LC* lectures on religious belief. First, there are philosophical difficulties here which are connected with the way Wittgenstein presents his case: the disjunction between the religious and the empirical is overstated and is far too rigid. Secondly, and this is a matter of some conjecture, these difficulties may be related to problems which Wittgenstein might have felt at that time (around 1938), and which arose directly from his novel thinking on logic. And, finally, there seem to me to be insuperable difficulties with what may described as Wittgenstein's 'theology', as it is reflected in the examples given in the *LC* of religious assertions.

Perhaps it is something of a surprise that someone who espouses Wittgenstein's later philosophy should find aspects of his thought in the *LC* unacceptable. Why is this the case? Is not Mulhall perfectly correct when he states that the whole of Wittgenstein's enterprise in the *LC* has to do with highlighting the differences between empirical statements and religious statements? And is not this emphasis, on showing differences, wholly in character with Wittgenstein's thesis in the *Philosophical Investigations*? It is readily conceded that the whole burden of Wittgenstein's later logic was 'to show differences' between different ways of speaking, or of language uses. He wished to destroy the kind of false unity that he has ascribed to language in the *Tractatus* by making that unity formal – 'the common or general form of proposition'. But, as it has already been suggested, the point of referring to different language games was to show that 'saying something' differs from context to context, from one activity to another. But, in the *LC*, at this comparatively early stage in the development of the later thesis, there are dangers inherent in the way Wittgenstein presented his case, and these may be partly responsible for much of the confusion that is often seen in the writings of Wittgensteinian philosophers of religion, and particularly the charge that their standpoint is fideistic.

What we are presented with in the *LC* is a dichotomy – between two ways of speaking, between the empirical and the religious. It may be asked, 'Why only two?' Is our speaking, our language, divided in such a dichotomous way? Granting that it was Wittgenstein's intention to demonstrate the distinctiveness of a religious way of speaking, why did he ground it on a single comparison? And why did that comparison have to be based on differences with empirical propositions? Would not, and does not such a contrast immediately and inevitably remind us of the *Tractatus* dualism? My impression is that the *Tractatus* casts a heavy shadow on the *LC*. This may be discerned in the way Wittgenstein proceeds to make the distinction between these two ways of speaking, and especially by the kind of language that he uses to make and describe the distinction. It is not that one questions the validity of the distinction itself between the empirical and the religious, but the language that is used echoes clearly earlier ideas. If one may adopt and adapt one of Wittgenstein's later analogies of language – that of a city without a high road – what we have in the *Tractatus* was, not so much a city, but a single throughfare. In the *LC*, we do have a city, but one that does have a high road – and that is the thoroughfare we had in the *Tractatus*. This high road in the *LC* is there variously alluded to, and described, as 'the normal', 'the ordinary everyday', and 'the reasonable'. In the first of the three lectures alone, the terms 'normal', 'ordinary everyday' and 'reasonable' are used on numerous occasions, and on each of these the purpose is to contrast such a way of speaking with the religious way of speaking. I do not think for a moment that the author of the *Philosophical Investigations* would have portrayed matters in this way. There clearly, language is portrayed as a city without a high road. Naturally, if only two things are sharply contrasted with each other, inevitably a dichotomy is created. But what is objectionable in the *LC* is that the one side of the dichotomy is exclusively identified with 'the ordinary', 'the normal' and 'the reasonable', and hence marking it distinctly as the high road. That cannot but be highly reminiscent of the *Tractatus* position – except, of course, that now the religious way is accepted as intelligible. But merely by describing *one* way of speaking as 'normal', 'ordinary', 'everyday' – even without identifying the precise nature of that way – Wittgenstein has, perhaps unwittingly, relegated *all* other ways of speaking to a suburban status in our lives. In the *Tractatus*, religious discourse was altogether outside the world, outside the city. In the *LC*, this way of talking is just somewhere within the city's periphery. Furthermore, by formulating the dichotomy in the way he does, Wittgenstein creates the impression that what he refers to as 'the ordinary everyday' way of speaking is a single or unified way of speaking – and that it stands in stark contrast with the religious way of speaking. It is an odd city indeed, with one major thoroughfare, and one distant side road which at no point intersects with that thoroughfare. How different this image is from that created in the *Philosophical*

Investigations where there is insistence on both diversity of ways of speaking and on their relatedness!

The manner then in which Wittgenstein makes and sustains his distinction between the empirical and the religious in the *LC* implies that, from a certain standpoint called 'normal', 'ordinary' and 'reasonable', religious beliefs are to be thought of as being entirely outside these categories. Prima facie, it would appear that the implication is that such religious beliefs are abnormal, extra-ordinary and even unreasonable. Indeed, he explicitly states of religious believers, 'I would say, that they are certainly not reasonable, that's obvious.' But then he proceeds to remark, ' "Unreasonable" implies, with everyone, rebuke.' And clearly, Wittgenstein does not, for logical reasons, wish to describe religious belief as 'unreasonable'. But he does want to say that religious belief is not within the realm of reason. In the *Tractatus*, religion is not in the realm of the intelligible. In the *LC* religion is not in the realm of reason.

Again, there are strong reasons for believing that the Wittgenstein of the *Philosophical Investigations* would not have expressed himself in this way. Here, in the *LC*, he seems to adopt an essentialist conception of 'reason', which is synonymous with 'the ordinary' and 'the usual'. Not that his remarks appear thoroughly consistent in the *LC*. For, as Mulhall points out, the distinction which Wittgenstein makes at one point between 'reasons' and 'normal reasons' (*LC*, p. 56) suggests that there are different kinds of reasons. Yet, what a strange distinction and dichotomy again! Are reasons that are not 'normal reason' to be thought of as abnormal? What would that mean? But the concession that there are different kinds of reasons does at least reflect a position which is slightly closer to that which we find in the *Philosophical Investigations*. What he ought to have maintained here is that which he made clear in his later writings – that there are multiple criteria of 'reason' or 'rationality'. But, here in the *LC* he proceeds to say: 'I want to say: they, (that is, religious believers) don't treat this as a matter of reasonability' – a remark which is patently false. This, it seems to me, reflects an essentialist conception of rationality, which is completely incompatible with Wittgenstein's later thinking.

Unfortunately, Wittgenstein goes on to attempt to fortify his claim by making the remark: 'Anyone who reads the Epistles will find it said: not only that it is not reasonable, but that it is folly' (*LC*, p. 58). Wittgenstein's exegesis of the Biblical text is patently wrong. The mistake he first seems to make is connected with the logical point that I wish to underline. In the text, to which I assume Wittgenstein is referring (1 Cor. 1), it is the *religious* unbeliever that calls the religious beliefs in question 'foolishness'. But to those who believe in the Christian faith, what they believe in – that is, redemption through the cross of Christ – expresses the very wisdom of God. Of course, this wisdom is very different from, and contrasts sharply with 'the wisdom of the wise' – (although, it would be a massive error to understand this wisdom here as something which is synonymous with 'the empirical'. The issue is essentially religious and concerns salvation. Is salvation through man's own wisdom or through divine grace?) But there is a huge gap between, on the one hand, recognizing that there are different kinds of wisdom or 'reasonability' and maintaining, on the other hand, that believers don't treat their beliefs 'as a matter of reasonability'. Or that believers 'don't use *reason* here' as Wittgenstein remarks. To extradite himself from his confusion at this level all that he needed to say is what St Paul himself was maintaining in this context, not that wisdom is one thing, but that God's wisdom is entirely different from 'the wisdom of the wise'. Indeed, had Wittgenstein followed strictly the apostle's reasoning, then he would have been led to say something that is to some degree more in agreement with his *Philosophical Investigations'* view, namely that these two forms of wisdom are wholly different from each other. For not only is the *logos* of the cross foolishness to those who do not believe, but it is also the case that God is said to pronounce the 'wisdom of the wise' to be 'foolishness'.

Now is 'the normal', 'the ordinary everyday' therefore, to be deemed to be outside this divine reasonableness? This question is merely indicative of the absurdity of the strict dichotomous way that Wittgenstein has presented his case. Indeed, Wittgenstein's error is even deeper than what has already been suggested. For the 'wisdom of the wise', in the Scriptural context, is not contrasted at all, as Wittgenstein has wrongly assumed, with a non-religious form of wisdom, but with a rival form of religious wisdom. For if the 'wisdom of the wise' is at all at variance with 'divine wisdom' both forms of wisdom are within the complex of religious thought, and are essentially at odds with each other on the issue of human salvation. In the relevant Scriptural text, both the Jews and the Greeks seek salvation in one way or another. But the wise, we are told, *have failed in their efforts to know God* through their wisdom – and that, we are told, is as a result of divine wisdom. They have failed therefore, in what is an essentially religious quest – that of salvation. The whole text and its reasoning has nothing whatsoever to do with anything like 'empirical evidence' or 'verification' and the connection between such concepts and the logic of propositions. Wittgenstein has completely misunderstood the text!

My second point is this. I believe that some of the difficulties I find with these lectures may be connected with the fact that what we have here belongs to an intermediary period in the development of Wittgenstein's later philosophy. Wittgenstein was constantly reviewing, modifying and developing his position, and the thinking reported in these lectures does not reflect the implications for religion of Wittgenstein's more mature standpoint as we have it, say, in the *Philosophical Investigations*, or in *On Certainty*. These lectures on religious belief were delivered in 1938. *The Blue and Brown Books*, which contain the earliest versions of Wittgenstein's later philosophy, were notes of lectures delivered in the academic years 1933/4 and 1934/5 respectively. The notes contained in the *Brown Book* were revised in 1936. Yet, despite the fact that these two books of notes are only separated by a short gap in time, there appear to be, as Rush Rhees explains in the Preface to these books, substantial modifications in Wittgenstein's views – in the way Wittgenstein speaks of language games, for instance. And there are differences again when we come to the *Philosophical Investigations* itself. These differences are not peripheral either, but belong to central notions in Wittgenstein's later thinking. They are connected with the whole question of the nature of the unity of language and the interrelationships between various ways of thinking – issues which also have a direct bearing on our understanding of the logic of religious propositions.

This may help us to explain why Wittgenstein underlined in such a rigid way the distinction between the empirical and the religious. Indeed, the rigidity of his position suggests that although he had rejected the formalism of the *Tractatus* he had embraced a new formalism – one that allowed for diversity in terms of multifarious language games, but now these forms of language have a rigidity of their own and are wholly autonomous. There seems to be nothing whatsoever in common between the empirical and the religious. Every way of speaking is distinct. Everything again, it seems, must be crystal clear! Logic demands it! Again, I am suggesting that the *Tractatus* casts its shadow on the way the dichotomy between the empirical and the religious is presented in the *LC*. This is even more understandable also at this stage because Wittgenstein at this time might still have been wrestling with difficulties connected with his novel reasoning. For his new logic led inevitably to the acceptance of realities other than simply the one reality that is 'pictured' by the empirical sciences. Did not his new thinking, therefore, lead to the acceptance of the reality of God? And did this mean that he had to embrace this reality? I suspect that Wittgenstein must have been troubled by these questions. They might have appeared to him as rather unfortunate consequences of his novel view that the criteria of intelligibility are internal to human practices. They certainly presented a challenge. For religion, after all, is not a universally embraced form of life – like, say, the language of talking about physical objects, or the language of mathematics, or even moral language. All these forms of discourse evidently have an unquestioned reality of their own. But religion? It would seem that the most effective strategy Wittgenstein could adopt, to extradite him from this logical dilemma, would be precisely the one that we find in the *LC* – that is, the strategy of underlining that religion is so different from the 'ordinary' or 'the reasonable' that it is not a matter of reasonableness at all to embrace it. On the contrary, religion is a matter of passionate belief without reason. All this, I admit is a matter of conjecture on my part. But I am looking for possible reasons why Wittgenstein created such an unbridgeable gulf between the empirical and the religious.

It is no wonder that, partly as a result of the use by Wittgenstein of such expressions as 'they (religious believers) are not reasonable – meaning they don't use *reason* here', Wittgensteinians have been labelled 'fideists'. If religious believers do not use reason, then they are fideists. They have faith 'without reason' – and what kind of faith is that? Mulhall discusses this issue in the second part of his paper. I suspect that the primary reason why fideism has been condemned by most Christian theologians is because they are rightly suspicious of emotion. And the Scriptures, in one of the most famous parables in the New Testament, that of the sower, warn against a faith that is based upon an emotional response. Emotions, we are advised, are fleeting and cannot withstand the trials and tribulations of life. As the strength of the emotion diminishes, so the faith disappears with it. Historically, of course, fideism has been connected with the rejection of natural theology, and natural theology has been seen as an external justification of religion through 'the natural light of reason' – whatever that means. If we base our assessment of Wittgenstein's position *re* these issues solely on the basis of what we find in the *LC*, then, in my view, he is rightly accused of being fideistic. However, in the light of the *Philosophical Investigations*, this view has to be radically revised. For if 'fideism' simply means 'faith without reason' then religion, like all other meaningful practices, has its internal rules that determine what does, and what does not, make sense. As Rhees once put it: 'Theology is the grammar of religious belief.' Furthermore, as it has already been emphasized, Wittgenstein in the *Philosophical Investigations* insisted that our 'language-games' are related to each other – and it is because our practices are related to each other that they are intelligible in our lives. Religion is not an exception and hence is not fideistic in terms of the *Philosophical Investigations* criteria – if 'fideism' means 'faith without reason'. However, if fideism means 'faith not *based* on reason', Wittgenstein's position is more complex. For he argues that our language games are not based on anything. Indeed, the whole meaning of the expression 'the natural light of reason', on which, according to traditional natural theology, faith is supposed to rest, becomes meaningless – for it implies that there is some rationality that is independent of, or transcends the particular practices in our lives. But, again, our reasons are internal to the activities: each 'game' has its own rules. This is the way we count. These are our moral values. This is the way we speak about physical objects. This is our religious faith. In each instance, in each 'form of life' or activity, we use reason – or rather we reason in different ways. What then becomes of natural theology? Does this mean that it is necessarily meaningless? It is possible to understand the arguments of natural theology in a different way – not as some proofs of faith based on considerations external to the realm of faith, but rather as exercises in the grammar of faith – and as bridges that may be used to attempt to relate the language of faith to other forms of discourse. For instance, without the theology of 'revealed religion', which contains references to 'the eternity of God', that He is 'from everlasting to everlasting', the Ontological argument would have no meaning at all. Similarly, if it were not for the religious belief in the goodness of God as Creator, both the Teleological and the Cosmological arguments would be religiously worthless. For the idea of everything depending on some impersonal Cause is a religiously futile idea. What the believer seeks is not a causal explanation of existence, but rather the assurance that existence is essentially good and, hence, meaningful. Natural theology is not a matter of making inferences from the world, from outside faith, to God, but rather it is an attempt to show how, from the standpoint of faith, the world is perceived.

Thirdly, let us turn to Wittgenstein's 'theology'. There is something profoundly wrong with Wittgenstein's characterization of religious beliefs in the *LC*. What we are presented with here are religious beliefs as caricatures of empirical hypotheses and predictions. Again, the influence of the *Tractatus* is undeniably evident. In the *Tractatus*, only propositions which belong to the natural sciences have sense. In the

LC, only the propositions which are supported by evidence are reasonable. If you make predictions, say about the weather or about the strength of the pound sterling in a year's time, you may be asked to justify your belief in terms of certain evidence. The predictions may be said to be reasonable or unreasonable depending on the evidence or weight of probability. And, evidently, if you make predictions without reference to any evidence, that is clearly an example of irrationality. Now, it is significant to note that almost every example provided by Wittgenstein of a religious belief has a form which resembles a prediction. They are supposed to be religious utterances but they have the appearance of empirical predictions – with this crucial difference. They appear to be without evidence and thus totally baseless. Hence, they have the appearance to being wholly irrational. This is Wittgenstein's ground for saying that they are 'not reasonable'. Now consider the following examples of 'religious' remarks made by Wittgenstein in this context:

'I shall think of you after my death, if that should be possible'.
'Suppose someone believed in the Last Judgement.'
'Suppose ... another says, 'No. Particles will join together in a thousand years, and there will be a Resurrection of you.'
'I believe that so and so will happen ...'
'What we call believing in a Judgement Day or not believing in a Judgement Day ...'
'Suppose someone dreamt of the Last Judgement ... and said to me ...' 'It will be in about 2000 years ...'
'Dead undergraduate speaks ...'
'He said that this was, in a way, proof of the immortality of the soul.'

'Death', 'speaking after death', 'immortality of the soul', 'Last Judgement', 'Judgement Day', 'Resurrection' – these concepts reappear time and time again in Wittgenstein's remarks on religion in this context. And this is profoundly misleading in two respects. First, these examples are formulated in such a way, deliberately or out of sheer ignorance, to appear as predictions. The references to 'a thousand years' and '2000 years' reinforces this view. Yet, in a profound sense, such allusions to a time-scale make them clearly pseudo-religious remarks – remarks which one normally associates with weird and superstitious cults. Secondly, they are given such, almost exclusive, prominence by Wittgenstein in this context, that the impression is created that they are, is some sense, typical of religious beliefs and central to the religion that is being characterized. But, they are certainly not concepts that are central in Christian belief. On the contrary, religious believers that give such prominence to eschatological ideas in their thinking are normally associated with peripheral, heterodox sects or cults that seem to appear and disappear as regularly as their false predictions! Wittgenstein's preoccupation with such examples is grossly unfortunate and betrays a sad misunderstanding of the Christian faith. This is not the place to discuss the meaning of Christian eschatology, but it is at least meaningful to ask whether or not these doctrines are, in any sense, connected with time, or whether any eschatological beliefs are essentially concerned with future events. There are some Christian theologians who advocate a belief in 'a realized eschatology'; that is, the Judgement Day is ever-present. However, even if these examples given by Wittgenstein are to be regarded as some kind of predictions, then they are religious predictions made within a religious conceptual framework. This would make them not unlike, say, an Old Testament prophet's prediction that Jerusalem would fall to an enemy attack. Such predictions were made, not because the prophets had some paranormal view of the future, but simply because they believed the words of the divine covenant. God would visit his people for their sins. The 'given' here is a belief in a divine covenant. It was believed that what happened to the nation was wholly predictable – for its fate depended on its obedience or disobedience to the Law of the covenant. Such predictions, within that conceptual framework, were not at all unreasonable, but were expressions of the prophets' religious reasoning and faith.

Yet in the *LC* context, whatever these beliefs mean, they are said to be unconnected with evidence. This, apparently, is partly what gives them their religious character and gives them the appearance of being outside the category of the 'reasonable'. I do not believe that the Wittgenstein of the *Philosophical Investigations* would have ever maintained this argument, for, as it stands, it is again contaminated by a form of essentialism. It is as if 'evidence' can only be one thing. But if we speak of different language games and practices, we may also speak of different kinds of evidence, and not only of evidence as we have it in science, or in 'everyday beliefs' as referred to in the *LC*. Wittgenstein's whole argument militates against the language of the Christian Scriptures, in which constant reference is made to 'witnesses' 'testifying' to the truth of their claims. For instance, one of the central concepts in the Fourth Gospel is that of 'witnesses' who 'testify' to the divinity of Jesus. Again, this is not to identify the evidence of such witnesses with what we call 'empirical evidence'. That would be wholly mistaken. The conceptual framework of New Testament-time observers that made it possible for them to 'see' God in Jesus is radically different from the conceptual framework that enables us to forecast tomorrow's weather or to see that inflationary pressures within the economy will affect the value of money in a year's time. But that does not mean that the concept of evidence is to be proscribed within religious language. That, indeed, would be a piece of philosophical dogmatism!

It seems to me that an aspect of Wittgenstein's error in this context is to transgress one of his own more important lessons in the *Philosophical Investigations* – never to divorce assertions from their context. Whatever is meant by the eschatological concepts he so frequently referred to, they cannot be alienated from the central concepts of divinity as they are understood within the Christian religion. The religious poverty of the *LC*, as reflected in the examples of religious beliefs provided, is startling. There is nothing at all here about those things which are unequivocally definitive of the Christian religion, such as, divine mercy, forgiveness, love and compassion. Wittgenstein's version of Christianity is one that is clothed in, what appears to be, absurd predictions. It is a travesty of the Christian faith.

If there are difficulties with Wittgenstein's eschatological remarks there are comparable difficulties also with his remarks about the role of historical propositions. And, it appears to me, that this is crucial. The interrelationships between various forms of life constitute an essential condition of their intelligibility. The language games whose truths are those most closely related to the Christian religion are morality and history. Not that religious truth is identical with either of these, but there is a close relationship between them. (Unfortunately, there is very little about morality in the *LC*. Wittgenstein does suggest one connection between religion and morality when he refers to the fact that denying the existence of God is seen as 'something bad', and he probably would have also understood the notion of 'divine judgement' in some moral sense.) But Wittgenstein does raise the issue of historical truth, again in conjunction with the role of evidence in our thinking. He admits that, even in religion, 'we do talk of evidence, and do talk of evidence by experience. We could even talk of historical events. It has been said that Christianity rests on an historic basis.' What follows these remarks in the *LC*, and indeed, the way that Mulhall also deals with these issues, appears to me to be fundamentally wrong both in terms of logic and in religious terms. The issues have to do with the relationship between the historical and the religious. Here, however, we need to restrict the sense of 'religious' to the Biblical religions – for both the religions of the Old and New Testaments claim a certain unique relationship with historical claims – a relationship which has been widely either denied or misunderstood since the middle of the last century. Certainly, Christianity makes the claim (and I believe this is also true of Judaism), that it would be false if certain alleged historical events did not take place. (In Judaism this is connected with the Exodus experience or deliverance of the Hebrew people from slavery in Egypt. The identity of both the Jewish God and his people are bound with this event.) In Christianity, the historical is connected with certain events in the life of Jesus and, in particular, the claim that he was raised from the dead. 'If Christ be not raised, then is our preaching vain, and your faith is also vain. Yea, we are found false witnesses of God' (A.V.1 Cor. 15). In other words, Christian truth and historical truth are here so closely interwoven that the historical truth has become at least *one* condition of the truth of the religious. There is nothing comparable to this in the *LC*. Instead, what we find are ambiguous comments. Wittgenstein introduces a strange, unclear distinction between 'a belief in historic facts' and 'a belief in ordinary historic facts'. A distinction could not be more ambiguous. But let us suppose that he had in mind, when referring to 'a belief in historic fact', something as extraordinary as a claim that the historical Jesus was raised from the dead. Then, Wittgenstein maintains, belief in this claim is very different from a belief in an 'ordinary historical fact' – like, say, some facts about Napoleon. Wittgenstein's point seems to be that in the latter case, it is, in principle, possible to express doubts about what happened to Napoleon, while, even though what happened to Jesus is so extraordinary, and so vastly remoter in time than what happened to Napoleon, no doubts are ever entertained about those 'historic facts' that are at the heart of Christian doctrines. Propositions about Jesus 'are not treated as historical, empirical, propositions'. There is a problem with both the generality of this remark and also with its ambiguity. Its generality suggests either that *nothing* about Jesus is treated as either historical or empirical – or that propositions about him are *never* thought of in historical or empirical terms – or both, nothing and never. All three generalizations are patently incorrect. The ambiguity of the claim is connected with the related idea that the truth of both historical and empirical propositions are contingent: and it is the case that when assertions about Jesus are treated as *religious* or *theological* assertions, as dogma, then what happened to Jesus is not treated as 'historical, empirical, propositions'. Contingency is inadmissible within the context of faith. Religiously speaking, what happened to Jesus, as God's will, could not be otherwise, while, on the other hand, what happened to Napoleon is a contingent matter. The believer claims that there was divine necessity in the life of Jesus which removes all contingency from it. In a religious sense these propositions could not be untrue. But propositions about Jesus are not always treated as dogma, and any religious necessity dogmatic propositions possess does not preclude the possibility of asking the empirical, historical question: 'What did actually happen to Jesus?' – in which case we are engaged in an empirical enquiry – and we may ask all sorts of questions about the historical authenticity of the Gospel records, and so on. In one context therefore, what happened to Jesus is absolutely indubitable, while in another related context, that of an historical enquiry, what did actually happen to Jesus is still open to empirical investigation.

Of course, it would be wrong to separate the propositions about the Jesus of history from the fact that they are propositions which form part of church dogma whose truth is guaranteed by a body that claims infallibility. Or, if it is believed that it is not the church that is their guarantor, then the Scriptures themselves, believed to be God's Word, guarantees their truth. Hence, in this religious tradition, the truths about Jesus are guaranteed to be, in one way or another, incontrovertible by an authority or authorities that claim to be absolute. Indeed, it is only after the questioning of these traditional authorities of faith that doubts have been raised about the historicity of Jesus. But the fact that such doubts have been seen as an attack on the very basis of the Christian faith is indicative of the significance of the role of the historical in Christianity.

I suspect that when Mulhall argues that if believers put so much trust in historical truth they must be 'ludicrously irrational as to strain credibility'. He also seems to have forgotten that these truths are not believed *in vacuo*, but are beliefs shared by a religious community – a community that maintains that it has its origins in these alleged historical events. In this context, both the concepts of 'community' and 'continuity' are important. And although such concepts may have some role in secular history, they do not, in that context, have the same role as they have in the religious context. Mulhall writes: 'Religious believers base matters of great moment on evidence that seems exceedingly flimsy by comparison with the corroboration they require before accepting claims of far less significance for their lives.' But this is to exclude the central function of the role of the religious community in the propagation of its truths – both its religious truths and those historical truths that are believed to be inextricably connected with the religious truths. Mulhall's remark would appear to carry more weight if he were referring say, to the peoples of Ephesus or Corinth in the first century AD. Their conversion to a new faith appears more remarkable as they were asked to believe in certain alleged facts that took place in a distant land, a generation or so earlier, and without the weight of centuries of belief in such historical truths. (But is it at all correct to attempt to account for their religious conversions while omitting all reference to the central Reality of their faith? Is it not a religious doctrine that eternal life is given as a gift by God – and that the mystery of divine grace surrounds the whole process?) But, nowadays, most religious believers are believers in a historical, resurrected Jesus because of their upbringing. Within the religious context, these truths are regarded as the 'certainties' of faith – 'certainties' that religious believers were probably taught before they had been introduced to, say, the certainties of mathematics. If, however, the believer develops doubts about the validity of his faith and asks such questions as 'Why do I continue to believe these truths?' the fact that he is surrounded by a cloud of living witnesses, that he is part of a fellowship of saints, would appear to me to be of inestimable significance for him. He is not an isolated believer who possesses some private beliefs. By questioning his faith, he is questioning the faith of his fellow-believers – the faith, probably, of those who mean most to him as persons. He belongs to a community of faith that claims that it has its roots in history, and it authenticates its existence, in part, by demonstrating the continuity between itself and the Jesus of history.

Let us finally turn to some of the remarks which Wittgenstein made elsewhere in his writing, particularly those we find in *Culture and Value*. I do not wish to comment at any length on what is in the *Tractatus*, for, although such comments are often quoted by some Wittgensteinians when it is convenient, the remarks cannot be reconciled with anything that is Christian. 'God does not reveal himself in the world.' 'The world' here may refer to 'everything that is the case', to 'the totality of facts' – expressions which have a special meaning within the *Tractatus* thesis, but the import of these assertions is to place the reality of God outside intelligible language. Hence, little of religious significance can be deduced from the *Tractatus*. But elsewhere in Wittgenstein's writings, particularly in *Culture and Value* we have a variety of utterances that are deeply religious.

In most of them, Wittgenstein rightly underlines the relationship between religious belief and a person's understanding of the kind of life that she leads and the kind of character that she is. There is a deep understanding here of the kind of experiences that can reinforce religious belief, or can even lead a person to religious faith. Wittgenstein is correct to point out in the *LC* that it is often the case that 'the word "God" is amongst the earliest learnt – pictures and catechisms, etc.' (p. 59) and this is partly the importance of the role of a religious tradition referred to above. But he also states that 'Life can educate you to "believing in God"', (*CV*, p. 97e) that the religious unbeliever can come to faith through certain 'sufferings of various sorts'. 'Life can force this concept on us' (ibid.) and Wittgenstein adds 'So perhaps it is like the concept of "object"' ' – by which I suppose he means that the concept becomes unavoidable, the concept becomes a fundamental part of a person's seeing and understanding. God becomes 'a certainty'. When Wittgenstein characterizes such experiences he invariably thinks of man becoming deeply aware of his limitations, his moral limitations and also his inability to cope with life's difficulties. Man can be beaten by circumstances and may feel that he is being destroyed by them. He can succumb to endless temptations which lead to a sense of hopelessness and despair. In such contexts, a person who has no faith may come to see that faith offers hope and acceptance and, through faith she may see new possibilities, including the possibility of some form of renewal. (Of course, it is also the case that the person who has faith may lose it when faced with the vicissitudes of life. A tragedy may be felt so deeply that the language of religious gratitude, of thanking God, has become empty and meaningless for him or her.) In one of these contexts, Wittgenstein explains why he is tempted to believe in the resurrection of Jesus. It is, perhaps, the most orthodox of Christian remarks in his whole writings – for here he does imply that salvation, in the Christian sense, is related to a belief in a relationship with the resurrected Christ. It is not just the case that Christians are followers of the Jesus of history who taught a certain moral code, but that they have faith, a trust, in a person who sustains them in their weaknesses and fortifies them through grace against temptation. It is a religiously wonderful passage and it is astonishing to find it in Wittgenstein.

> What inclines even me to believe in Christ's Resurrection? I play as it were with the thought. – If he did not rise from the dead, then he is decomposed in the grave like every human being. *He is dead and decomposed.* In that case he is a teacher, like any other & can no

longer *help:* & once more we are orphaned & alone. And have to make do with wisdom & speculation. It is as though we are in a hell, where we can only dream & shut out of heaven, roofed in as it were ... (CV, p. 38e).

Wittgenstein goes on to refer to the soul and its passions and states,

Only *love* can believe the Resurrection. Or: it is *love* that believes the Resurrection. One might say: redeeming love believes even in the Resurrection; holds fast even to the Resurrection (CV, p. 39e).

The ideas and the language used here are reminiscent of Kierkegaard. And it is important to note that this is one reason why it is correct to claim that the meaning of 'believing', in the Christian context, changes in the light of the fact that the believer believes, first and foremost, in a person – in the living Christ – and believing in a person is a very different form of believing from, say, believing in any theory or in any historical truths. To believe in a person is to say something about a relationship with that person, and in the Christian context, this relationship is determined by its theology. Hence, the constant use of such concepts as, 'Lord' and 'Saviour', 'God' which indicate that the believer sees himself respectively as servant or slave of his Lord, as the one who has, is, will have to be rescued from sin by his Saviour, and as one sees his life in terms of submission to and the worship of God. It is within relationship that religious passion is to be understood, for the relationship is one of love, trust and dependence. But these passionate beliefs are not unconnected with the belief in One who is not 'dead and decomposed'. So although Kierkegaard was perfectly correct to underline the passionate character of religious faith, it was his error to deny that one condition of this faith was a belief in the truth of certain historical propositions – that Jesus is not 'dead and decomposed'. 'Thou wilt not suffer thine holy one to see corruption.' (Acts 2)

In the final part of his paper, Mulhall raises questions about the human condition and develops an analogy, if not something more than an analogy, between human sinfulness and the roots of philosophical confusion. He does this in the context of Malcolm's now famous analysis of Wittgenstein's claim that he could not help 'seeing every problem from a religious point of view', and Winch's critical response to Malcolm's essay. Again, there is a great deal that is religiously edifying in this third part of his paper. Like Mulhall, I very much approve of Winch's critique of Malcolm's elucidation of Wittgenstein's comment – although, personally, I have no clear understanding at all of what Wittgenstein meant by this confession. There is no difficulty with the first part of Wittgenstein's admission that he was 'not a religious man' and this I find is easy to accept. For I do not find much in Wittgenstein's writings that would tempt me to describe him as 'religious' – particularly if 'religious' means 'Christian'. There is a super-abundance of evidence, of course, that Wittgenstein had a passionate concern for moral ideals and that he strove for some kind of moral perfection. But that is very different from being, say, a worshipper of God or a man of prayer. A religious man, in the Christian sense, is a holy man – a man of God, who believes and knows that 'as many as are led by the Spirit of God, they are the sons of God (Romans, 8). Yet, there are different forms and conceptions of spirituality and some of these may encompass Wittgenstein's religiosity. However, the problem with that is that Malcolm's four analogies between philosophy and faith are based on possible parallels between *Christian* doctrines, as understood by Malcolm, and Wittgenstein's philosophy. I accept *in toto* Mulhall's approval of Winch's criticisms of Malcolm. But then, towards the very end of his essay, he proceeds to make the point that there may be more to Malcolm's third analogy than what Winch had appreciated. Here I have failed to follow Mulhall's argument. But, if I have not failed, then Mulhall seems to me to be confused.

This third analogy, it will be recalled, was 'between the religious attitude of regarding oneself as radically imperfect or "sick", and the idea that philosophical puzzlement is a symptom of a "disease" of our thinking' (RPV, p. 110). Mulhall interprets Wittgenstein's notion of 'the grammar or criteria of our ordinary words' as constituting the 'limits or conditions of the human capacity to know, think or speak about the world and the various things that are in it'. And the argument is developed as follows. We see these limits as limitations. 'Limitations' implies imperfection and it is on this sense of imperfection that scepticism thrives. This scepticism is analogous with our 'inability or refusal to acknowledge the fact that human knowledge…is necessarily conditioned'. 'The desire to speak outside language games is an inflection of the human pride to be God.' So it would seem to follow that conceptual confusion is a sin – part of our degenerate nature, of 'Original Sin'. And, it is further argued that salvation from sin, in the religious context, is paralleled by salvation from conceptual confusion in a philosophical context. We need a personal relationship with Christ to save us from sin by his grace. We need a personal discourse with someone in philosophy to deliver us from the 'sin' of conceptual confusion.

Although I approve every theological remark by Mulhall, I believe that his religious enthusiasm has clouded his normal philosophical perspicuity at this point. Of course, from a religious point of view, any sort of imperfection – physical, spiritual, moral and intellectual *may* be understood in terms of man's fallen nature and state. But it is equally the case that in the same context, all human goodness and perfection are seen as revealing the general grace of God. But part of the difficulty of amalgamating such a perspective with philosophical considerations – quite apart from establishing some identity between the religious and the philosophical – is with the generality of the religious assertions. One might argue, from a religious standpoint, that all crime is the result of sin. But that belief does not in any way help us to understand why certain crimes are connected with, say, social or economic conditions. The general does not help us to understand the particular in this context. And, it seems to me, that the religious perception of universal human depravity does not help us to understand either the nature of the distinction between sense and nonsense or what conceptual clarity amounts to, or what are the roots of conceptual confusion. And I suspect that Wittgenstein did not mean anything like what we have here by his admission that he saw everything from a religious point or view.

I believe that in this context, Mulhall has, to some degree, misrepresented some of the ideas found in the *Philosophical Investigations*. First and foremost, he misconstrues the function of the notion of a 'language-game'. As I tried to make it plain in my introductory remarks, my own conviction is that Wittgenstein introduced this notion in his work to fulfil two specific functions only: first, to demonstrate the diversity and complexity of the criteria of intelligibility – and thus to contrast this view sharply with what he had said in the *Tractatus* about the single, general condition of intelligibility, and, secondly, to underline the connection between language and human practices or activities. In the *Philosophical Investigations*, saying something does not always amount to the same thing: there is a diversity of language games. And language must never be separated from our doings, from human practices. Now it may be correctly maintained, as Mulhall states, that these language games 'constitute the limits or conditions of the human capacity to know, think or speak about the world'. Yet there are dangers here which arise through the use of the concepts of 'limits' and 'conditions' – for there is a temptation to think of these, particularly in the way Mulhall argues here, as boundaries that are strictly set, fixed and formal. And such a view would bring us back to the idea of language games being rigidly autonomous. But this is to overlook the fluid character of language and practices – the fact that there is something fundamentally indeterminate about our practices and lives. There is constant flux. Constantly, there are new ways of saying and doing things. Furthermore, what becomes of the point, emphasized by Wittgenstein, that practices and saying things are closely interrelated? What I am suggesting is that Mulhall misrepresents the character of the boundaries of language games. Again, it seems to be the case that we are confronted with a new formalism – whereas the thesis presented by Wittgenstein is one of logical informality.

When anyone is conceptually confused *one* root of such a confusion is that we have taken a concept out of its natural setting, out of its grounding activity, without realizing it, and possibly, draw wrong conclusions on this basis. (Incidentally, this happens to all and sundry, and it is not only to 'competent speakers' who 'suffer such a loss of control when under pressure to philosophize'. It is difficult to reconcile the specific nature of the circumstances indicated here with what Mulhall has written just a few lines earlier about philosophical confusion not being 'restricted to inhabitants of certain disciplines'.) The confusion, of course, is not in the taking of a word or concept out of its natural habitat, but the failure to realize that when we are doing so, we *may* be using the concept in an entirely new way, perhaps metaphorically, or even misusing the word entirely, and consequently drawing false inferences on that basis. Through extending the use of words we can easily become confused. But I am at a loss to see how such a simple common error 'is an inflection of the prideful human craving to be God'. We also make all sorts of other intellectual errors, like miscalculating when doing mathematics, or committing the fallacy of the undistributed middle term in a piece of syllogistic reasoning. Are these also aspects of our pride and depravity? Furthermore, if my language has gone on holiday, it may suddenly occur to me that this is the case. I may retrace my steps, and analyse my use of the relevant concepts, and save myself from conceptual confusion – without the intervention of either a friend or a philosopher. I will have saved myself. But in religious language, as Mulhall underlines, the self cannot save itself from its egocentricity. Finally, not all my thinking, hopefully, is wholly confused. But, religiously speaking, my depravity is total – and if, by chance, I perform any good, that is the result of the intervention of the grace of God: 'it is not I, but the grace of God that was given to me'. Here there is no analogy between the occasional conceptual virus that one's thinking is susceptible to, and the religious condition of sickness that leads, without the intervention of grace, to spiritual death.

Notes

1. L. Wittgenstein, *Philosophical Investigations*, tr. G.E.M. Anscombe, Blackwell, 1958.
2. *Wittgenstein, Lectures and Conversations on Aesthetics, Psychology & Religious Belief*, ed. C Barrett, Blackwell, 1978.
3. L. Wittgenstein, *The Blue and Brown Books*, Blackwell, 1975.
4. L. Wittgenstein, *Culture and Value*, ed. G.H. von Wright, Revised Edition, Blackwell, 1998.
5. N. Malcolm, *Wittgenstein: a Religious Point of View*, ed. P. Winch, Routledge, 1993.
6. All Biblical references are from the King James Authorized Version.

9
Voices in Discussion

D.Z. Phillips

J: In the first part of what I had to say I concentrated on Wittgenstein's own comments on religion. In his *Lectures on Religious Belief*, he contrasts religious beliefs with historical and empirical beliefs. He did this in order to rebut misunderstandings. It is tempting to think that you can investigate the existence of God as though it were a prior, independent belief. Wittgenstein thought this was question-begging because everything depends on what 'existence' means.

In the second part of my criticism I discuss Wittgensteinianism. Here, in the presence of D.Z. Phillips at Claremont, I felt I was bringing coals to Newcastle. I addressed the accusation of fideism, and especially the charge that Wittgensteinians claim that religion is immune to criticism. It is impossible to sustain that charge, as Phillips has pointed out. First, there are terms of criticism within religious traditions. Second, there are religious responses to aspects of life that strike everyone. Some of these responses may be superstitious and, hence, criticizable. Third, Phillips makes use of common moral responses to criticize certain treatments of the problem of evil. Fourth, although Phillips does not press this, there is the kind of criticism that Nietzsche, Freud and Marx made of religion. Certain forms of religion may indeed turn out to be unhealthy masochism, economic exploitation, social and political oppression, or dependence on a father figure. So possibilities of criticism are not denied by Wittgensteinians. What is denied is that the whole of religion could be shown to be meaningless.

The third part of my paper is the most controversial and I doubt whether it would be acceptable to Phillips. I try to see what Wittgenstein meant when he said that although he was not a religious man he could not help seeing every problem from a religious point of view. This remark is discussed by Norman Malcolm in *Wittgenstein – a Religious*

Point of View? And by Peter Winch in his Response in that work. I do not think Malcolm's analogies between philosophical concerns and religious concerns work for the reasons Winch provides, but Winch does not dismiss the issue of spiritual concern in this context. But I am not altogether convinced of what he goes on to say. He says that lack of clarity has important consequences for life, but distinguishes, somewhat artificially in my view, between 'importance for the sense of life' and 'importance for the sense of one's own life'. Take as an example of the difference between first person and third person statements in the philosophy of psychology. Conceptual confusion can lead to views about private access; that there is something unique about one's experience that others can't have access to. But is it not also possible to live that confusion, to think that one is unique beyond the reach of others? I think Winch's distinction makes it look as though there are difficulties which only belong to an exclusive class of people called philosophers, as though others were not vulnerable to them.

But why do I think there is a genuinely religious aspect to this philosophical concern? First, the confusion comes from the attempt to speak outside all language games; to speak outside the conditions of sense. This can be seen as a profound dissatisfaction with life, and aspiration to transcend the human, an impulse to go beyond it.

Second, there is an interesting comparison between the philosopher and his or her interlocutor, and Christ and the believer. I suggest that there is a parallel between original sin and the role Cavell assigns to scepticism – the issue of what is involved in the denials of scepticism. Spiritual issues are involved in the denial of the human. One's concerns may be philosophical, but the motivation can be spiritual, just as, in political theory, Rawls can advance a theory of justice, inspired by neutrality, and still be moved by a passion for justice. So I am suggesting that Wittgenstein's combating confusion can have a spiritual aspect.

K: I am critical only of the third part of *J*'s paper. I don't object to the religious comments he makes there, but I do not see how he can link them to a philosophical position.

When I read Wittgenstein's *Lectures and Conversations* I was unhappy from the outset. I listened with two ears: one philosophical, the other trained by my religious upbringing. It seemed to me that his remarks on religion are tied too closely to the *Tractatus* view of language. It is unfortunate, therefore, if defenders of Wittgenstein use these very remarks as a general account of his views on religion. I have in mind the claim that God does not reveal himself in the world, and that the mystical is not how the world is, but that it is. Rhees in *Wittgenstein and the Possibility of Discourse* says that even in the *Investigations* Wittgenstein is still influenced by the analogy between language and a calculus. If Rhees is right, there is an interaction between language games and there is not the sharp distinction between the empirical and the spiritual that we have in the *Lectures and Conversations* where the concepts of 'knowledge' and 'truth' are simply given up to the empirical realm. Truth and falsity belong to activities and thus when we pay attention to divine activities we open up an entirely new field of enquiry.

The charge that Wittgensteinianism has no room for notions of 'truth' and 'falsity' is absurd. Here are just some examples.

First, Paul argued that circumcision was not necessary to be a member of the Church. To think otherwise, he said, was an error. Paul said that this was false doctrine. So this is doctrinal falsity.

Second, the Jews would condemn calling Jesus 'Lord' or 'God'. To them this is idolatry. That is another form of falsity.

Third, we have hypocrisy – another form of error.

Fourth, there is superstition. I had never flown before I came to this conference. I took my New Testament with me on the plane. I found myself wondering whether I was indulging in superstition, thinking that the mere possession of the Testament would save me from harm. So superstition is another kind of error.

Fifth, the Pharisees committed a terrible error. They were not hypocrites. They prayed sincerely, but what they said was, 'We thank thee that we are not as other men are'.

Sixth, to say that Jesus is not risen is false. Wittgenstein says that to believe in the resurrection is to believe that Jesus did not decompose in the grave like other teachers. The belief has an empirical element: god did not suffer his holy one to see corruption.

These are simply some examples of uses of 'truth' and 'falsity', and yet Wittgensteinians are said to deny the distinction.

J: The claim that a general distinction between the empirical and the religious is too sweeping is important. I was less worried about that distinction, than with bringing out the religious and ethical significance of notions like the Last Judgement which is lost if it is treated as a merely empirical event. But I agree with *K* that before we say that an event is this or that, we must look to contexts to see the sense in which they might be taken together.

B: You spoke of 'theistic metaphysics'. What do you mean by that? Is it to be dismissed and not taken seriously?

J: I didn't make much use of that term. I did refer to Hyman's tendency to think that religious practices presuppose metaphysical beliefs. I argued against that. But there is little doubt that in Wittgenstein, 'metaphysics' is a term of abuse. Metaphysics is an attempt to solve problems that don't need solving because they are the product of conceptual confusion.

H: Isn't that because, for Wittgenstein, what is real in religion is found not in relation to reason, but in relation to Christ?

C: I think we have to be careful here. First, I would agree with *K* that at the time of the *Tractatus* or the *Lecture on Ethics* for that matter, the religious expressions he wants to use are linked to the *Tractatus* view of language. I agree that he is struggling to work his way out of that position in the *Lectures and Conversations* without wholly succeeding. That is why he can't make sense of the expressions in the *Tractatus* and the *Lecture* while thinking, nevertheless, that they are extremely important. The importance of some of the remarks, therefore, survives the philosophical position from which they were made. So I don't agree with *K* that they have little religious significance. For example, the view that when one comes to believe in God, the world changes as a whole is extremely important.

In response to *B* I'd say that there are times when Wittgenstein gives the impression that he is the unconfused one, whereas the metaphysician is confused, as though he learnt nothing from the discussion of metaphysical theses. True, he thinks these are confused, but this is something which he comes to see through struggling with metaphysical voices in the *Investigations* which are voices within himself. In the main he never dismissed metaphysical questions. He called them the deepest worries in philosophy, albeit worries which we should strive to overcome.

K: My main criticism is of the third part of *J*'s paper. I see no justification for his analogy between scepticism and sin. The source of the former is philosophical, whereas the latter comes from the want of a proper relationship with God. Coming to terms with scepticism doesn't turn one's life around or bring salvation in the way in which receiving grace does.

J: I wasn't so much equating them as suggesting that there is an issue here to be addressed, both in relation to Christianity and Cavell's model of perfectionism. Cavell used the term 'recognition' and wanted to explore what it or resistance to it involves.

C: But, then, what kind of recognition are we talking about? I think the similarity comes from the fact that 'the spiritual' is wider than 'the religious'. Wittgenstein said that we must suffer in philosophy. There is an analogy with moral problems here because there is a question of the obstacle of the will involved – we will not give up certain ways of thinking. But, having said that, what we are asked to recognize is wider than what we appropriate personally. For example, compare St Francis saying that the way flowers gave glory to God put him to shame, with Spandrell in Huxley's *Point Counter Point* slashing a field of flowers with his stick saying, 'Damn their insolence.' What is it to see the world in these ways? What sort of disagreement exists between them?

Philosophy itself is a spiritual determination to see the world as it is in all its variety, but, for that very reason, it does not underwrite any perspective. Cavell seems to want to advocate specific perspectives. I do not think that he, or any other philosopher, can take that moral weight on himself.

J: I agree with a great deal of that. I can see why you say that taking on that moral weight cannot be part of a philosophical project. On the other hand, I was thinking of how ethical and spiritual concerns enter that philosophical discussion which is a love of wisdom. After all, in some sense, you have to admit that you've been lost. Why does that repeat itself again and again? Some conceptual confusions are very specific, but they may still express the impulse to violate criteria, to speak outside language, and, therefore, to deny the human.

E: Aren't you referring to human problems, not philosophical problems? Or are you saying that 'the human' includes 'the philosophical'?

J: Well, having rejected Malcolm's analogies, Winch does not deny that philosophy can have a spiritual concern. He thought that Wittgenstein's investigations are suffused with it. So does a context emerge where there is a connection between a conception of philosophy and a conception of life? There is at least an issue here to be addressed.

S: I was puzzled why K said that belief in the Resurrection involved an empirical element. Does he mean that you could settle the matter by checking whether the tomb was empty? Suppose someone said that Hitler had walked out of an empty tomb. So what? What religious significance would it have?

P: I think we need to recognize that language games overlap in this context. There is no sharp distinction between the empirical and the spiritual.

K: Exactly. The empirical is the condition of the spiritual. If Christ is not risen, then, indeed, our faith is in vain.

A: If one is a religious believer one must ask what sort of person would have brought about such an event, just as one asks what sort of person would have committed a crime. If you say there can't be any such thing as a resurrection you'll need a lot of evidence to show this. But if you have a belief that it is probable that there is a God, then you must ask whether it is reasonable and probable that he would do such a thing.

T: Wittgenstein says that religious believers walk a tightrope with beliefs of this kind. If you over-emphasize some aspect you fall off, but people do manage to walk the tightrope.

C: One way of falling off the tightrope is to say as K does that the resurrection is the empirical condition of religious faith. That cannot possibly be right because 'resurrection' is itself a religious notion.

K: But for you 'raised' simply means 'exalted'. You believe the bones of Jesus are somewhere in Palestine.

C: You referred to Wittgenstein endorsing your view. I don't think he does. I believe there is a change of direction in the passage you referred. He says, at first, that he plays with the thought that to be saved he needs Jesus not to have decomposed in the grave like any other teacher. Now, I have no idea where the bones of Jesus are, but it does not take love to believe that they are not in Palestine. And when Wittgenstein turns away from the thought that he was playing with, that is what he says – that it takes love to believe that the crucified one has been raised on high, exalted to the right hand of God the Father. Now if you think this invites the empirical question, 'How high was he raised?' that is your problem. Are you going to ask the same empirical question of the Ascension? These are religious terms and must be understood as such.

F: Christianity is an historical religion – things happen at a certain time. But it doesn't follow that what happened is itself to be deter-mined historically. The writers of the Gospels were not writing an his-torical report, but proclaiming Good News. C is right, the Resurrection is part of that Good News. It's not as though a video camera could have picked it up. They are not CNN reporters.

D: How do you know a video camera could not have picked it up?

F: That wasn't my claim – it couldn't.

E: *K*, you were referring to I Corinthians 15. There, for Paul, without a doubt, resurrection and exaltation come to the same thing.

A: That's a disputable view; we'd need to look at the texts.

K: It is certainly disputable. Paul refers unequivocally to the post-resurrection appearances, on which the faith of the believers depends.

E: And he says that he is passing on what he, too, has received.

C: In other words, the sense in which Jesus appeared to him is the same sense as that in which he appeared to others.

D: I think that if you ask most Christians whether they think that they would deny it.

C: But what makes you think you can do philosophy in that way? If I knocked on a door in Claremont and asked the lady of the house what she meant by 'thinking', would I take her answer to settle the matter? One cannot do philosophy by Gallup poll.

D: Why not? Wittgensteinians always claim to tell us what we really mean. Why not ask Christians what they do mean? If the majority says they mean such-and-such, that settles the matter. You can do this kind of philosophy by Gallup poll.

C: No you can't, because <u>when reference is made to what people mean</u>, <u>the reference is to the role the words play in their lives, not to the</u> <u>account they would give if asked</u>. <u>Notoriously, in giving that account</u> <u>our own words can lead us astray</u>. That is why Wittgenstein said that though a picture, including a religious picture, is in the foreground, its actual application may be in the background. The matter can only be resolved, if at all, through discussion with one's interlocutor. It cannot be settled by Gallup poll.

Part IV
Postmodernism

10
Messianic Postmodernism

John D. Caputo

The word 'postmodernism' has come to mean many things. So before addressing the principal objections that have been made against it, particularly as regards its usefulness as a framework for a philosophy of religion, we would do well to specify the sense in which we are using this term. Very broadly conceived, I would argue that postmodernism is a philosophy of 'difference', that it emphasizes the productive role of difference, as opposed to the 'modern' or Enlightenment predilection for universality, commonality, consensus, and what modernists (rather presumptuously) call 'rationality'. Speaking very broadly still, I would say that, for our purposes here, there are (at least) two different varieties of this philosophy of difference, depending on which of its two nineteenth-century predecessors – Nietzsche or Kierkegaard – one favours. These I will call, only slightly tongue in cheek, 'Dionysian' and 'messianic' postmodernism.

It is the thesis of the present essay that most of the objections that are made against postmodernism have in mind the Dionysian version, but that they fall wide of the mark of the messianic version, about which the critics of postmodernism often seem badly informed. The line of objections that are raised against postmodernists bear a family resemblance: relativism, subjectivism, scepticism, anarchism, antinomianism, anti-institutionalism, nihilism and despair. In my view, this line of complaint takes its lead from the highly Nietzscheanized face of the first version of postmodernism, but it does not come to grips with the Kierkegaardian (and Levinasian) face of the second version. Clearly, were all or most of these objections valid, postmodernism would not be of much help to the philosophy of religion, or to anything else for that matter, and it would be rightly denounced as inimical to God and religion. Although I will argue that when these complaints are legitimate, they hold of its Dionysian version, I would insist that a more nuanced understanding of this version also reveals very interesting possibilities for religious reflection. The danger of the present 'good cop/bad cop' strategy is that it tends to sell the Nietzschean version short, to throw it to the wolves of postmodernism's critics, and to let it take a hit for the rest of us. But be that as it may, this string of objections against postmodernism is, as regards the second or messianic version, false on its face and very likely betrays the critic's unfamiliarity with its religious and even biblical provenance.

Dionysian postmodernism

The Nietzschean version of postmodernism has grabbed most of the headlines and has dominated its popular reception. In this version of the philosophy of difference (*heteros*), difference has the sense of *diversitas*, the variety of forms. Here the emphasis is placed upon the affirmation of multiplicity, a multiplication of forms, a polymorphic or 'heteromorphic' pluralism of many different kinds. This goes hand in hand with a love of novelty, of the invention of as many new kinds as possible. Philosophically, this view draws upon Nietzsche's 'perspectivalism', that is, his critique of 'truth' and the 'ascetic ideal'. Nietzsche was critical of the classical metaphysical ideal that there is a firm centre which holds, a firm and immutable foundation or principle, to which all lovers of the true or the good, of science or ethics, must rigorously ('ascetically') hold – whether one takes that principle to be God, the laws of physics, or even the laws of grammar. Indeed, when Nietzsche said that '*God* is dead', he meant this entire metaphysical order, any notion of an absolute centre or foundation. That explains why he said we would not be rid of belief in God until we had dispelled our belief in grammar, our belief that what are for him the 'fictions' – or conventions – of Indo-European grammar somehow give voice to the very order of being (the grammatical subject arousing faith in the personal self, and so forth). In the place of this absolutism, Nietzsche put his notion of perspectives, that every belief, including the propositions of physics, is an interpretation.

For Nietzsche, the perspectives issue from the play of forces asserting themselves, each with greater or lesser strength, each expressing its own immanent life force to a greater or lesser extent. Our own 'beliefs' are the perspectives we cognitive beings impose on things to promote the flourishing of our own life, rather the way the trees in the forest struggle for light. When Nietzsche complained, 'if there were a God, what would there be left for us to create?' he pressed the view that the maximization of the invention of the perspectives required the dismantling of the idea of a *summum bonum* or *primum ens* in which every such possibility would be already realized. For Nietzsche no belief or idea enjoyed eternal or timeless validity; every such idea is invented – historically constituted – to promote the needs of life. Indeed, one is tempted to argue that for Nietzsche such ideas are biologically constituted, so long as one does not forget that biology too is another perspective and ought not to be turned into another ascetic ideal, that is, a rigorous, absolutely true, non-perspectival science to which everything can be systematically reduced. Everything is surface, surface is what is deep; the distinction between depth and surface, the true world and apparent, being and appearing, comes undone. God is dead.

The most prominent 'Nietzschean' postmodernists are Gilles Deleuze and Michel Foucault and nowadays, after their death, Jean Baudrillard, who uses Nietzschean presuppositions in a 'postmodern' theory of 'images'. Baudrillard represents a very important, more broadly 'cultural' dimension of postmodernism, one which forces us to distinguish it from a more technical philosophical position called post-structuralism. In Baudrillard, postmodernism is the articulation of the culture of the world-wide web and 'virtual reality' upon which we have all entered, where the distinction between image and reality, surface and depth, dissolves. As his recent CD-Rom, *The Réal: Las Vegas, NV*, illustrates very well, this is the 'postmodern' world that today interests radical theologian Mark C. Taylor.[1] Feminist theologians like Sharon Welch and Rebecca Chopp have made interesting use of Foucauldian inspired 'genealogical' analyses to criticize the historically constituted constellations of power and sexuality that have been used to oppress women and minorities, inside the church and without. In still another direction, Bataille had taken up Nietzsche's notion of the overflowing of the will to power to formulate a theory of an expenditure without return as the essence of the religious act.

On the whole, this version of postmodernism has been greeted with hostility by a wide variety of thinkers on both the left and the right, by scientists and humanists alike. The right wing tends to think Nietzsche is the devil himself, having utterly relativized, God-Motherhood-and-Apple-Piety. But then again so does the 'old' (liberal, modernist) left, which has no interest in religion at all, as witness physicist Alan Sokal, who wants to restore the left to its pre-Nietzschean senses, has made a reputation for himself denouncing the 'cultural studies' movement, made up of postmodernists of the Dionysian stripe, who on his view are ill-informed charlatans attempting to relativize the results of mathematical physics while knowing little mathematics and less physics. Even Richard Rorty, who thinks that Nietzsche is good for use on weekends when we are inventing our private selves, is highly critical of letting Nietzsche into the workaday public sphere, with the confusion besetting the new left, as he argues in his recent *Achieving our Country*.[2] Philosophical theologians like Brian Ingraffia have roundly criticized Nietzsche for having a defective understanding of Christianity and on this basis have denounced any attempt to mix Christianity and postmodernism.[3] That is, I think, an overreaction, but it is an understandable reaction that this version of postmodernist thinking tends to bring down upon itself. At its best, Nietzscheanized postmodernism has opened up important genealogical investigations into the historical constitution of power clusters that can have emancipatory effects for the oppressed, and have paved the way for the new or what Allan Bloom grumpily called the 'Nietzscheanized left', a political result that would, needless to say, have profoundly saddened Nietzsche himself who was deeply antipathetic to modern democratic movements and who deeply regretted the passing of the *ancien régime* in France. At its worst, postmodernists often give us the impression that they have utterly jettisoned any standard of reason, intelligibility or argumentation; they give everyone the distinct impression that 'anything goes' just because their texts are written precisely as if anything does indeed go. They make themselves easy targets for people like Sokal who have neither the time, the training, nor the taste for trying to decode and decipher the excesses of their jargon. They write for an inside group of 'po-mo' academics, bolting from one conference on postmodernism to the next, presenting the worst but most public face of this movement.

Messianic Postmodernism

But 'postmodernism' is capable of assuming a second and quite different form, one whose nineteenth-century predecessor is not Nietzsche but Kierkegaard. Here the notion of 'difference' takes on a significantly different sense, where it means not *diversitas*, or heteromorphic diversity, but rather *alteritas*, the alterity of the 'other one', that one 'over there'. In the second version, difference demands *transcendence*, the movement from the 'same' to the 'other', a movement first announced in philosophy by Plato, who said that the Good is *epikeinas tes ousias*, beyond being, at the end of a steep ascent, and in religion by the transcendence of the Most

High, the Holy One of Second Isaiah, Who said that His ways are not our ways. Here difference means the One Who is 'wholly other' (*tout autre*), to use the expression that Levinas borrows from Vladimir Yankelévitch, who was writing about the One in Plotinus, although that expression is also found in Kierkegaard.

By the wholly other these thinkers mean the 'paradox' – by which they do not mean not some simple logical contradiction (*x* and ~*x*) – of a concept of something inconceivable, a concept whose very meaning or conceptual function is to indicate something beyond, something we cannot conceive and comprehend, not just because of present limitations but always and in principle. A classical example of this is the Anselmian God, *id quo major nequit cogitari*, the concept of what we cannot conceive, of something so surpassingly great that it is always and in principle better than anything we can conceive. Such concepts have a principle of self-surpassal built right into them. So, too, the Cartesian notion in the Third Meditation of an idea of something of which I can have no idea, an idea that has been implanted in me that I cannot understand, viz., of an infinite God. The 'wholly other' is always like that. It is not going to turn out upon further investigation to be an instance of a type of which I already have an idea, so that I am already schematically familiar with it. It has an unreachability, an unattainability – an alterity – built into it, like a shore for which I set out but never reach. I am in relation with it, heading for it, but the 'wholly other' is also always withdrawing from this relation, so that, in principle, I never get there. The paradox is encapsulated nicely in Levinas's phrase, 'a relation in which the terms *absolve* themselves from the relation, remain absolute within the relation',[4] or in Blanchot's French quip, *le pas au-delà*, taking the 'step (*pas*) beyond', which is also prohibited, the 'no-beyond' (*le 'pas au-delà'*), the step not beyond, the step I am always taking but not quite making. There is both a relation and a breakdown of the relation, like a desire to have what cannot be had, or to know what cannot be known. So if in the Dionysian version of postmodern difference, 'infinite' tended to mean the unregulatable and uncontrollable play of differences spreading across an infinite horizontal surface, 'rhizomatically', as Deleuze would say (which means like crab grass), in this second version, infinite difference has the sense of unreachable depths or heights, like the Ancient of Days or the Most High in the Tanakh.

If the Dionysian version of difference takes the form of a certain 'heteromorphism', this second version, which I am calling 'messianic', is best thought of as a certain 'heteronomism', where everything turns on the *law of the other*, on the disruption visited upon the 'same' by the 'other', which is the language Levinas uses, adapted from Plato's *Sophist* and *Parmenides*, to express a very biblical notion. In this version, what matters is the 'responsibility' that I incur when the other overtakes me, taking me by a kind of deep surprise, one that is older than I can say, prefigured in the very structure of *creatio ex nihilo*, in which, in Levinas's beautiful phrase, the creature answers to a call that it never heard. The heteronomic version is structured around the notion of a call in which the other lays claim to me, has always and already laid claim to me. Its model and prototype is no one less than father Abraham himself, who, called forth from the land of his fathers never to go home again, and called upon to sacrifice the seed of the very future he was promised for this uprooting, could only say *'hineni'*, *'me voici'*, see me here, here I am. In the Dionysian version of postmodernism, modernity's autonomous subject is dispersed and disseminated into a Dionysian plurality of many selves, each one of which is historically, even grammatically constituted. In the heteronomic version, the modern autonomous subject is taken from behind, overtaken, by a call which it never heard, by a command of which it is not the author, by a past that was never present, and reduced – 'led back' – to a level of deeper subjection and accusation, radically singularized by an inescapable, irrecusable responsibility. The Cartesian 'I' of modernity becomes a biblical 'me', in the accusative, accused by the call which claims it. 'Abraham!' 'See me here!'

Thus far from being the nemesis of religion and ethical responsibility, which is the complaint directed at its Dionysian cousin, the figures of *this* postmodernism, where the term 'postmodern' marks a meditation on 'alterity', are distinctly ethical, biblical and, as I will show, messianic. Indeed, this discourse has been described by Derrida as 'a non-dogmatic doublet of dogma … a *thinking* that "repeats" the possibility of religion without religion'. This 'thinking', Derrida says, is 'developed without reference to religion as institutional dogma,' and concerns 'the essence of the religious that doesn't amount to an article of faith', representing a body of 'discourses that seek in our day to be religious … without putting forth theses or *theologems* that would by their very structure teach something corresponding to the dogmas of a given religion'.[5]

Although Derrida is speaking of Kierkegaard and Levinas,[6] among others, I have argued elsewhere and at some length that this 'religion without religion' also befits Derrida himself, particularly as regards the works that have appeared since 1980.[7] This claim is anathema both to secularizing deconstructionists, who on the question of religion repeat deeply modernist critiques of religion with perfect loyalty, and to religious thinkers, who, like Brian Ingraffia, mistakenly identify deconstruction as a form of Dionysian rather than of messianic post-modernism. But to the surprise and chagrin of many, Derrida, it turns out, has religion, what he calls 'my religion', and it can be ignored only at the cost of systematically misreading his work. Indeed, time and time again the most outrageous and, one is tempted to say, the most irrespon-sible misrepresentations of his work appear regularly in print, grotesque distortions of a thinker whose principal interest these days lies in such notions as the messianic, hospitality, friendship, testimony and forgive-ness. That is due to the fact that in Derrida there are important veins of both versions of postmodernisms, very roughly approximating his ear-lier and later writings, and that too many commentators go by second-hand accounts of the earlier work. Indeed, getting one's reading of Derrida right is a good case study in being able to identify these different tendencies in postmodernism and the way they interact.

The principal document in which the religious, or as we shall shortly see, the messianic element in Derrida's work most clearly emerges is his *Circonfession*, an autobiographical book woven together with St Augustine's *Confessions*, which appeared in 1990, on the dual occa-sion of reaching his fiftieth year and of the death of his mother.[8] Here Derrida recounts his upbringing as an Algerian Jew and a *pied noir*, as an Arab/Jew who speaks 'Christian Latin French' in the land where Augus-tine was born (he was raised on the *rue Saint Augustin*). *Circonfession*, the confessions of a circumcised Augustine, a Jewish Augustine, is an attempt, he says, to 'leave nothing, if possible, in the dark of what related me to Judaism, alliance broken in every respect'. Of this alliance, 'without continuity but without break', he says 'that's what my readers won't have known about me', 'like my religion about which nobody understands anything', and the result is that he is 'read less and less well over almost twenty years'. Jacques is also the *filius istarum lacrymarum*, whose mother Georgette/Monica, now dying on the shores of the other side of the Mediterranean in Nice/Ostia, wept and worried over whether Jacques still believed in God, never daring to ask Jacques himself, 'but she must have known that the constancy of God in my life is called by other names', even though he 'rightly passes for an atheist' (JD, pp. 154–5).

Nothing better embodies and illustrates the convergence of religion and postmodernism than the emergence of the 'religion' of Jacques Derrida, his 'religion without religion', and nothing more effectively lays to rest the misguided idea that religion is irrelevant to 'deconstruc-tion' – the version of postmodernism I will focus on now – and that deconstruction is irrelevant to religious reflection. The central interest of the debate about Derrida and religion up to now has been the question of negative theology. It is certainly true that Derrida loves negative theology, because it constitutes a paradoxical discourse organized around a self-effacing name – the name of God – a name that is betrayed as soon as it is uttered. Nothing pleases Derrida more than Meister Eckhart's beautiful and famous prayer, 'I pray God to rid me of God.' Derrida stands in loving awe of the resources of negative theology, of its attempt to 'go where you cannot go', as the mystical poet Angelus Silesius wrote. Negative theology is for him an ancient archive of the deepest attempts that have been made to learn how to avoid speaking, to speak without speaking, how not to speak. *Comment ne pas parler?* But he differs fundamentally with negative theology, which he regards, in one of its voices at least, as inevitably 'hyperousiological'. However much it protests that it does not know, negative theology always knows in a certain way just what it does not know, and always manages to affirm something all the more essentially by way of its negations. Negative theology, Derrida says, always knows where to direct its prayers.[9]

Derrida is more interested in its 'other' voice, the darkest night of its soul, when it truly does not know for what it prays and weeps. *Quid ergo amo cum deum meum amo?*, St Augustine writes. Derrida says that he has been asking this question all his life: what do I love when I love my God? It is not a question of whether he loves God – who would be so cold of heart to deny that? – but of what he loves when he loves his God. He has, Derrida says, all his life long been 'hoping sighing dreaming' of something *tout autre*, something marvellous to come, something 'undeconstructible' which is the heart and soul, the prayers and tears, the impulse and the point of deconstruction. Deconstruction, to the consternation of its Nietzscheanizing, secularizing admirers, and to the no lesser consternation of its conservative religious critics, turns out to be a religion of the *tout autre*, a religious affirmation of what is to come, hoping and sighing, dreaming and praying for the coming of the wholly other.

But this religion is to be understood not in terms of negative theology but in more Jewish, 'messianic' terms. The present preoccupation with deconstruction and negative theology fails to see that deconstruction is more prophetic than mystical, more preoccupied with messianic peace and justice than mystical union, more Jewish than Christian-Platonic. Deconstruction, Derrida says, is best conceived as the affirmation of the *undeconstructible*, which he also describes as the affirmation of '*the* impossible'. *The im*possible is to be distinguished from the 'possible', which means for him the 'relatively' other, what is no more than a new move in an old game, the future that is foreseeable, plannable, programmable. Deconstruction is the affirmation of the 'wholly other', of a new game altogether, of an unforeseeable surprise, in virtue of which the current order is kept in principle 'open' or 'deconstructible'. To the coming of this wholly other, we say 'yes', and 'yes' again, *oui, oui*, since every yes demands a follow through which keeps its hands to the plough, lest the resolve slacken or the repetition become rote. Deconstruction says yes to '*l'invention de l'autre*', where *invention* should not be translated as 'invention', which would suggest the Dionysian play of Nietzschean fictions, but rendered rather in messianic terms, as the 'in-coming of the other', in keeping with its Latin roots, *in-veniens*. In the military if someone shouts 'incoming', everyone heads for cover. But, in messianic postmodernism to shout 'incoming' is to proclaim the good news, which is why the proper response to the incoming, and the first, last and constant prayer of deconstruction, is to shout, to pray, '*viens, oui, oui*'.

According to an old rabbinical story that Derrida finds in Blanchot, the Messiah never arrives. His very meaning is to be always, structurally *to come, à venir*, so that if he ever showed up, ever actually appeared, he would ruin everything.[10] The coming (*venue*) of the Messiah, Blanchot said, must never be confused with his actual presence (*présence*). Indeed, if one day he did show up incognito, we would ask him 'When will you come?' The coming of the Messiah belongs to what Derrida calls the 'absolute' future, the future which is structurally futural, always to come, not the future present, the future that will roll around into presence sooner or later. For if the Messiah ever came into the present, history would close and we would have no more future, no more hope. What would there be left to *come*? (to adapt Zarathustra's complaint). Even in Christianity, which from the point of view of the rabbis is too impatient, where it is believed that the Messiah actually did come, everyone now wants to know, 'when will he come *again*?' For it belongs to the very idea of the future, of hope, of history, that the Messiah is still to *come*. Furthermore, and this is a point of great importance for Derrida, if the Messiah were actually to come, to become present, a war would surely break out over what language he spoke, what nation he visited, where his capital is to be installed, who is to be his vicar and hold his keys, who is authorized to speak in his name, who is authorized to say what he said and what he meant, or to translate it into other languages, and who has the power to exclude and excommunicate those who disagree with the authorized interpretation of what he said. (If the absolute truth ever arrived, who could be trusted with it?). The affirmation of the in-coming of the wholly other, Derrida will now say, is the affirmation of the 'justice' to come, where justice has the sense not of a Greek universal but of the justice due to the 'singular' one, to the one whose every tear and every hair has been counted by God, to the outcast, the outsider, the 'widow, the orphan, and the stranger', to use the biblical figure that Levinas invokes. In deconstruction, the 'kingdom of God' would be a kingdom of nobodies, of what Paul called *ta me onta*. The point of Derrida's messianic is to hold the present up against the white light of absolute future, of absolute justice, which means the justice which is always to come, which prevents the present order from closing over on itself and declaring itself just, or well on the way to justice, in a perfidious asymptotic progress that tolerates an intolerable amount of misery.[11] The affirmation of justice in deconstruction is the affirmation of 'hospitality' to the other, of making the other welcome. But to offer hospitality to the 'wholly other' is to expose yourself to a 'surprise', to being overtaken by what you did not see coming, to get more than you bargained for, since hospitality is not supposed to be a bargain but a gift. The notion of hospitality puts a stress on the idea of a 'community' which on one etymology means *com-munire*, to build a defence (*munire*) around (*com*) oneself, to protect oneself against the other. That is the very opposite of deconstruction whose very idea is to make the other welcome, the wholly other, the other whom I cannot circumscribe in advance by preconditions. But how can one welcome the other 'unconditionally'? Are we to open the banquet to every passer-by? Whoever heard of such a thing? But then again, how could one be conditionally hospitable, 'welcoming' only those whom one has carefully chosen in advance and only subject to certain conditions? That is not a true welcoming but a closing off, a private list, a closed circle of invitees. Conditional hospitality is as incoherent as conditional love, as loving someone but only up to a point, after which we lose interest.

Thus, far from being a philosophy of despair, as its critics claim, this form of postmodernism turns on messianic hope (*viens*). Far from being nihilistic, it is deeply affirmative, *oui, oui*. Far from being relativistic and capricious, it insists upon the uncircumventable responsibility of the subject to the other. From reducing everything to subjectivistic play of traces or signifiers, it is organized around alterity, indeed around the wholly other.

A problem

The largest sticking point, the main difficulty, which messianic postmodernism poses to 'the philosophy of religion' has to do with Derrida's intractable suspicion of what he calls the 'concrete messianisms', the historical religions of the Book, which on Derrida's account have a history of violence built right into them. The power of the messianic on Derrida's accounting is precisely its indeterminacy, its structural emptiness, the resistance it puts up against the closure of the present or prevailing order, that blocks off in advance any claims of *exclusivity* on the part of any religion or of any determinate body of dogmatic claims that may take itself to be *the* revealed word of God. As an Algerian (Arab) Jew who speaks (Christian Latin) French, Derrida is deeply impressed by the capacity of the religions of the Book to wage war on one another, on the ability of the children of Abraham to slaughter one another in the name of God. If his distinction between the concrete messianisms and the formal messianic does not *reduce* to a distinction between war and peace, that is at least an important part of its import. The *im*possible, the justice *to come*, precludes in advance the claim of any confession or any tradition to exclusive or definitive truth. One needs to proceed with caution here. On the one hand, one needs to avoid dismissive gestures that would ignore the powerful force for justice that stirs within the concrete messianisms, a force that nourished Dietrich Bonhoeffer, Martin Luther King, and Dorothy Day and countless others, famous and unknown alike. On the other hand, such witnessing strengthens faith, but it does not pass over into knowledge, because people can witness with their lives and deaths to entirely different things. In a deconstructive philosophy of religion, the concrete messianisms might be *unique* but never *exclusive* or *definitive*, each longing and sighing in its own way for the *tout autre*, each praying and weeping in its own way over the name of God. But none of them is relieved of the need to ask, without having a secret answer up its sleeve, *quid ergo amo, cum deum meum amo?*

Convergences

The line of thought that runs through this second, messianic version of postmodernism converges with other approaches on at least two points.

(1) Postmodernism does not reject reason, as its critics charge, but rather, like *critical theory*, postmodernism has redescribed 'reason' in

intersubjective terms. Reason in postmodernism is not a subject–object relationship enacted within the solitary, monological confines of a 'pure' reason, whose very purity removes it from history, language and the human community. Rather, like critical theory, 'reason' for postmodernists is a relationship of speaking subject with speaking subject and so reason has the sense of 'reasoning together'. But by rejecting the solitary ahistorical subject, postmodernism, unlike critical theorists, go on to reject the *transcendentalism* of Habermas's notion of communicative rationality, the notion that intersubjective communication is guided from within by ahistorical laws of rationality, which it regards as just so much ahistorical modernism or neo-Kantianism. Furthermore, postmodernists regard consensus not as the goal of communication, but simply as a temporary pause in the conversation. Otherwise, the goal of communication would be silence. Were everyone saying the same thing, there would be no reason to say anything. The idea behind the multiplication of voices – the story of Babel – can hardly be to speak *una voce*, for where there is one voice there is no voice, where there is only one interpretation, no interpretation is allowed. The idea of 'reason' that is astir in postmodernism turns on the idea that the *language* of the wholly other is the language of the *wholly other*, that the wholly other always offers a surprise. These words come to me from the other shore; they are not *my* words, not something I already know in principle. The idea of reason in postmodernism is deeply opposed to any version, direct or indirect, of Socratic *majeutics*, but rather, like Kierkegaard, it turns on the model of the *teacher*, the one who comes over me with something I do not know, so that reason means learning how to welcome the wholly other, and reason is a form of hospitality.[12]

(2) The attempt to open up a post-secular discourse, to repeat or reinstitute religion in a post-critical or post-modern way, to re-establish the rights of religious discourse after modernist critiques have run their course, is closely tied up with the notion of language games in *Wittgenstein*. That claim is documentable in Derrida's early interest in Austin, which Searle utterly confounds, and it is quite explicit in Lyotard, who makes extensive use of Wittgenstein in *The Postmodern Condition, Just Gaming*, and *The Differend*. The point is plain. Religious discourse is another and irreducible way to think and speak, religious practices another, irreducible way to be. Postmodernism resists mightily the hegemony of overarching discourses or metalanguages into which other discourses are to be assimilated, reduced, or translated without remainder. Postmodernists are committed to the irreducible plurality of

discursive practices and rules, and they resist at every turn the notion that there is a privileged access to the things themselves that is the exclusive province of a particular discipline, natural language, tradition, mystical experience, or religious faith, which is why in postmodernism 'religious discourse' itself refers to a plurality of language games, to many different traditions, saying many different things. Postmodernists think that there are many ways for things to be and many ways to speak. The story of the tower of Babel is one of their favourite biblical narratives, putting God, as it does, on the side of the deconstructors of tall towers, monolingualism, and univocity.

In the end, to come back to my initial distinction between Dionysian and messianic postmodernism, one would not get things right until one could see the porousness of this distinction, the way these two bleed into and communicate with each other, the way, if I may say so, the postmodern religious sage would have to take the impudent form of a Dionysian rabbi.

Notes

1. Mark C. Taylor and José Marquez, *The Réal: Las Vegas, NV.* A CD-ROM. (Chicago: University of Chicago Press, 1998).
2. Cambridge: Harvard University Press, 1998.
3. Brian Ingraffia, *Postmodern Theory and Biblical Theology* (Cambridge: Cambridge University Press, 1995). Contrary to his title, Ingraffia presents us with a rigorous either/or: *either* postmodern theory *or* biblical theology, but no mixing! His criticisms of Derrida make the standard mistake of assimilating Derrida to Nietzschean postmodernism and missing Derrida's 'messianic' side.
4. Emmanuel Levinas, *Totality and Infinity*, trans. A. Lingis (Pittsburgh: Duquesne University Press, 1969), p. 64.
5. Jacques Derrida, *The Gift of Death*, trans. David Wills (Chicago: University of Chicago Press, 1995), p. 49.
6. In these thinkers both premodern religious and postmodern themes are made to intermingle in a fascinating way, an intermingling aptly captured by the phrase 'post-secular'. Post-secular thinking rejects the narrow, abstract and ahistorical concept of rationality put forth by the Enlightenment, and in particular the reductionistic tendencies of Enlightenment rationality. Totalizing, eliminationist, reductionistic critiques of religion, whether based upon the universal sweep of physics (naturalism), economics (Marx), or the unconscious (Freud), are just more tentacles of the *Aufklärung* trying to consume everything on its plate.
7. At this point I am only adumbrating an argument developed in detail in John D. Caputo, *The Prayers and Tears of Jacques Derrida: Religion without*

Religion (Bloomington: Indiana University Press, 1997); for a correlative but more introductory study to the later Derrida, which is where these religious thematics are to be found, *see Deconstruction in a Nutshell: a Conversation with Jacques Derrida*, edited with a commentary by John D. Caputo (New York: Fordham University Press, 1997).

8. *See* Jacques Derrida and Geoffrey Bennington, *Jacques Derrida*, trans. Geoffrey Bennington (Chicago: University of Chicago Press, 1993), pp. 153–5. For a lengthier commentary on *Circonfession, see* my *Prayers and Tears of Jacques Derrida*, VI, 'Confession'. To this postmodern interest in Augustine should be added the work of the late Jean-François Lyotard, who at the time of his death was writing a book about St Augustine's *Confessions*, the work of the English theologian John Milbank, and the recent publication in the *Gesamtausgabe* of Heidegger's 1920–21 lectures on the *Letters to the Thessalonians* and the Tenth Book of the *Confessions*, commentaries which lie at the heart of the 'genesis' of *Being and Time*.

9. *See* Caputo, *The Prayers and Tears of Jacques Derrida*, I, 'The Apophatic'.

10. *See Nutshell*, pp. 24–5, 156–80.

11. That is the argument of *Specters of Marx* (New York: Routledge, 1994) against the liberal euphoria of the new world order, invoking the spectre of Marx in messianic terms that go back to Walter Benjamin.

12. *See* Levinas, *Totality and Infinity*, pp. 201–4, 216–19, 252.

11
The Other without History and Society – a Dialogue with Derrida

Anselm Kyongsuk Min

Let me begin by congratulating Professor Caputo for his very lucid presentation of postmodernism and its potential as a philosophy of religion. I also want to thank him for writing two very helpful introductions and commentaries on Derrida, *Deconstruction in a Nutshell: a Conversation with Jacques Derrida* and *The Prayers and Tears of Jacques Derrida: Religion without Religion*.[1] *Prayers and Tears*, especially, is a masterpiece of exposition, analysis, and composition, which I would enthusiastically recommend to all students of Derrida. So much of what he says in the paper presupposes his much more elaborate and extensive analyses in these two works. My dialogue will be primarily with Derrida and his works, and with Professor Caputo in his two works as interpreter and defender of Derrida.

The spectre of Derrida has been haunting the western intellectual world for some three decades now. His message has been getting across. Totalities tend to totalize and oppress. Identities tend to exclude and marginalize. Dogmas dogmatize, and systems produce closure. Messianic claims spill blood. Fundamentalist claims to certainty and definitiveness create hell on earth. Hence the need to subvert totalities, disrupt the same, complicate simplicities, problematize the complacent, contaminate the pure, and destabilize all systems and fundamentalisms, by exposing them to the shock of alterity, the demand of the other, the trauma of the unexpected. That is, to deconstruct. Deconstruction is 'the delimitation of totalization in all its forms',[2] the thought of 'an absolute heterogeneity that unsettles all the assurances of the same within which we comfortably ensconce ourselves'.[3]

In the area of religion Derrida's deconstruction has been most challenging in his treatments of negative theology and the messianic, the first showing what God should not be, the second what God should be without being.

Derrida's deconstruction of negative theology

Derrida discerns two different voices in negative theology. The first voice is hyperousiology. Even though negative theology denies the possibility of attributing names to God and places God beyond all names, it does not stop at negation but affirms God precisely in God's hyperessential reality. It is a higher, more refined modalization of ontotheology, a variation on the metaphysics of presence.[4] For all its negations, it claims deep down to 'know' what God is. The God of negative theology, in fact, turns out to be 'a transcendental signified, the dream of being without *différance*, of being outside the text, outside the general text, outside the play of traces'.[5] Negative theology feels as secure in its possession of an object as positive theology; it is a triumph of presence over representation.[6]

There is, however, another voice in negative theology. As an irruption from the depth, it expresses a yearning, a movement, a passion for the wholly other of which we all dream and by which we feel addressed, a deeply affirmative desire for 'something always essentially other than the prevailing regime of presence, something *tout autre*'.[7] It embodies a passion for the impossible, a movement of transgression over and beyond the present, a response to a primordial promise. It embodies the spirit of relentless critical negation in pursuit of an ultimate that always remains wholly other, a kind of a generalized apophatics, a 'kenosis of discourse'.[8] Everything must pass through 'the aporias of negative theology', and only a discourse 'contaminated' by negative theology can be trusted.[9]

What does deconstruction do for negative theology? Deconstruction does not provide a secure foundation or a horizon for the intelligibility of the content of negative theology. Instead, by reinscribing or resituating negative theology within the general movement of the trace, *différance*, and undecidability, within all the multiplicities and ambiguities of language and history, the basic situation of all human experience according to Derrida, deconstruction preserves faith as faith, as something 'blind', without the privilege of *savoir, avoir, and voir*, both accentuating the passion of faith as faith struggles to take a leap and decide for the impossible in the midst of the very undecidability that constitutes its very structure, and maintaining faith as an indeterminate, open-ended groping and hope in the wholly other. *Différance* precludes the possibility of knowledge, vision, or face-to-face union with God, as it always recontextualizes faith, exposing it to indefinite substitutions, translations, and interpretations. Ontotheology takes faith as a mode of presence outside the movement of *différance* and the play of traces and turns it into something secure, positive and closed, generating the pernicious dangers of absolutism and triumphalism inherent in all fundamentalisms and all 'determinable' faiths. 'Closure spells trouble,...closure spells exclusion, exclusiveness; closure spills blood, doctrinal, confessional, theological, political, institutional blood, and eventually, it never fails, real blood.'[10]

Religion as messianic hope

For Derrida, religion is a response to the call and demand of the wholly other, an invocation or prayer ('come!') for its advent, and the messianic praxis of justice here and now corresponding to that invocation and demand.

The 'object' or 'God' of this religion remains the 'wholly other' resisting all reduction to a human concept, category or horizon. It lies beyond all human imagination, credibility, graspability or determinability, beyond all human logos, teleological, eschatological and otherwise. In contrast to the God of ontotheology who remains 'infinitely and eternally the Same'[11] and in fact 'the name of indifference itself',[12] the God of deconstruction is:

the name of *the* impossible, of novelty, of the coming of the Other, of the *tout autre*, of what is coming with the shock of an absolute surprise, with the trauma of absolute heterogeneity. Cast in a deconstructive slant, God is not the possible but the impossible, not the eternal but the futural.[13]

There is no transcendental horizon within which God can be awaited, expected, or made knowable; God shatters all human horizons.

Derrida is especially insistent that the wholly other is beyond all determination or determinacy. A determinable future, with a determinable telos, is a future that can be anticipated within the horizon of a particular aim, of what is possible, and thus a future as present. Presence, possibility, determinacy: these are, for Derrida, one and the same. The future of the wholly other is an 'absolute' future, a future absolved from the regime and horizon of presence and identity, from whatever is presentable, programmable, imaginable, foreseeable, beyond the traditional dualisms of essence and existence, universal and particular, ideal and real. The wholly other is 'structurally' and therefore 'always' to come. It is precisely the function of the wholly other to shatter and shock the horizon of the same and foreseeable and open up the promise and possibility of something wholly other. The wholly other is identifiable with neither a determinable faith nor a determinable messiah nor a determinable end of history nor a determinable degree of justice. It is also to be distinguished from any utopian or Kantian regulative ideal, which too has its own determinate content. The wholly other is simply the beyond, the *au-delà*. It is impossible to measure the extent to which the wholly other is being approximated or realized in a society.[14]

Religion addresses its prayer, its 'come!' to this wholly other in response to the latter's solicitation and demand.

> To call upon God, to call God's name, to pray and weep and have a passion for God is to call for the *tout autre*, for something that breaks up the hohum homogeneity of the same and all but knocks us dead. The name of God is a name that calls for the other, that calls from the other, the name that the other calls, that calls upon us like Elijah at the door, and that calls for things new.[15]

The invocation is a primordial affirmation based on faith and hope that the impossible will be possible, the impossibility of a saving breach in the chain of presence and totality, of a liberating breakthrough in the oppressive horizon of the same, of the messianic emergence of the *novum* beyond all human expectations and calculations.

> Outside all human mastery and control *viens* hopes for a break within the interstices of the laws of regularity, an outbreak of chance within the crevices of the continuous flow of presence.

It 'silently tears open lived time and ordinary language,' 'renders them always already structurally open to what is coming', and 'prohibits (*pas!*) closure while soliciting transcendence (*le pas*)',[16] It is 'the order, or disorder, of messianic time, of *venir* and *avenir*, that disturbs the order of presence'.[17] This messianic invocation of the wholly other embodies 'a certain structural wakefulness or openness to an impossible breach of the present, shattering the conditions of possibility, by which we are presently circumscribed'.[18]

For Derrida, *tout autre est tout autre*. The wholly other is every other. The wholly other is not only God but also every human being. As Levinas says, 'infinite alterity' or 'absolute singularity' belongs to both God and human beings. For Derrida, this invalidates both the Kierkegaardian distinction between the ethical (the finite relationship to the finite) and the religious (the infinite relationship to the infinite) and the Levinasian distinction between ethics and religion.[19] Religion is not separable from ethics nor, for that matter, from political and legal matters. Wherever infinite alterity is at issue, there is religion. This is why the hope in the wholly other is also a messianic hope for a 'universal culture of singularities'[20] in which justice will be done to the other in its irreducible singularity.

Messianic time interrupts the living present with the demand for justice. Messianic time is prophetic time, the time of justice which is always to come yet issues a call for justice here and now. Justice deferred is justice denied. Deconstruction 'is not meant to be a soft sighing for the future, but a way of deciding now and being impassioned in the moment',[21] *Différance*:

> does not mean only deferral, delay, and procrastination, but the spacing out, the extension between memory and promise or *a-venir*, which opens up the here-now in all of its urgency and absolute singularity, in the imminence of the instant. The call of what is coming calls for action now.[22]

Justice does not tolerate present injustice in the name of a gradual approximation of an ideal but demands justice here and now. It is by definition 'impatient, uncompromising, and unconditional. No différance without alterity, no alterity without singularity, no singularity without here-now.'[23]

The freedom of the wholly other from all determinate contents makes Derrida's religion 'a messianism without religion,... even a messianic without messianism',[24] a faith without dogma, a religion without religion. It is a commitment to the wholly other in all its nominalist freedom and absolute heterogeneity without an equal commitment to the determinate content of a particular religion, dogma, institution or programme. Such a commitment to determinacy, for Derrida, entails totalitarian reduction of the other to the same and generates violence and war.[25] The 'call for a fixed and identifiable other, foreseeable and foregraspable... would release the manic aggression of a program, the mania of an all-out rush for a future-present.'[26] Thus, deconstruction 'keeps a safe distance from ever letting its faith be a faith in a determinate thing or person, from ever contracting the *tout autre* within the horizons of the same'.[27] The invocation for the coming of the other is an apocalyptic prayer for the advent of messianic time, but it is an apocalypse without (determinate) vision, truth, or revelation, an apocalypse without apocalypse. This description of Derridean religion should also make clear the minimal character of its content. The heart of that religion lies in its messianicity or its prophetic passion for justice, 'the infinite respect of the singularity *and* infinite alterity of the other'.[28] This is where religion and deconstruction converge. It is the very nature of messianicity, however, to shatter all determinate horizons with their determinate contents and thus to exclude all determinate, particular, historical religions and messianisms. Derrida's messianic hope and promise always remain 'absolutely undetermined' and 'eschatological'.[29] To endorse a determinate religion is to spell closure and to spill blood. It is important to purify the messianic of all determinate contents by *epoche* and abstraction so as to intensify its urgency, but this also amounts to 'desertification' or rendering of religion into a dry and barren desert, deprived of its specific comforts and intelligibilities and reduced to a universal, formal structure with a minimal content, 'the messianic in general, as a thinking of the other and of the event to come',[30] 'the opening to the future or to the coming of the other as the advent of justice, but without horizon of expectation and without prophetic prefiguration',[31] a primordial idea of justice and democracy to come – to be distinguished from any of their current conceptions – as the irreducible and undeconstructible ultimate. Religion is reduced to the bare minimum of an atheological, open-ended, negative, or apophatic process of justice, a movement toward a New International as 'a community without community'[32] or 'the friendship of an alliance without institution'.[33] Particular religions are nourished by their 'place', their history, tradition, nation, language and people, and generate the 'politics of place and the wars over place'.[34] Derrida seeks to liberate the messianic of universal justice from such politics and wars by turning it into a desert, 'a kind of placeless, displacing place – or a place for the displaced',[35] a postgeographical, universal religion, a 'religion for all and everywhere',[36] a Derridean equivalent of the Kantian 'religion within the limits of reason alone', although reason is never without faith.

Living together with those who are different, especially with respect for their difference, has always been a central problem of human history. Individually and collectively, our instinct has been to subjugate them to our system of identity that makes no room for their difference, and to reduce and violate them in their integrity as the other. This occurs at all levels of human existence, individual and social, in all spheres of society, economics, politics and culture, and with consequences in all areas of philosophy, ontology, epistemology, ethics, aesthetics and philosophy of religion. What Emmanuel Levinas calls the 'horror of the other'[37] and its correlative, the terror of the same have been as pervasive, as destructive, and as compelling as any original sin in human history. The two global wars of the present century, the many regional and local conflicts from the Korean War to Bosnia, the countless racist, ethnic and religious strifes from the Jewish holocaust to South African apartheid and racism in the United States to the bloody struggles between Jews and Arabs in Palestine, and the growing recognition of the sexist violation of women throughout human history: all of these have deepened our awareness, and intensified the urgency in dealing with the problem of the other in our century. On the eve of the twenty-first century most societies also increasingly face the problem of living together under conditions of religious and cultural plurality. Global capitalism has been bringing together different cultures and making them interdependent, relativizing all cultural absolutes, compelling all to become aware of the problem of the other, and imposing the political imperative of dialogue.

Given these historical urgencies, it is no exaggeration to say that today we cannot live without a heavy dose of what deconstruction stands for, its critique of the terror of the same in all its forms, and its vision of justice and democracy. All modern philosophies have been critical of the given, from Descartes through Kant, Hegel and Marx to pragmatism and critical theory. Deconstruction has few peers, however, in the single-mindedness of its attention to the problem of the other, in its universalization of that problem, and in the radicality with which it subverts all traditional ideologies from Plato to Heidegger. To enter the world of deconstruction is to enter a world without absolute principles, horizons, foundations, and centres from which to judge the other, to reinscribe or resituate all our beliefs within the general movement of *différance* that renders all identities heterogeneous and defers all presences to the play of traces, and to live accordingly, without nostalgia for absolute certainties but also with respect for difference and always with hope – in the case of messianic postmodernism – in the coming of the absolutely other. Nothing can boast of pure identity, nothing can insist on pure presence, all reality is marked by differentiation and deferral. In an age that has suffered so much from the terror of the same, at a time when a pluralist sensibility is *de rigueur* for survival and peace on earth, in a world where the 'sacrifice of Isaac continues every day',[38] deconstruction should remain, even for those of us who do not accept it, a thorn in our side, a perpetual reminder of the dangers into which monocentrism can plunge the world, keeping us in a state of 'vigilant insomnia' (Levinas)[39] for the cry of the other.

In this spirit, much of Derrida's philosophy of religion deserves and demands attentive and respectful meditation. His deconstruction of negative theology and determinate religions, his description of the messianic as the wholly other, his refusal to separate religion and politics, messianicity and justice: these are important antidotes against the terror of the same lurking in religion, in its claim to closure, its dogmatism, its fundamentalism, its totalitarianism. Left to themselves, religions, including believing philosophers and theologians, delude themselves into thinking that they 'know' who God is, with only lip service to the classical thesis of the 'incomprehensibility' of God. Augustine's question, which is also Derrida's, remains and should remain compelling in its very challenge: What exactly is it that I love when I love my God? In this regard, Caputo is quite right in locating the specific contribution of deconstruction in providing for the religious believer 'a saving apophatics, a certain salutary purgation of the positivity of belief, which reminds us all that we do not know what is coming, what is *tout autre'*.[40] A periodic 'contamination' of religion with negative theology should be a wholesome exercise that would also challenge each religion to transcend its determinacy and probe its own messianic depth for the impossible possibility of the wholly other.

What can we say about Derrida's 'religion without religion'? Derrida's religion is deliberately minimal in its content. It consists in an existential commitment to the impossible possibility of the absolutely other, in a prayerful invocation for the advent of the wholly other beyond all human reason, calculation and imagination, and in the praxis of justice in response to the call and demand of that other. It is a deliberate, extreme abstraction from the content of all determinate and determinable religions, their dogmas, rituals and institutions, and therefore also an intellectual and emotional desert without the nourishing comforts of tradition and community. It places itself beyond the distinctions of theism and atheism, religion and secularism, as different therefore from the atheism of Enlightenment rationalism as it is from traditional religious faith. One could say that it is the 'logical' expression of the faith of the modern Western intellectual who has been thoroughly alienated from all institutional religions as well as from all traditional rationalities yet who cannot simply surrender themselves to sheer, destructive nihilism and irresponsible relativism. Even in thorough alienation and utter blindness one still hopes and gropes, beyond all reason and faith, for the possibility of the impossible, for something ultimate and undeconstructible, the advent of messianic justice, without quite knowing what to call it. It is 'a search without hope for hope', 'in a space where the prophets are not far away'.[41] Derrida's religion is perhaps the last refuge of the Western intellectual elite committed to both the protest of modern atheism and the Blochian spirit of utopian hope.

I do not say this in disparagement. The cultural situation Derrida depicts is not fictional. It is a situation that has been facing Western intellectuals for some time and that is now increasingly facing intellectuals in the rest of the world as well. It is no wonder that Christian theology has likewise been trying to cope precisely with that situation in some of its representatives such as Paul Tillich and Karl Rahner. It is quite relevant here to mention Tillich's deconstruction of traditional faith into 'absolute faith', which is not faith in a determinate object but a state of being grasped by the power of being-itself, which in turn is neither personal nor pantheistic but goes beyond both, which can only be called 'the God above God'.[42] Rahner's increasingly negative reference to God as 'absolute', 'incomprehensible mystery' and 'absolute future' is likewise an attempt to make Christianity credible in the present intellectual climate, as is his minimalist, existential definition of the Christian content as the commitment that 'we are ineluctably engaged by the incomprehensible mystery whom we call God, and who ceaselessly and silently grasps us and challenges our hope and love even when we show little concern for him in the practice of our lives or even actually deny him in theory'.[43]

This is also, however, precisely where the issue lies. Neither Tillich nor Rahner goes on to propose, as does Derrida, an extreme abstraction from the concrete content of determinate Christian faith. They may try to criticize and sublate the determinate historical content of Christian faith into something more credible and relevant through existential or transcendental hermeneutic; it is not their intention to do away with the essential mediation of faith by determinate historical contents and produce a religion without religion, which Derrida does. Granted that we cannot live *without* deconstruction today, as I believe we cannot, granted that we have to reinscribe religion and politics within the general movement of *différance*, can we live *on* deconstruction alone?

I do not think we can. The very strength of deconstruction, the radicality of its negations, may also be its very weakness. Let me begin with Derrida's depreciation of determinate religion. Derrida has nothing but aversion for concrete, determinate religions with their historical content. They are simply identified with reification and closure and as so many sources of absolutism, triumphalism and bloody conflicts. It is not that *some* determinate religions are triumphalistic or that all determinate religions *sometimes* generate triumphalism and absolutism; it is rather that the very idea of determination or determinability entails presence, identity, and the imperialism of the same. Even though Derrida himself derives his concept of the messianic from existing, determinate Jewish and Christian eschatologies by bending and repeating them 'with a difference', and even though Caputo himself admits that Derrida's own messianic religion has all the marks of a determinate religion and can survive only with the support of determinate, institutionalized messianic eschatologies,[44] still, determinate religions remain only 'consummately dangerous',[45] with no positive virtues to show. As a non-essentialist, Derrida may not say, but he does imply, *pace* Caputo, that 'theology or religion always and essentially means bad news, the *ancien regime*, a reactionary, world-negating, and fear-driven pathology'.[46]

This means two things. On the one hand, the wholly other of messianicity cannot and *should not* become actual and concrete through incarnation in a determinate religion. The only relation between messianicity and determinate messianic religions is one of relentless negation, period. The messianic is *not* what a determinate religion is. The messianic is nowhere embodied because it is not in principle embodiable. It is not only that the messianic always transcends any of its concretizing historical mediations but also that it should *not* be so mediated because such mediation necessarily involves a fall, a corruption.

On the other hand, it also means that determinate historical religions have no positive mediating function to provide precisely in the service of the messianic, the wholly other in terms of nourishing faith and praxis. As modes of frozen presence and identity, determinate religions have no principle of self-transcendence, self-criticism, and self-reform within themselves; there are no resources of a dialectic between the present and the future, the determinate and the determining in historical religions. Between the wholly other and historical religions there is no mediation, only radical otherness.

Derrida's own religion without religion, therefore, can remain pure and holy only because it is nowhere embodied or institutionalized in a determinate religion. It engages in the deconstruction of *all* determinate religions from the transcendent height of pure, disembodied, angelic ideality, just as Enlightenment rationalism has been engaging in the critical dismissal of all religions from the self-legitimating height of pure, uninstitutionalized, ahistorical reason. Instead of advising concrete religions, therefore, on how to bear better witness to the wholly other under the conditions of history and necessary institutionalization, it simply says no! indiscriminately to all determinate religions regardless of their differences in the degree and kind of witnessing they do. It is a yes! to the messianic but a no! to all historical attempts to embody it. Derrida's messianic reservation, like the Christian eschatological proviso, is more interested in condemning religions for what in any event they *cannot* do, that is, achieve a perfect realization of the messianic on earth, than in empowering them to do what they *can*, that is, bear a more effective witness to the messianic even if no witnessing will ever measure up to the full demand of the messianic. Derrida's religion without religion remains an ahistorical abstraction.

The messianic wholly other impinges on our history, therefore, only in the mode of interruption, disruption, discontinuity, surprise and opposition, and only in the experience of the impossible, unimaginable, unforeseeable and unprogrammable. What we can do by our own power and with our own foresight and planning and what we experience within the realm of the possible and the foreseeable, within what Derrida calls, with sweeping generality, the horizon of the same: these have no messianic or religious significance. That is to say, our moral and political actions in history have no religious weight because we undertake most of them with our own responsibility, with our own knowledge of what is possible and what is not, and with our own freedom to risk the unknown but always with caution and prudence. The ancient dualism of body and soul returns in the guise of a new opposition of what is determinate and what is indeterminate, what is possible and what is impossible, what is foreseeable and what is unforeseeable. We encounter the God of deconstruction only as a matter of 'absolute surprise'.

What Derrida says about determinate religions also applies to determinate political praxis. The messianic as such – the 'universal culture of singularities'– or justice and democracy are 'structurally' and therefore 'always' to come, and should not be identified with a determinate present form of law or political structure. Although the perfection of the messianic lies in the 'absolute' future, not in a future that can become present, its demand is for justice 'here and now'. The messianic provides the light in which all present forms of justice and democracy, however perfect, will be judged and challenged to transcend themselves. Messianic politics lies in the hope for 'an impossible breach of the present, shattering the conditions of possibility by which we are presently circumscribed'.[47]

The messianic rhetoric of 'shattering', 'new', 'unforeseeable', and so on creates the impression of a 'radical' politics as appropriate praxis for the messianic hope that deconstruction constantly evokes. When it comes to political praxis, however, it is anything but radical. Deconstructive politics involves operating *within* the conventions and rules of the prevailing order – there is no other place to operate – 'bending' and 'repeating' them 'with a difference', and 'twisting free of the same, altering it just enough to let a little alterity loose', which is different from 'straightforward opposition, confrontational countering, which succumbs to dialectical assimilation'.[48] Furthermore, we 'can only prepare for the incoming of the other, but we cannot invent it, cannot effect it, bring it about, by a cunning deconstructive agency. We are called upon, paradoxically, to prepare for the incalculable, to prepare without calculating in advance'. The 'only' concern of deconstruction is the time to come: 'allowing the adventure or the event of the *tout autre* to come'.[49]

Deconstructive political praxis, then, comes down to 'hoping' for an impossible breach of the present, 'bending' and 'twisting free' of the present rules and conventions to 'let a little alterity loose', and thus 'preparing' for the coming of justice, which we cannot 'calculate' or 'program' or 'control'. It is opposed to 'confrontational countering' because it would 'succumb to dialectical assimilation'. At best, we have a 'politics of exodus, of the emigre', 'a subversion of fixed assumptions and a privileging of disorder', or 'responsible anarchy'.[50] Just as deconstruction reduces religion to a minimal content, so it reduces politics to the passive minimum of hoping, bending a little, and waiting. There is no substantive, systematic reflection on the dynamics and trends of contemporary history, on the possibilities they contain for liberation and oppression, on prospects for political mobilization for the liberation of the oppressed and marginalized others that deconstruction seems so much to care for, nor on political structures that mediate between the messianic ideal always to come and present political praxis that will concretize for a society and for a time at least the demand of the messianic.

This is not accidental. Politics in the classical sense presupposes that human beings can, collectively, as a community, acquire the knowledge of their historical situation and mobilize themselves to produce a political structure that will best embody their (prevailing) ideals of justice in that situation according to their knowledge. This is predicated on faith and hope in the possibility of collective human action and collective human wisdom. This faith and hope have sometimes been vindicated by history, as witness the gradual, often uphill, but, by historical standards, truly significant achievements in democratic institutions, as they have also sometimes been contradicted by history, as witness the many violations of human rights and the often incalculable suffering brought about by totalitarian regimes. We do not, however, have much choice here. It takes precisely collective action and collective wisdom to combat the terror of totalitarian oppression, as history has also amply demonstrated; the only alternative to the oppression by a totalitarian regime is to set up a democratic regime. In any event, classical politics presupposes this faith and hope in collective action and collective wisdom.

It is precisely this faith that Derrida lacks, as is evident in his 'historical and political' investigation into the secret of responsibility in *The Gift of Death*.[51] Derrida defines duty or responsibility as a relation between a person in his or her 'absolute singularity' and the other in his or her equally 'absolute singularity'.[52] This ethical relationship, however, immediately exposes me to the risk of absolute sacrifice because I cannot at the same time respond to the call of all the other others, an infinite number of them, who are also addressing an absolute appeal to me in their respective 'infinite singularities'. This is the paradox, scandal and aporia of the concept of responsibility, which reveals the concept at its limit and finitude.

'As soon as I enter into a relation with the other, with the gaze, look, request, love, command, or call of the other, I know that I can respond only by sacrificing ethics, that is, by sacrificing whatever obliges me to also respond, in the same way, in the same instant, to all the others. I offer a gift of death, I betray, I don't need to raise my knife over my son on Mount Moriah for that. Day and night, at every instant, on all the Mount Moriahs of this world, I am doing that, raising my knife over what I love and must love, over those to whom I owe absolute fidelity, incommensurably. Abraham is faithful to God only in his absolute treachery, in the betrayal of his own and of the uniqueness of each one of them, exemplified here in his only beloved son.'[53]

Fulfilling an obligation to an other entails sacrificing and betraying all other obligations to all the other others including those dying of starvation and sickness. Everyone is being sacrificed to everyone else in 'this land of Moriah that is our habitat every second of everyday'.[54] The aporia of responsibility is that there is no justification for sacrificing all these others, the 'ethical or political generality'.[55] Derrida asks, 'How would you ever justify the fact that you sacrifice all the cats in the world to the cat that you feed at home every morning for years, whereas other cats die of hunger at every instant? Not to mention other people?'[56] In this sense, then, the sacrifice of Isaac, a beloved son, the infinite other to whom I owe an absolute duty, is 'inscribed in the structure of our existence'.[57] Likewise, behind the appearances of normality and legitimacy, of moral discourse and good conscience, society organizes and participates in the death and sickness of millions of children through the very structure of its market, mechanisms of its external debt, and other inequities. We allow the sacrifice of others in order to avoid being sacrificed ourselves.[58]

What, then, can one do about this ethical scandal? That Derrida provides no answer is perhaps indicative of the limits of his horizon. One can say that he provides no answer because 'this land of Moriah' is 'our very habitat', because such a scandal is 'inscribed in the structure of our existence', about which, therefore, we cannot do anything. His interest is in accentuating the aporia of moral experience and complicating our moral simplicities, within the structural limits of our existence. Is such a sandal, however, really 'inscribed in the structure of our existence'? Or, does it point, rather, to the limits of Derrida's own deconstructionist horizon?

Derrida's horizon, as that of his two mentors, Kierkegaard and Levinas, is that of the individual in her 'absolute' and 'infinite' 'singularity'. As a moral agent each of us is 'infinitely other in its absolute singularity, inaccessible, solitary, transcendent, nonmanifest, originarily nonpresent to my ego'.[59] From this perspective of the isolated individual, Derrida goes on to ask, What can *I* do, precisely *in my absolute singularity and isolation*, to avoid the suffering of millions of starving children and millions of cats other than mine, since I cannot respond 'in the same way, in the same instant, to all the others'?[60] The answer, of course, has to be 'not much'. An individual as such cannot respond to all these moral appeals in the same way at the same time, nor does she have the resources to respond to many of them with any adequacy even if she has the time to respond. The assumption, however, is false.

Modern history amply demonstrates that in situations where what is at stake is the welfare of a large number of people serious enough to constitute the 'public' interest or common good, the appropriate agent is not the isolated individual but the political community as such. Whenever our serious welfare is at stake and we cannot attend to that welfare as isolated individuals, we do so as united individuals, together, that is, as a community. We cannot protect our security individually, so we do so as a community by instituting the police and the military as organs of the state. We cannot provide education for ourselves individually, so we do so as a community by establishing public education. We cannot guarantee minimum welfare for ourselves individually, so we do so as a community by making sure that the economy is adequately functioning through monetary, fiscal and other policies, by establishing minimum wage laws, and by instituting social security for old age and times of sickness. This common or collective care for the common good is precisely what is meant by politics in the classical sense. What we cannot do individually, we do together, that is, politically.[61]

If we change the horizon from that of the isolated individual to that of the political community, from the lone 'I' to the 'we', and ask not, 'What can *I* do *as an individual?*' but rather, 'What can *we* do *together?*' the moral aporia that Derrida weeps over need not be as great or as scandalous as he makes it out to be. We together, that is, various countries and private associations including the United Nations, have been alleviating the suffering of millions of starving and sick children. I as an individual do my part by paying my fair share of taxes and making my fair share of contributions, which will both hire and enable other individuals, that is, relief workers and government agents, to provide the relief. If so many cats other than mine are suffering as to constitute their relief a matter of the public interest, we can, through the government, organize such relief by setting up shelters for cats, as many communities are already doing. The fact that our existing political means are not adequate to match outstanding needs is no argument against the political solution; it is an argument for improving it.

This 'political' approach does not eliminate the moral aporia that so concerns Derrida. In some sense, given the existential limitations of the moral and material resources of humanity, such a moral aporia will indeed always remain. Such an aporia, however, can be exaggerated when it is approached only from the individual perspective, and become ideologically pernicious when it is used as an argument for political fatalism and neglect of available political means. It is critical to remember how much humanity has achieved by working together, collectively, that is, politically: elimination of hunger, illiteracy and many forms of epidemic in many parts of the world is, by historical standards, an achievement too great and too noble to be merely humiliated by a misplaced messianic or eschatological proviso, although it is not great enough and often too ideologically tainted to serve moral complacency among us.

However, it is precisely this 'political' horizon with its faith and hope in the possibility of collective action and collective wisdom that Derrida lacks. Derrida's emphasis on the 'infinite singularity' of the individual and his deconstructionist distrust of totality, community and unity for fear of 'fusion'[62] do not provide confidence in the possibility of 'collective' action: such an action is either too ridden with otherness and division to be genuinely collective or too totalitarian to respect the infinite alterity of the agents.[63] Derrida is more interested in unmasking hidden oppressions in a totality than in encouraging wholesome collective action. Likewise, his emphasis on the absolute transcendence of the messianic and its radical discontinuity with any determinable political structure or institution or law does not encourage mobilization of collective wisdom in the interest of a determinate reform or revolution as a historically appropriate institutionalization of messianic justice. Instead, Derrida is more interested in condemning current institutions for *not* being a perfect model of justice than in providing a vision of better institutions that they *can* become or judicious reflections on the *how* of the justice that must indeed be done here and now. As 'infinite asymmetry of the relation to the other', as 'incalculability of the gift and singularity of the an-economic ex-position to others',[64] justice lies in principle 'beyond' all right, calculation, commerce, beyond 'juridical-moral rules, norms, or representations, within an inevitable totalizing horizon'.[65] In this sense, it is difficult to disagree with Richard Bernstein when he accuses Derrida's idea of a 'democracy to come' of being 'an impotent, vague abstraction', or with Thomas McCarthy when he accuses Derrida of being more interested in destabilizing universalist structures than in reconstructing protective institutions for rights and dignity.[66]

William James once spoke of two attitudes towards truth and error. One attitude is that of the sceptic, who is driven by an obsessive fear of falling into error and does not want to believe in anything except on sufficient evidence. The other is the attitude of the pragmatist, who is more driven by the hope of finding truth than by the fear of falling into error and is therefore willing to risk even believing in error in order to find truth.[67] Deconstruction is more like the sceptic than the pragmatist. It is fundamentally fearful of all determinate embodiments of human sociality in history because of the terror of the same. It may offer prayers and tears for the coming of the wholly other and its messianic justice, but it does not want to dirty its hands by working at establishing determinate institutions of religion and politics. In the name of *différance* it flees from the historical determinacy of matter, body, senses, objectivity and sociality, the world of presence, identity and totality, and takes refuge in the dream of the impossible. Perhaps deconstruction should inscribe itself in the quite possible dialectic of the determinable within history so as to keep its *différance* human, not angelic. Please remember: in human history all negations are *determinate* negations.[68]

Notes

1. John D. Caputo (ed.), *Deconstruction in a Nutshell: a Conversation with Jacques Derrida* (New York: Fordham University Press, 1997), and John D. Caputo, *The Prayers and Tears of Jacques Derrida: Religion without Religion* (Bloomington: Indiana University Press, 1997).
2. *Prayers*, 126.
3. Ibid., 5.
4. Jacques Derrida, *Margins of Philosophy*, trans. Alan Bass (Chicago: The University of Chicago Press, 1982), 6; Jacques Derrida, *On the Name*, ed. Thomas Dutoit and trans. David Wood, John P. Leavey, Jr. and Ian McLeod (Stanford: Stanford University Press, 1995), 68; Jacques Derrida, 'How to Avoid Speaking: Denials', in Harold Coward and Toby Foshay (eds), *Derrida and Negative Theology* (Albany: SUNY Press, 1992), 77–83.
5. *Prayers*, 11.
6. Ibid., 6–7, 10–11.
7. Ibid., 28.
8. *On the Name*, 50; *Prayers*, 27–8.
9. *On the Name*, 83 and 69.
10. *Prayers*, 6; also 11,12, 47–8, 57, 63.
11. Ibid., 113.
12. Jacques Derrida, *Of Grammatology*, trans. Gayatri Chakravorty Spivak (Baltimore: The Johns Hopkins University Press, 1974; corrected edition), 71.
13. *Prayers*, 113.
14. Ibid.,73–86, 118, 129.
15. Ibid., 113.
16. Ibid., 86.
17. Ibid., 86.
18. Ibid., 96.
19. Jacques Derrida, *The Gift of Death*, trans. David Wills (Chicago: University of Chicago Press, 1995), 83–4.
20. *Prayers*, 155.
21. Ibid., 125.

22. Ibid., 124; *see also* Jacques Derrida, *The Specters of Marx*, trans. Peggy Kamuf (New York: Routledge, 1994), 31.
23. *Specters of Marx*, 31.
24. *Specters of Marx*, 59; *Gift of Death*, 49; Jacques Derrida, 'Faith and Knowledge: the Two Sources of 'Religion' at the Limits of Reason Alone', in Jacques Derrida and Gianni Vattimo (eds), *Religion* (Stanford: Stanford University Press, 1998), 17–18.
25. *Prayers*, 128.
26. Ibid., 99.
27. Ibid., 150.
28. *Specters of Marx*, 65.
29. Ibid.
30. *Prayers*, 128.
31. 'Faith and Knowledge', 17.
32. *Prayers*, 131.
33. *Specters of Marx*, 86.
34. *Prayers*, 154.
35. Ibid.
36. Ibid., 155.
37. Emmanuel Levinas, 'The Trace of the Other', in Mark C. Taylor (ed.), *Deconstruction in Context: Literature and Philosophy* (Chicago: University of Chicago Press, 1986), 346.
38. *The Gift of Death*, 70.
39. Sean Hand (ed.), *The Levinas Reader* (Oxford: Blackwell, 1989), 28.
40. *Prayers*, 150.
41. Jacques Derrida, 'Deconstruction and the Other', in Richard Kearney (ed.), *Dialogues with Contemporary Continental Thinkers* (Manchester, UK: Manchester University Press, 1984), 119.
42. Paul Tillich, *The Courage to Be* (New Haven, CT: Yale University Press, 1952).
43. Karl Rahner, *Prayers and Meditations* (New York: Seabury Press, 1980), 35.
44. Caputo, *Prayers*, 128 and 150.
45. Ibid., 128.
46. Ibid., 148.
47. Ibid., 96.
48. Ibid., 75.
49. Ibid., 76.
50. Derrida, 'Deconstruction and the Other', 120.
51. *The Gift of Death*, 33.
52. Ibid., 68.
53. Ibid., 68.
54. Ibid., 69.
55. Ibid., 70.
56. Ibid., 71.
57. Ibid., 85.
58. Ibid., 86.
59. Ibid., 78.
60. Ibid., 68.

61. For an elaboration of the concept and morality of collective action as distinguished from those of individual action, *see* Anselm Kyongsuk Min, *Dialectic of Salvation: Issues in Theology of Liberation* (Albany: State University of New York Press, 1989), 104–15.
62. *On the Name*, 46.
63. *Deconstruction in a Nutshell*, 13–14.
64. *Specters of Marx*, 22–3.
65. Ibid., 28; *Deconstruction in a Nutshell*, 17–18, 134–5.
66. Richard J. Bernstein, 'An Allegory of Modernity/Postmodernity: Habermas and Derrida', in Gary B. Madison (ed.), *Working through Derrida* (Evanston: Northwestern University Press, 1993), 227; Thomas McCarthy, 'The Politics of the Ineffable: Derrida's Deconstructionism', *The Philosophical Forum* 21: 1–2 (Fall–Winter, 1989–90), 146–68.
67. William James, *The Will to Believe and Other Essays in Popular Philosophy* (New York: Dover Publications, 1956; originally published by Longmans, Green & Co., 1897), 17–19.
68. For my similar critique of Emmanuel Levinas, *see* my 'Toward a Dialectic of Totality and Infinity: Reflections on Emmanuel Levinas', *The Journal of Religion* 78:4 (October 1998), 571–92.

12
Voices in Discussion
D.Z. Phillips

F: Derrida is well received by theologians, but among philosophers he is not so fortunate. Perhaps this is because he attacks eighteenth-century rational theology, an attack which extends into a criticism of Platonic and Aristotelian metaphysics. He talks in terms of postmodern Heideggerian reflections, and his work has been influenced by Levinas. His work can be related, with profit, to that of J.-L. Marion.

What are the main objections to his views? It is better to leave the term postmodern to itself, since it is used so loosely now. It is better to talk of post-structuralism. In this the philosophy of *difference* is the main heuristic device. It falls under two denominations. One emphasizes polymorphic plurality and goes back to Nietzsche. The other goes back to Kierkegaard and is influenced by Levinas who is anything but postmodern. Levinas is a conservative, Jewish Rabbinical scholar.

For Nietzsche we are confronted by the innocent play of forces, both noble and ignoble. This is the play of necessity for which no one is responsible. Nazis are like waves which crash on the shore and break houses down. Some try to democratize this on the Nietzschean left.

Nietzsche shows us what we do not want Christianity to be. Here we can be self-destructive with the notion of guilt. Much of the abuse is aimed at this tradition.

The other tradition goes back to Kierkegaard and emphasizes God as the wholly other to which we are subject as the measure of truth. Levinas introduced the prophets to Paris of all places, where so many exotic philosophical plants grow. If the Bible makes sense it should make philosophical sense, and so Levinas uses Plato to emphasize the ethical relation to the neighbour. He says that the face of the other is the trace God leaves of himself as he withdraws from the world. Philosophers took notice of these Biblical categories, among them Derrida. He is seriously interested in Levinas in his emphasis on justice, the gift (grace) and hospitality, the most venerable of the Nomadic virtues. This year he is to give a series of lectures on forgiveness. He is interested in matters that can be put to work. He is not interested in the philosophy of religion.

I: I have no quarrel with *F*'s interpretation of Derrida, so I will go straight to my criticisms.

First, 'living with the other' is central in Derrida's work. It is a problem which is likely to increase in our global world. No one has raised this problem so intensely as Derrida. Levinas stressed that a concern with the other cannot be reduced to self-interest. For Derrida the other has a self-negating transcendence, and so purifies us of dogmatism and cultural particularity. So he seeks a 'religion without religion'. Religions are criticized for not living up to this ideal. Derrida tends to ignore possibilities for self-transformation within specific faiths. Instead, he criticizes them for what they cannot be. He doesn't tell us how to improve them. Derrida's speculations are beyond positive law and positive rights. So he has been accused of impotent deliberations. These problems are not resolved in *The Politics of Friendship* because he has a fear of community, hence his emphasis on *difference*. The social is always seen as an oppressive, exclusive singularity. Derrida cannot have a theory of political action.

How do I relate Derrida to liberation theology? In this latter context I emphasize the infinite dignity of the individual, as in the classical tradition. By 'totality' I mean any system of identity. It may or may not be oppressive depending on the attention it gives to infinity. Finally, I emphasize 'solidarity', the mutual response to our dependence on each other. But without totality, informed by infinity, this becomes an empty ideal.

I distinguish between the sceptic who, because of the fear of error, denies truth, and the pragmatist who will risk error for the sake of truth. Derrida is more like the sceptic. He flees from our difficulties and takes refuge in a dream of the impossible. *Difference* is not human, but angelic.

F: I liked your paper up to a point; that point was when you began criticizing me! I don't recognize Derrida in your criticisms. He does not have a dream of the impossible. On the contrary, he insists that speculation should begin from where we are. The singularity he emphasizes is not that of the self, but of the other. He is seriously concerned with justice, but it is not a goal which can be specified once and for all and then sought after. It is a never-ending ideal. He is not condemning particular institutions, but he is critical of crude solutions and anxious to see that they are not thought to be the ideal. Our institutions are forever answerable to an unending ideal.

C: I want to compare Derrida's emphasis on *difference* with Wittgenstein's promise to teach us differences. Michael Weston in his *Kierkegaard and Continental Philosophy* argues that Nietzsche, Heidegger and Derrida, although avowedly anti-metaphysical, cannot resist the temptation to put some general attitude in its place. This something is sublimed above the differences. Do you think that is a just accusation?

F: Decision in Derrida is neither wanton nor pointless. The 'sublime' is welcomed since it is what we are not. The new age is not here. We must always respond critically to the present.

J: Isn't there a difference in the later Derrida? In his early work he responds to specific texts and destabilizes them. But now comes a concern with justice. Why justice? Justice presupposes particular institutions, whereas his general position only supports destabilization.

F: I don't think the early texts are wanton, but he did not think they could be made objective by closed rules.

J: Which is why he thought Searle was so awry.

F: Exactly. How many ways can a text be opened up? He finds as many as he can. But the expectation of a new way saves it from being played around.

G: But hasn't an act of subversion taken place in *The Gift of Death*? I feed my cat while thousands of other cats are starving. So it is with humans. So I cannot fulfil my obligation at all if I start with one. I also make the other dependent on me.

F: The late writings are often said to be open to this objection. But Derrida wants to describe a self-limiting set. What we want from a gift makes it impossible. What I actually do is to produce a debt of gratitude in the recipient, and a feeling of generosity in myself. But his argument is not: therefore no gift, but a recognition that this is the human situation, a self-limiting set. Derrida is telling us to understand this and then act – understanding our limitations. If we ignore the logic of the gift it has an unfortunate effect on us. Know what it is to give; know the inherent difficulty in a gift. The limitation is structural, not personal.

G: But as long as there are cats I can't feed, guilt is built in, structurally, to my act.

F: But I must act.

G: I doubt that is his view.

F: I don't accept that.

D: Are you saying that these insights into our limitations are better achieved by his philosophy than any other kind of philosophy, say, Process Thought or analytic philosophy?

F: No, I didn't mean to. But Derrida does attack the notion of the autonomous subject in philosophy which you find from Descartes, through Kant to Husserl. In Levinas we are called forth by the law, but this is not equated with reason as it is in Kant.

B: But responding to the other is not independent of rules, is it?; rules that can be extended in various ways to meet new situations?

F: Derrida has broken with the Heideggerian conception of language. He wants to say that we must go beyond rules in recognizing that the other may surprise you. You have to listen to something you didn't see coming. The other knows something you don't. So the Messiah cannot turn up, for then there would be no more surprises. Derrida is always open to a new game.

B: Is what is to be accepted as a new game entirely up to me?

F: No, it depends on the conditions of discourse.

B: That sounds like Rorty.

F: No, I do not find Derrida's seriousness in Rorty.

O: Why should my relation to the other be ethical? What about sexual relations?

F: Derrida is more political than ethical. We'd have to look at the details of particular cases. Unjust laws are answerable to the demands of hospitality.

E: Aren't the terms of the equation in Derrida too simplistic? On the one hand, you have certain demands which belong to specific religious traditions. On the other hand, you have his emphasis on 'religion without religion'. How are these to be combined? There seems to be an unresolvable tension between them.

F: There is no reason why one shouldn't consider the relation between these emphases in specific contexts. He is not talking of an abstract impossibility. The difficulty of the other is always in the present. We must begin where we are. Derrida detests the late twentieth-century view of democracy, as though the answer has arrived. What he wants us to do is to view any situation in a critical tension between what we are and what we are not.

Part V
Critical Theory

13
Critical Theory and Religion

Matthias Lutz-Bachmann

The 'Critical Theory' of the Frankfurt School was conceived in particular by its founders Max Horkheimer and Theodor W. Adorno, as an 'open project': that is, more a philosophically funded search for a theory of society than a unified doctrine or teaching. It is not therefore surprising that the positions taken by critical theorists on the question of religion differ significantly from one another in their details.

In my paper, therefore, I wish to examine a few selected texts by proponents of the 'Critical Theory'. I shall first discuss the critical impulse of the philosophy of Max Horkheimer from his early period in the 1930s (1); second, the fundamental aims and philosophical programme in the 'Dialectic of Enlightenment' by Horkheimer and Adorno (2); third, the relation of the later critical theory of Horkheimer and Adorno to religion and what they called 'theology' after the Second World War (3) and fourth, I shall refer to a criticism of these general theses of Horkheimer by Jürgen Habermas (4).

1

Max Horkheimer in 1957 wrote:

> Critical Theory displaced theology but has found no new Heaven to which to point, not even an earthly Heaven. But critical theory cannot erase the memory of Heaven and will always be asked the way that leads there, as if it weren't already a discovery that a heaven, to which one can point the way, is none at all.[1]

This short description of his philosophical convictions makes clear the importance of the theme of religion in Horkheimer's work. It penetrates his entire thought and cannot be separated from his central concerns. If in his final creative period he was perhaps more clearly concerned with the object of religion than previously, it can be argued conversely, that the religious problematic is already closely connected with his writings of the 1930s.

Horkheimer's early work for the *Zeitschrift für Sozialforschung*, like his programmatic inaugural lecture at the University of Frankfurt and his 1931 lecture as Director of the Institute for Social Research, are characterized by the attempt to reflect philosophically on an empirical and at the same time historical conception of social research. Horkheimer sees 'the present situation of social philosophy' as the title of his 1931 lecture puts it, as characterized by an unfruitful side-by-side of positivistic social science, on the one hand, and a kind of social philosophy, on the other, which looks to a 'transpersonal sphere' of ideally constituted state or humanity or a 'value in itself' and views these as 'more essential, meaningful and substantial' than the empirically accessible ordinary world of the individual. For Horkheimer the criticisms of a positivistic philosophy modelled on the social sciences that were advanced by the Marburger neo-Kantians as well as by Hans Kelsen, Max Scheler or Nicolai Hartmann were insufficient since they criticized neither its methodology nor its concept of facts, but rather they 'set them more or less constructively, more or less "philosophically" over against ideas, essences, totalities, independent spheres of objective Spirit, unities of meaning, "national characters" etc, which' they considered 'equally foundational – indeed, "more authentic" – elements of being.'[2]

Horkheimer opposes such a concept of philosophy since the relation:

> between philosophical and corresponding specialized scientific disciplines cannot be conceived as though philosophy deals with the really decisive problems … while on the other side empirical research carries out long, boring, individual studies that split up into a thousand partial questions, culminating in a chaos of countless enclaves of specialists.[3]

In contrast, for the Institute for Social Research, Horkheimer proposes a programme of 'a continuous, dialectical penetration and development of philosophical theory and specialized scientific praxis'[4] to which:

> philosophers, sociologists, economists, historians, and psychologists are brought together in permanent collaboration to undertake in

common that which can be carried out individually in the laboratory in other fields. In short, the task is to do what all true researchers have always done: namely, to pursue their larger philosophical questions on the basis of the most precise scientific methods, to revise and refine their questions in the course of their substantive work, and to develop new methods without losing sight of the larger context.[5]

With the concept of a dialectical mediation of the individual sciences and the philosophical question about the totality, Horkheimer returns to some basic elements of Hegel's philosophy, insofar as these had been incorporated into Marxist theory. In contrast to Georg Lukács, Horkheimer's reception of Hegel's philosophy does not extend so far as to ground a materially oriented universal history and an 'absolute knowledge' of it. Horkheimer's relation to Hegel is much more determined by the insight that the doctrine of identity has long broken down and with it Hegel's system of idealistic philosophy. But, as Horkheimer points out, 'it is easily forgotten all of what it buried with it'.[6]

For Horkheimer an accurate concept of history must take as its starting point a historical-material analysis of human labour in history such as that of Marx and Engels. In his essay *History and Psychology* published in 1932 in the first volume of the *Zeitschrift für Sozialforschung*, Horkheimer wrote:

> Marx and Engels took up the dialectic (of Hegel) in a materialist sense. They remained faithful to Hegel's belief in the existence of supraindividual dynamic structures and tendencies in historical development, but rejected the belief in an independent spiritual power operating in history. According to them, there is nothing at the root of history, and nothing is expressed in history that could be interpreted as comprehensive meaning, as unifying force, as motivating Reason, as immanent telos.[7]

It is not difficult to see in such formulations the revival of the thought of Marx and Engel's *German Ideology*. When Horkheimer describes historical materialism as that view of history in which 'the turn from metaphysics to scientific theory' is realized, he acknowledges that even such an accurate interpretation is vulnerable to being torn apart by dogmatists. Such dogmatism is always a threat to historical materialism as Marx understood it. Against Marxist orthodoxy Horkheimer points out: 'Marx insists that no insight logically prior to history offers the key to its understanding.'[8] He underscores both the continuing indecisiveness and the historical conditionedness of a materialist view of history as well as its critical function. This is evident when Horkheimer, in the face of an economic determinist view of history continued to maintain that human beings are producers of the entire historical shape of their human life even if this takes place in a constrained and irrational form. In this way, Horkheimer shows that the economic necessity proclaimed by Critical Theory is not as invariant natural or historical law but the diagnosis of a wrong structure of society which has to be overcome. In his programmatic article 'Traditional and Critical Theory' Horkheimer explained that the concept of necessity is not a descriptive concept but a normative one. That means it presupposes the idea of human autonomy as historically possible but not yet realized in a capitalistic economy. Here Horkheimer returned to insights of Kant's philosophy of history, holding to the idea of a future society as a community of free men.[9] Kant's employment of reason for the purpose of judging and grounding correct action is, like for Hegel and Marx, retransported into the sphere of historical development. Horkheimer explains that Critical Theory is linked to the interest of the oppressed in overcoming the class rule. For him that is the negative circumscription of the materialistic content of the idealistic concept of reason.

Reason and truth are concepts that Horkheimer's Critical Theory does not wish to do without, while not thereby simply returning to the version of these concepts worked out by Kant and Hegel. Horkheimer is nevertheless aware of the inevitable problems posed to historical materialism by historical relativism and pragmatism which inform his critique and renunciation of metaphysics. He attempts to avoid these problems by holding to a negative notion of truth in the form of a true theory of a false state of affairs. The model of such a theory is, as he writes in his 1935 essay, 'The Problem of Truth', Karl Marx's systematic presentation and critique of the bourgeois economy. For Marx 'reason' takes the form of a dialectical critique of the determinations of 'understanding' and the economic categories. This process is in principle infinite since in theory there is no possibility of reconciling the contradictions which arise in society. Horkheimer goes beyond the theory itself and looks to the historical stage when he writes that:

> the truth advanced because the human beings who possess it stand by it unbendingly, apply it and carry it through, act according to it, and bring it to power against the resistance of reactionary, narrow, one-sided points of view.[10]

The question of the truth of thinking has now widened to include the problem of the truth of historical reality. The question of the historical form of religion and its claims to truth is discussed in a series of essays published by Horkheimer in the *Zeitschrift für Sozialforschung* against the background of his reception of historical materialism. In this respect they differ from Horkheimer's earlier literary essays, for instance the anonymously published collection of aphorisms *Dämmerung* in 1934. Hence Horkheimer could write in his short 1934 article entitled 'Thoughts on Religion' that the concept of God includes the idea of a better world. And he concludes that if justice has to be thought of as identical with God it could not be present in the world: 'If justice resides with God, then it is not to be found in the same measure in the world. Religion is the record of the wishes, desires, and accusations of countless generations.'[11] Ludwig Feuerbach's theory of religion as espoused in the *Essence of Religion* is reproduced by Horkheimer in terms of an analysis of history. Marx in his *Introduction to the Critique of Hegel's Philosophy of Right*, had already referred to religion as the expression of the suffering of the creature and the protest against it and so attempted to describe its relative justification and at the same time illusory character. Horkheimer's own formulations in these years come relatively close to such judgements. But in contrast to Marx, Horkheimer's reflections on the illusory character of religion do not stop there in order to move on to a critique of law or politics. Horkheimer holds to a notion of God which is not solely reducible to psychological anthropology, psychology or socially critical praxis. He writes that we find in 'God' the picture of the idea of 'a perfect justice', but that idea can never be realized in history since a better society would never compensate for the suffering of the past. For Horkheimer, the idea of 'God' represents certainly an illusion, but the concept of God at the same time articulates the lasting universal human hope for fulfilment beyond the bounds of nature and history: 'What distinguishes the progressive type of man from the retrogressive is not the refusal of the idea but the understanding of the limits set to its fulfilment.'[12]

The theoretically important idea of the 'infinite' points to a historical openness, indeed a metaphysical pessimism already evidenced in his essays from the 1930s, which is not easy to reconcile with the Marxist faith in the progressive march of history. In his 1936 review of Theodor Haecker's book *The Christian and History*, Horkheimer notes that the striving for a universal justice is something about which Marxists agree with religious people. Horkheimer's critique of religion in the 1930s did not lead to a new dogmatism or a confession of atheism, which was propagated by the official Marxism of the day. Rather it was more a part of his efforts to contribute to a philosophical critique of the limits of human theoretical or metaphysical knowledge in general. This moves his philosophy, still concerned as it is like Marx's with the capacity of human beings to change the course of history through their actions, in the direction of Arthur Schopenhauer. It is the dogmatic optimism of an 'absolute knowledge' and the human pride reflected in the attempt to overcome the limits of human knowledge which Horkheimer criticizes, in Hegel's philosophy and in doctrinal religion as well as in a dogmatic understanding of Marxist theory. His materialism reflects the 'consciousness of the finitude of human action and human insight' and the 'bitterness of the death' as he formulated it. Precisely such knowledge belongs to the 'essence' of materialistic thinking, since the indignation at the suffering of the majority of human beings originates in the experience of the uniqueness of human life and happiness. Horkheimer opposed 'the ideas of the resurrection of the death, the last judgment and eternal life as dogmatisms' while nevertheless holding to them as expressions of the general human wish for 'eternal beatitude', 'universal justice and goodness', enabling a critique of the status quo and 'infinitely increasing the solidarity with all living things'.

2

Horkheimer's further philosophical development is marked by the consciousness of an unavoidable sadness and an attitude of enlightened pessimism. This mentality mirrors the historical catastrophes of the twentieth century: the terror and state-organized Holocaust by National Socialists in Germany but also Stalin's regime and the machinery of annihilation of the Second World War which continued until the dropping of the atom bomb on Hiroshima and Nagasaki in 1945. These events form the backdrop for the 'Dialectic of Enlightenment' which Horkheimer wrote, together with Theodor W. Adorno, while in exile in California. The book begins with the assertion:

> In the most general sense of progressive thought, the Enlightenment has always aimed at liberating men from fear and establishing their sovereignty. Yet the fully enlightened earth radiates disaster triumphant.[13]

Hence it is the intention of Max Horkheimer and Theodor W. Adorno to investigate the connection between the catastrophes of the twentieth century and the programme of Enlightenment. Mistakenly, the essays in the 'Dialectic of Enlightenment' have repeatedly been linked to the post-modern attack on the modern (Cartesian) notion of the subject and the ideals of the European and American traditions of the Enlightenment.[14] By contrast, Horkheimer and Adorno are concerned with salvaging the programme of the Enlightenment in the face of their current ambivalence and internal contradictions. Thus they write in their introductory chapter:

> The dilemma that faced us in our work proved to be the first phenomenon for investigation: the self-destruction of the Enlightenment. We are wholly convinced – and therein lies our *petitio principii* – that social freedom is inseparable from enlightened thought. Nevertheless, we believe that we have just as clearly recognized that the notion of this very way of thinking, no less than the actual historic forms – the social institutions – with which it is interwoven, already contains the seed of the reversal universally apparent today.[15]

Therein the authors draw the conclusion:

> If enlightenment does not accommodate reflection on this recidivist element, then it seals its own fate. If consideration of the destructive aspect of progress is left to its enemies, blindly pragmatized thought loses its transcending quality and, its relation to truth.[16]

Horkheimer and Adorno seek to secure the relation of their thought to 'truth' through recourse to Hegelian philosophy: from an analysis of the 'Concept of Enlightenment' its inner 'dialectic' as well as its historical and social reality is to be reconstructed. This method of intellectual reconstruction of central concepts is taken from Hegel and attempts to encapsulate the entire historical epoch of modernity and demonstrates the fundamental contradictions within this concept. Hegel too speaks of a conceptual unity of 'presentation and critique' and employs the notion of a 'determinate negation'. But in contrast to Hegel – and here once again Horkheimer and Adorno follow Marx – they do not expect a 'determinate negation' to overcome and reconcile all contradictions in the manner of a speculative concept.

In the fundamental programmatic first chapter of the *Dialectic of Enlightenment* entitled 'The Concept of Enlightenment', Horkheimer and Adorno identify three historical forms of reflection and knowledge which they recognize as having the potential to break through the blind inextricable development of the contradictory processes of Western rationality: these are 'art', 'critical thinking' and 'religion'. Here too we have an analogy with Hegel and the stages of 'absolute Spirit' found in his *Encyclopedia*.[17] Yet in contrast to Hegel, these moments do not form a reflectively closed whole, whose highest form is represented by philosophical thinking. As a result of their critique of Hegel, Horkheimer and Adorno give a different valuation and assessment of these concepts from those of Hegel. By 'art' they mean authentic 'works of art' which were to be found especially but not exclusively in Modern Art and its abstract form of representation. Commenting on such 'authentic' works of art, they write: 'With the progress of enlightenment, only authentic works of art were able to avoid the mere imitation of that which already is.'[18] It is evident that Horkheimer and Adorno recognize in art a claim to knowledge, in accord with an acknowledgement of the biblical injunction prohibiting graven images: 'The justness of the image is preserved in the faithful pursuit of its prohibition.'[19] That quality links modern art with the tradition of religion. It is above all this insight into the Jewish tradition that appears to be capable of breaking through a false enlightenment which Horkheimer and Adorno see in the positivistic creed prevalent in modern scientific enterprise. This has become a new myth and led to an enormous increase in domination. In contrast, Jewish religion broke the power of the ancient pagan myths by their negation in the name of God:

> Jewish religion allows no word that would alleviate the despair of all that is mortal. It associates hope only with the prohibition against calling on what is false as God, against invoking the finite as the infinite, lies as truth. The guarantee of salvation lies in the rejection of any belief that would replace it: it is knowledge obtained in the denunciation of illusion.[20]

These two forms of knowledge, 'art' and (Jewish) 'religion' point the way to a philosophical 'critique' of the unreason of the positivistic science and have the power to break through the system, 'the absurdity of a state of affairs in which the enforced power of the system over men grows with every step that takes it out of the power of nature'.[21] This critique 'denounces the rationality of the rational society as obsolete. Its necessity is illusive, no less than the freedom of the entrepreneurs who ultimately reveal their compulsive nature in their inevitable wars and contracts.'[22]

In conclusion, the goal of Horkheimer and Adorno's study is to show that:

a thinking, in whose mechanism of compulsive nature is reflected and persists, inescapably reflects its very own self as its own forgotten nature – as a mechanism of compulsion.[23]

This de-mythologization of positivistic thinking is an expression of the hope by Horkheimer and Adorno to transcend what they call 'the false absolute' that means the principle of domination.

3

After his return from exile one searches in vain in Horkheimer's philosophical writings for a programmatic work expressive of his primary philosophical concerns. His countless essays and lectures from the period, often occasional pieces dictated by the demands of the moment, are materially closely related to his writings in the 'Dialectic of Enlightenment'. This holds true for his personally reflective 'Notes: 1949–1969' which despite their lack of systematic character are not without philosophical sharpness.

In his writings after 1950 one is confronted with an increasingly radical epistemological scepticism and a pessimism about the prospects of theoretical and practical philosophy. Here one must not forget that Horkheimer's interest in philosophy was awakened by his early reading of Schopenhauer. It was only after his confrontation with Edmund Husserl and Immanuel Kant that the young Horkheimer turned to Hegelian philosophy and its critical reception by Marx. His philosophy remained indebted, even in his appeal to the notion of 'critical social research', to Marxian materialism, Kantian criticism and Schopenhauerian pessimism. The resulting enlightened 'sceptical materialism' forms the foil to his philosophy of religion.

Horkheimer's concept of philosophy shows itself, in consequence of his critiques of both a too narrow concept of European Enlightenment and of the positivism of the sciences, as beholden to a notion of rationality which holds to the idea of an absolute truth is nevertheless in principle unattainable to finite human understanding. This corresponds to Schopenhauer's epistemologically critical insight that the world is appearance. The 'in itself' of things – that is, their essence remains unknowable. For Horkheimer every form of metaphysics which makes claims to knowledge of essences is fundamentally impossible since it does not correspond to the capacities of finite human understanding. However Horkheimer sees that this epistemological scepticism is subject to an objection which for good reason he does not wish to contest. Writing with a view to his critique of knowledge he notes that the entire reflection on the impossibility of philosophy falls under its own verdict of which it itself consists.[24] He admits philosophy against itself is impossible because it asserts the truth of that which it nevertheless denies.[25] Yet this aporetic insight into the impossibility of something like a final truth for philosophy, is not itself claimed to be a final truth. That conclusion would be an 'idealistic dead-end', a trespassing of the limits and competence of finite human understanding. 'Can we conclude', Horkheimer asks:

> that because scepticism contradicts itself that some non-sceptical philosophy, religion or some faith is perhaps justified? No, there is another conclusion to be drawn: to keep silent. That which has always been said, is never really said, since he who ought to hear it, the Infinite One, does not hear it.[26]

Since Horkheimer ties the philosophical idea of a positive fulfilment of truth claims in human language to the attainment of 'The Infinite' but thinks that this is something reason can neither prove nor positively deny, human language loses its claim to truth even while ordinary language and the positive sciences remain bewitched by such language. As he writes in his 'Notes':

> language in the emphatic sense, language that wants to claim truth, is babbling silence, nobody speaks and language does not speak to anyone. Therefore nothing is true. Not even that we are in the darkness of night is true, not even that it is not true, is true.[27]

Horkheimer interpreted the logical positivist denial of a transcendental meaning to the world and the binding character of truth as a sign of the inevitable decline of the grand tradition of European philosophy. That this critique of positivism was not linked to the Western tradition of metaphysics is owing to his epistemological scepticism. His scepticism resisted affirming that being has the same extension as goodness and truth, a conviction of Thomistic as well as Hegelian philosophy. In accord with the finite constitution of human beings and the conditions of human knowledge which makes the metaphysical knowledge of essences impossible, the philosopher cannot presuppose any final unity of being, truth and goodness. That this was done, especially in the neo-Platonic tradition of metaphysics, is to be explained by the human desire for consolation taken over from religion by philosophy. But the fundamental fact of conditioned finite human knowledge is the fact of death which is constitutive of the 'essence' of human knowledge. In continuity with the ancient tradition of materialistic philosophy, Horkheimer contends that his philosophy does not over-look human mortality.

Kant's theoretical philosophy is for Horkheimer in a decisive respect more honest than the tradition of rationalistic metaphysics, against which Kant's 'Critique of Pure Reason' is directed. But Schopenhauer's metaphysical pessimism which Horkheimer recognizes as having a high degree of initial plausibility in the face of the actual course of historical events, trespasses the limits set by Kant's epistemology in finding 'solace' in the apparent unity of the 'essence of the world as will'. Schopenhauer's metaphysical pessimism turns into its opposite, namely into an 'optimistic' philosophy.

In contrast, Horkheimer, in his 'Notes' defends a sceptically grounded pessimism, which alone corresponds to the materialistic foundations of philosophy. But in contrast to the essentially 'religious' pessimism of Arthur Schopenhauer, he insists on a 'philosophical reflection' which forthrightly acknowledges the limits of the realization of human striving toward knowledge and happiness. Assertions about a reality other than the apparent, real world refer to a region into which one is in principle unable to enter.[28]

For Horkheimer, the philosophical doctrine of the unknowability of essences or the things themselves and the impossibility of 'absolute knowledge' does not mean that a philosophical notion of truth should be replaced by a pragmatic notion of 'correctness'. First, maintaining the philosophical pursuit of 'idea of absolute truth' while recognizing the impossibility of its attainment, qualifies Horkheimer's thought as pessimistic, as if characterized by a persistent sense of sadness. Horkheimer speaks, in reference to his thought of a philosophical 'insight into the powerlessness of the intellectual'.[29] He interprets this as the 'last and final' insight of which critical philosophy is capable 'this is the point at which materialism and serious theology coincide'.[30] What Horkheimer means by this might be explained by a remark he made in reference to Paul Tillich's notion of the concept of a 'boundary'. In his essay 'Remembering Paul Tillich' Horkheimer writes:

> I have always understood the concept of boundary such that the philosopher should always see reality as relative which means, that all of our judgments about reality are not absolute and that the world, itself relative, presupposes an absolute that we nevertheless are unable to grasp.[31]

Yet precisely his philosophical insight into the inevitable relativity of human knowledge presupposes the idea of an 'absolute truth' which the sceptic must nevertheless regard *as* 'pure idea', that is, as beyond the fulfilment of finite individuals. This pessimistic or sceptical strain in Horkheimer's philosophy, viz., of an absolute truth as a non-relativistic 'other' to the space–time world has affinities with theology and stands in contrast both to an idealistic metaphysics and a positivistic science. Horkheimer argues that without the idea of an absolute truth and its conditions, knowledge of its opposite, that is 'the desolateness of the human being', is unthinkable. Horkheimer's philosophy is pessimistic, but not cynical. Cynical, by contrast, are those philosophical doctrines that beyond claiming the end of metaphysics, proclaim the end of 'reason', 'the subject' and the ideas of 'humanity' and 'justice'.

The idea of truth, to which Horkheimer holds despite his insight into its unattainability takes on a critical function within scientific discourse. Philosophy rejects the assertion of the finite reality as an ultimate determination and the fulfilment of the concept of truth. This indispensable and yet unattainable notion of truth is indebted at least to the concept and the idea of God. With the notion that the unconditioned truth corresponds to the concept of God, Horkheimer transcends behind the contrast between belief and denial of God, or in his words: the false alternative between theism and atheism. In the past, atheism sometimes has been thought of as a document of freedom of spirit as 'a witness to the inner independence and indescribable courage', but today theism has taken its place. And indeed, compared with atheism, theism has had at least one decisive advantage in terms of its inner conceptual determination: in principle, theism never allowed hatred in the name of God while hatred and murder can in theory coexist with and sometimes follow from an atheistic view of the world. This judgement does not undo the injustices perpetrated in the name of God, but it allows a degree of criticism which does not seem possible for an atheistic reign of terror. Atrocities committed in the name of atheism do not necessary conflict with its fundamental philosophical tenents.

The concept of God like that of 'the truth itself' cannot be given a definite content, indeed it is fundamentally unknowable. Therefore for Horkheimer, assertions about the existence of God, the Creator of the world and the Saviour of humanity are philosophically illegitimate. But according to Horkheimer within our knowledge of the finite state of the world an idea of an Infinite is already presupposed. This idea gets its practical relevance in the 'human desire for the totally Other' as well as in the political struggle for justice and a better world. The practical relevance of the idea of God which totally coincides with the ideas of the good and the just does not concede anything to his fundamentally sceptical position. Horkheimer's philosophical objection to a positive human knowledge of God articulates the central concern of his epistemological scepticism and his Schopenhauerian and Marxist-oriented materialism, namely the philosophical insight into the finitude of human knowledge, the limits of reason and limits to human self-realization as a whole.

In his principal philosophical work, 'Negative Dialectics' published in 1966, Theodor W. Adorno speaks of a 'Passage to Materialism'[32] which runs like a thread through his entire philosophy. This turn to materialism is for Adorno a result of a successful search for the true form of the objectivity of the world, as it is realized in metaphysics and idealistic philosophy: 'The innervation that metaphysics might win only by discarding itself applies to such other truth, and it is not the last among the motivations for the passage to materialism.'[33] And Adorno does not shy away from describing his philosophical position in paradoxical terms: 'If negative dialectics calls for the self-reflection of thinking, the tangible implication is that if thinking is to be true – if it is to be true today, in any case – it must also be a thinking against itself.'[34] Thus for Adorno the concept of 'matter' is a place holder for a concept of reality, idealistic philosophy can only formulate as something non-intellectual. For Adorno, the concept of 'nonidentity still obeys the measure of identity. Emancipated from that measure, the nonidentical moments show up as matter, or as inseparably fused with material things.'[35]

This insight allows Adorno's passage to materialism in the sense of a priority of the object within the mediation of Subject–Object. This position agrees with theology insofar as it holds to a hope in a resurrection of the deaths. 'At its most materialistic, materialism comes to agree with theology. Its great desire would be the resurrection of the flesh, a desire utterly foreign to idealism, the realm of the absolute spirit. The perspective vanishing point of historic materialism would be its self-sublimation, the spirit's liberation from the primacy of the material needs in their state of fulfilment.[36]

4

In his discussion of the philosophical development of Horkheimer and Adorno's thought since the 1940s, Jürgen Habermas points to some fundamental difficulties and aporetic arguments of the so-called 'older critical theory'. It is primarily these difficulties which make Horkheimer and Adorno's appeal to the concepts and symbols of religion understandable; nevertheless Habermas attempts to avoid the difficulties involved in Horkheimer and Adorno's arguments by appealing to a universal pragmatics of language. As a result, Habermas comes to a different conclusion about the function of religion. In his understanding 'religion' is not able to compensate for the difficulties or limits of philosophy as it seems to do in the case of Horkheimer and Adorno. For Habermas, 'religion' neither competes with philosophical rationality nor claims the ability to resolve the problems of a post-metaphysical theory of reason.

Habermas offers his critique of Horkheimer's philosophy of religion in his criticism of the representative essay 'Theism-Atheism' published in 1963. There Horkheimer contends that it is 'vain to attempt to try to preserve absolute meaning without God'.[37] Habermas rejects Horkheimer's argumentation as inappropriate. According to Habermas, Horkheimer's philosophical position is based on the practical idea that the darkness which casts its long shadow upon world history should not have the last word. In Habermas's view, Horkheimer thereby shifts the burden of explaining the historical catastrophes of the twentieth century to the concept of reason itself so that, indebted to Arthur Schopenhauer as he is, he no longer trusts a philosophical concept of reason to be able to positively ground the morally good or at least the morally better act. So, in Horkheimer's thought, it is the task of a critical theory of society to describe historical wrongs or injustices. In accordance with the view that historical materialism is a theory that describes successive conditions that need to be overcome, it is the task of Critical Theory to contribute to the improvement of the conditions of society by identifying societal evils and their 'determinate negation'. It is the weak point in Horkheimer's argument that he doesn't realize that the possibility of describing something as evil already presupposes the capacity to define the content of the concept of the good or to describe the differences between 'good' and 'evil'.

Nevertheless, Habermas believes this type of argument confronts Horkheimer's philosophically funded Critical Theory of society faced with a serious dilemma. In comparison with his earlier and seemingly less presumptuous moral philosophy, the language about an injustice or wrong which is abolished through a 'determinate negation' nevertheless presupposes, simply at the level of the description of just or unjust conditions, the validity of a normative measure of value that must be philosophically explicated. However, Horkheimer, in Habermas's view, fundamentally denies human understanding such a capacity because it falls under the rule of an entirely formal, instrumental rationality. Since Horkheimer nevertheless does not want to give up his intention to contribute to the amelioration of social conditions through a critical theory of society yet no longer trusts human reason to provide a justification of such improved or normatively valid conditions. Hence Horkheimer must, according to Habermas, borrow the now antiquated forms of rationality from a concept of theology amalgamated with an at least neo-platonic philosophy. This protects the inheritance of an already obsolete form of 'substantial reason'.[38] Even Horkheimer sees that his own notion of 'objective reason'[39] is an appeal to a form of rationality which had been surpassed by the critiques of eighteenth-century rationalism, transcendental philosophy and idealism and which would never again gain ascendancy. Hence Horkheimer is not oblivious to the philosophical problems of implementing his own proposal. Yet he sees no alternative to such an 'anamnetic recourse to the substantial reason of metaphysical and religious views of life'[40] in the attempt to search for an alternative to instrumental reason. Since Horkheimer does not have any illusions about the inconsistency and fruitlessness of his appeal to 'objective reason', his philosophy offers an ambivalent message swinging, as it does, between his own complete despair in reason and a 'return to the faith of his forefathers'.[41]

In contrast to Horkheimer and Adorno, Habermas adheres to a concept of truth set in terms of his own language-based, pragmatic theory with the goal of 'interpreting the resolution of a claim to truth under the conditions of an ideal communication situation, that is, in an ideally extended social and historical community'.[42] In the context of an argumentative exchange between interlocutors whose goal is understanding, Habermas maintains that assertions or practical statements imply validity claims which extend beyond a particular time and place. In such utterances there is a 'moment of unconditionedness' that is 'deeply embedded in the process of understanding'.[43] For Habermas there is in the very character of the communicative situation, a transcendence of language which points to a possible understanding inclusive of future communication partners.

These few remarks about Habermas's pragmatic interpretation of reason and truth within the context of his 'theory of communicative action' suffice to make clear that for Habermas, in contrast to Horkheimer, 'post-metaphysical thinking' does not require recourse to 'God or an Absolute'[44] in order to preserve a 'meaning of the unconditioned'.[45] Rather this 'unconditioned' is immanent in the use of language itself and the claims to truth and to correctness implicit in the process of communicative acting. But the 'unconditioned' only has cognitive import if it is 'justified before the forum of reasoned speech'[46] or exposed to discursive scrutiny without qualification. Yet one must distinguish between what Habermas means by the 'meaning of the unconditioned' and what Horkheimer called 'the unconditioned meaning'; for Habermas, the failure of metaphysics since Hegel means that philosophy can no longer appeal to such a sense of the whole. Rather, this can only be mediated by religion where people provide comfort to each other, a task philosophy cannot and does not intend to replace. Such consolation is that which takes 'the unavoidable and innocent injustice, the contingency of misery, loneliness, sickness and death and throws a different light on it, teaching one to bear it'.[47] But in a further sense Habermas can imagine that talk of an 'unconditioned meaning' without reference to God is 'vain'. In that case we are not concerned with the possibility of gaining and grounding a fundamental normative insight, which is strictly the task of a communicatively constituted reason, but with providing a 'motivating answer' to the question why we should act according to our best moral insights, including the question: why be moral at all?[48] In view of this fundamental ethical problem, Habermas suggests he can 'perhaps' affirm the indispensable 'meaning of the unconditioned', explained within the work and through the tradition of biblical Religion.[49]

Translated by Michael Parker

Notes

1. *See* Max Horkheimer, 'Notizen 1950 bis 1969', in: *Gesammelte Schriften*, vol. 6, ed. A. Schmidt and G. Schmid Noerr, Frankfurt am Main, 1991, p. 253.

2. Max Horkheimer, 'The Present Situation of Social Philosophy and the Tasks of an Institute for Social Research', in: Max Horkheimer, *Between Philosophy and Social Science, Selected Early Writings*, trans. by G.F. Hunter *et al.*, Cambridge, 1993, p. 7.
3. Ibid., p. 9.
4. Ibid.
5. Ibid.
6. *See* Max Horkheimer, *Hegel und das Problem der Metaphysik*, Frankfurt, 1971, p. 90.
7. Max Horkheimer, 'History and Psychology', in: *Between Philosophy and Social Science*, op. cit., p. 116.
8. Ibid.
9. *See* Max Horkheimer, 'Traditionelle und Kritische Theorie', in: *Critical Theory. Selected Essays*, trans. by M.J. O'Connell *et al.*, New York, 1995, pp. 188–243.
10. Max Horkheimer, 'On the Problem of Truth', in: *Between Philosophy and Social Science*, op. cit., p. 193.
11. *See* Max Horkheimer, 'Thoughts on Religion', in: *Critical Theory. Selected Essays*, op. cit., p. 129.
12. Ibid., p. 130.
13. Horkheimer/Adorno, *Dialectic of Enlightenment*, trans. by John Cumming, New York, 1994, p. 3.
14. *See*, for instance, Jürgen Habermas, *Der philosophische Diskurs der Moderne*, Frankfurt, 1985, pp. 130–57.
15. Horkheimer, Adorno, *Dialectic of Enlightenment*, op. cit., p. xiii.
16. Ibid.
17. *See* G.W.F. Hegel, *Encyclopaedia of the Philosophical Sciences in Outline*, §§ 553–77.
18. Horkheimer/Adorno, ibid., p. 18.
19. Ibid., p. 24.
20. Ibid., p. 23.
21. Ibid., p. 38.
22. Ibid., p. 38 f.
23. Ibid., p. 39.
24. *See* Max Horkheimer, 'Notizen 1950 bis 1969', op. cit., p. 320.
25. Ibid.
26. Ibid., p. 321.
27. Ibid.
28. Horkheimer, 'Schopenhauer als Optimist', in: 'Notizen 1950 bis 1969', op. cit., pp. 387–8.
29. Horkheimer, 'Gegen die Philosophie', in: 'Notizen 1950 bis 1969', op. cit., p. 281.
30. Ibid.
31. *See* Horkheimer, 'Erinnerung an Paul Tillich', in: *Gesammelte Schriften*, Bd. 7, Frankfurt, 1985, p. 279.
32. Theodor W. Adorno, *Negative Dialectics*, trans. by E.B. Ashton, New York, 1992, p. 192.
33. Ibid., p. 364 f.
34. Ibid., p. 365.
35. Ibid., p. 193.

36. Ibid., p. 207.
37. *See* Max Horkheimer, 'Theism and Atheism', in: *Critique of Instrumental Reason*, trans. by M. O'Connell *et al.*, New York, 1974, p. 47.
38. *See* Jürgen Habermas, 'Einen unbedingten Sinn zu retten ohne Gott ist eitel', in: M. Lutz-Bachmann/G. Schmid Noerr, *Kritischer Materialismus*, Munich, 1991, pp. 125–42.
39. *See* Max Horkheimer, 'Zur Kritik der instrumentellen Vernunft', in : *Gesammelte Schriften*, vol. 6, Frankfurt/M., 1991, esp. pp. 27–74, 165–86.
40. Jürgen Habermas, op. cit., p. 134.
41. Ibid., p. 131.
42. Ibid., p. 139.
43. Ibid., p. 140.
44. Ibid.
45. Ibid., p. 141.
46. Ibid.
47. Ibid.
48. Ibid.
49. *See* Jürgen Habermas, 'Israel und Athen oder: Wem gehört die anamnetische Vernunft?', in: *Diagnosen zur Zeit*, Düsseldorf, 1994, pp. 57–64.

14
Critical Theory and Religion

Maeve Cooke

Critical theory is a theory of society with a 'practical intent': a theory concerned with investigating the potentials for freedom, justice and happiness in actual historical social systems with a view to transforming them accordingly. As a normative theory of society it both diagnoses the causes of social evils and points the way towards better – more rational – forms of social life. This holds both for early critical theorists such as Max Horkheimer as well as for contemporary heirs to the tradition such as Jürgen Habermas. Critical theory is thus not primarily a theory of knowledge or a theory of truth – indeed, not even primarily a theory of justice or of freedom – although such theories form an important part of its endeavours. Bearing in mind its practical orientation towards society as a whole, my essay initially focuses on the following question: what *distinctive contribution*, if any, does religion make to a critical social theory? Here I concentrate on the work of (the early) Horkheimer. In the second section, I consider some points of convergence between Horkheimer and Habermas. Here, the problem of truth emerges as a potential challenge for critical theory.

1

A concern with religion is evident throughout Horkheimer's writings although, as a number of commentators have observed, it appears to play a more prominent role in his later writings than in his earlier ones.[1] However, I leave aside questions concerning the development of Horkheimer's thought in the following. Instead I want to draw attention to the principal functions that he assigns to religion and to the idea of God, respectively, and consider their status within his critical theory of society. This will necessitate, in turn, a brief discussion of what he understands by materialism.

Dialectical materialism and the social contribution of religion

It is striking how often religion features in Horkheimer's essays of the 1930s. Although only a few of these are concerned primarily with the question of religion, references to religion can be found in almost all of his essays on topics as diverse as the 'problem of truth', 'philosophical anthropology', 'materialism and morality', 'materialism and metaphysics', or 'egoism and the liberation movement'. It is also striking that these remarks are almost equally critical of religion and favourable to it. This is at least partly explicable in terms of his dialectical materialist standpoint. In keeping with this standpoint, Horkheimer assesses religion as either a progressive or regressive social force, depending on the specific functions it assumes in concrete historical circumstances. Since in the present context we are considering the question of religion's distinctive contribution to a critical theory of society, my focus is on its progressive aspects. I argue that religion, even when it assumes progressive social functions, either makes no *distinctive* contribution to critical social theory as conceived by Horkheimer or makes one that is highly ambivalent. The idea of God, by contrast, plays a crucial role in his critical theory – but mainly, I contend, in a negative sense, released from a positive religious framework.

Horkheimer's assessment of the function of religion must be understood against the background of his dialectical materialism. His version of this theory owes evident debts to the thinking of Hegel and Marx. It follows Hegel in its adoption of the method of determinate negation as central for the process of ascertaining truth. Determinate negation is a critical method that starts by exposing the one-sided and conditioned character of concepts, proceeding then to re-examine and reinterpret these concepts in light of their limitations, through reference to a general (normative) theory.[2] It follows Marx in its rejection of idealism. Materialism rejects the view that conceptually grasping the conditioned and transitory nature of prevailing ideas is synonymous with overcoming them. Instead it emphasizes transformatory praxis: it insists on the necessity and possibility of overcoming existing conditions of suffering and oppression through collective human action.[3] However, Horkheimer not only follows Marx in his materialist, praxis-oriented, interpretation of the Hegelian dialectic, he also diverges from

Hegel in a second respect. In contrast to Hegel – and some versions of Marxism – he stresses that the dialectic is in principle open-ended.[4] When he writes that 'in materialism the dialectic is not deemed to be concluded', he not only rejects idealism: he also affirms the notion of a *negative* dialectic that maintains an insurmountable discrepancy between human thought and reality.[5] According to this negative interpretation of the dialectic, the progress of history is a struggle to realize human ideas in praxis that can *never* be concluded. As we shall see, this assertion of an ineradicable disjunction between concept and object is one reason why the idea of God is held to embody a moment of truth.

The starting point for Horkheimer's version of dialectical materialism is the need for a better order of things to be achieved through transformation of existing historical reality. This better order of things – which is the normative notion guiding the dialectical method of determinate negation – is conceived neither formally nor abstractly.[6] Rather, it is given a concrete content and shape by the interests and desires of actual human beings as they have been articulated in historical struggles to overcome suffering and oppression.[7] On Horkheimer's reading of history, human beings have historically been motivated by the desire for justice in the sense of overcoming inequality[8] – a desire that has been given a universalist interpretation only under conditions of modernity[9] – and by a longing for happiness and freedom.[10] There can, of course, be no guarantee that future generations will continue to be inspired by these aims[11] – this aspect of materialist theory is one reason for Horkheimer's pessimism in his later writings. However, in the essays written in the 1930s, Horkheimer is confident that affectively based motivation of this kind is widespread:[12] he discerns in bourgeois society a moral feeling akin to love that desires the free development of the potentialities of each and every human being, and that finds expression in the twin reactions of *sympathy* for neediness and suffering and a *politics* aimed at the happiness of human beings in general.[13]

Dialectical materialism is primarily a theory of transformatory praxis. Nonetheless, its view of knowledge as guided by human interests, which both arise out of, and have the power to transform, historical reality, has implications for the perspective it takes on religion. On the dialectical materialist view, the reciprocal conditioning of knowledge and reality has a double aspect: on the one hand, it has a *genealogical* aspect in that it refers to the origins of concepts and theories in historically specific social constellations; on the other hand, it has a *normative* aspect, for it requires ideas and theories to respond appropriately to the (historically specific) interests and desires of human beings. If we keep these two aspects distinct we can see that dialectical materialism does not *reduce* the spiritual to the material, even though it often gives a materialist explanation of the genesis and development of religious (and moral) beliefs and practices. For example, Horkheimer on occasion offers a materialist account of the historical connection between keeping promises and the economic relations of capitalism,[14] between the modern conception of God and the capitalist principle of exchange,[15] and between religious faith and the failure to transform undesirable social structures;[16] importantly, however, he distinguishes between a materialist account of the historical roots of morality and religion and the question of the value of the beliefs and practices he mentions. For Horkheimer, the value or significance of any ideas, principles, theories, knowledge, and so on depends on the overall state of society and on the concrete situation to which they belong.[17] More fundamentally, as we have seen, the ultimate point of reference for determining value or significance is a normative, historically grounded, theory of human interests and desires, and of the kind of social structure deemed appropriate for their satisfaction.[18]

It is clear from the foregoing, therefore, that, according to Horkheimer's materialist view, there can be no *abstract* answer to the question of whether religious faith is a positive or negative social force. The value or significance of religious beliefs and practices always depends on the historically specific social situation in which they are formulated. For this reason, it comes as no surprise that in his various writings Horkheimer both criticizes religion and draws attention to its positive potentials. For example, he is critical of religion insofar as it plays down the importance of insight into the earthly order of things (thus relegating social problems to second place), by turning the minds of human beings towards a more essential order.[19] Or, again, he questions Christian claims to selflessness, arguing that supposedly selfless Christians are in fact more egoistic than atheistic freedom fighters who, by renouncing the hope of reward in an afterlife, are willing to sacrifice their lives for the good of human beings in general.[20] In addition, he criticizes Christianity's unwillingness to acknowledge the brutality that has been part of human nature historically; instead it has justified its own brutal acts through appeal to the 'name of God', leading to a repression of brutality rather than an attempt to deal with it rationally.[21] On the other hand, Horkheimer acknowledges that atheism can be symptomatic of a kind of intellectual passivity that fails to recognize what is wrong with the bourgeois social order and lacks any desire to change it.[22] Implicit in this assessment of atheism is the basic yardstick used by Horkheimer to measure the social contribution of religion.

As he sees it, religion can be regarded as a positive social force on two main counts. The first has to do with its moral message, the second with its orientation towards an idea of the absolute.

Religion's moral message

Religion is a progressive social force insofar as it preaches a moral message of human dignity and universal solidarity that inspires criticism of prevailing suffering and oppression. For Horkheimer, the proclamation of the infinite value of the human person, of the innate rights of the individual, the fight against ideologies of race, nation and 'Führertum', are part of a humanistic message propagated by some strands of Christianity that can motivate social struggle for a better society.[23] It should be noted here that Horkheimer distances himself from the spiritual *justification* offered in support of religiously motivated messages of human dignity and solidarity, insisting that the struggle for a better order of things has no need of appeals to absolute meaning[24] or to an absolute demand (*Forderung*) upon human beings.[25] He sees 'man's striving for happiness [as] a natural fact requiring no justification'.[26] *Feelings* of revulsion against, and solidarity with, suffering and oppression are sufficient – feelings that neither require nor permit justification.[27] Indeed, Horkheimer is emphatic that morality cannot be justified – neither through intuition nor through arguments.[28] As he sees it, *all* value judgments are unfounded.[29] There are no binding moral commands: 'Materialism discerns no authority transcending human beings that could distinguish between helpfulness and greed for profit, goodness and brutality, covetousness and self-sacrifice.'[30] All religious attempts to find a divine justification of morality are thus ideological. Nonetheless, Horkheimer recognizes that under certain circumstances religious messages can serve to reinforce the desire for happiness and feelings of solidarity with suffering, thereby strengthening the incentive for social transformation. In such situations a temporary alliance between materialist thinkers and religious thinkers may be desirable – but only insofar as both aim for a better society.[31] For our present purposes, two points are particularly relevant. First of all, religion's progressive social function is *conditional*: the value of its moral message depends on whether or not it links up with the above-mentioned feelings to inspire transformatory praxis. In Horkheimer's view, this link is purely contingent for, like every idealistic philosophy, religious ideas can easily justify *any kind of* attitude to existing society – a critical or an apologetic, a reactionary or a rebellious one.[32] Second, religion is *replaceable* as the vehicle of the moral message of universal human dignity and solidarity. Even if, historically, religion has been one of the most powerful means of conveying this message, the truth of the message is dependent on religion neither for its justification nor for its dissemination. As we have seen, Horkheimer holds that morality cannot be justified. In addition, there is nothing about religion that makes it inherently better suited than non-religious belief systems to act as a vehicle for moral ideas; indeed, its intrinsic idealistic element makes it *less* suited to this task than materialism is. When, in 1935, Horkheimer writes that, today, 'good will, solidarity with misery and the striving for a better world have cast off their religious mantle', he clearly approves of the development.[33]

Religion's orientation towards the idea of God

Religion does, however, have one distinctive characteristic – a feature peculiar to religious belief – that makes it a potentially progressive social force. This is its orientation towards the idea of God. Unfortunately, it is precisely this characteristic that makes it equally a potential force for social *regression*. Horkheimer asserts an intimate connection between the idea of God and the idea of the absolute: that is, projections of absolute meaning, final knowledge, perfect justice, ultimate truth and so on. There is an oft-cited phrase from his later writings that runs: 'Without God one will try in vain to preserve absolute meaning.'[34] For the early Horkheimer, at least, the relationship between materialism and absolute meaning is highly ambivalent; furthermore, his approval of the idea of God, insofar as it is unconditional, is an approval of a negatively construed idea of God that is essentially non-religious.

From the point of view of Horkheimer's critical social theory, the idea of the absolute is both desirable and dangerous. On the one hand, the idea of the absolute expresses the longing of human beings for perfection – a longing that is the utopian counterpart to the feelings (of desire for happiness or of solidarity with suffering) that Horkheimer presents as historically articulated psychological attributes of human beings.[35] It is the idea of an alternative, better order of things: 'For a long time the concept of God preserved the idea that there are alternative standards to those that find expression in the operations of nature and society…Religion records the wishes, desires and protests of countless generations.'[36] Even materialists – who know that the idea of perfection is a potentially ideological illusion – long for eternal, perfect justice for all human beings.[37] The underlying impulse towards transcending the given – or even the possible – in thought is regarded by Horkheimer as part of what is to be human (which, of course, is a historical category).[38] As he sees it, what distinguishes the progressive type of human being from the retrogressive one is not rejection of visions of transcendence but rather recognition that perfection can never be achieved.[39] Thus, for example, like Walter Benjamin, Horkheimer maintains that perfect justice can never be realized in the world, for even if contemporary injustice were to give way to a more just social order, the misery of bygone generations would not have been made good and the suffering of the rest of nature would still remain.[40] In contrast to religious thinkers, materialists acknowledge that the demand for perfection can never be fulfilled; Horkheimer maintains that this accounts for a certain melancholy discernible in materialist writings, while insisting that melancholy feelings do not constitute a reason for continuing to embrace the illusion.[41] At least in his early writings, Horkheimer holds that materialists must acknowledge the illusionary character of their longing for perfection, retaining only the valuable impulse at the heart of it. This is the impulse towards social struggle to overcome the imperfections of existing social reality.

However, the idea of the absolute is also an illusion that is potentially ideological and dangerous. In affirming the idea of salvation in the hereafter, it directs attention away from suffering and oppression in concrete social reality and runs the risk of making religion a cog in the wheel of the totalistic state (*totaler Staat*).[42] Furthermore, the idea of the absolute as a meaningful object of human knowledge rests on the assumption of a possible reconciliation between concept and object that effects a closure of the dialectical process of history. To be sure, the idea of God can also prevent closure. As we shall see, when integrated within a materialist theory, the idea of the absolute *is* precisely the idea that there is no end-point of history. Paradoxically, however, the idea of God contains a moment of truth only when it is construed negatively and released from its connection with positive religious beliefs, rituals and practices.

Again, two points should be emphasized here. The first is that, for Horkheimer, the value of the religious idea of God is *conditional*: it is dependent on whether the idea of an alternative to the existing order translates into actual transformatory social action. To be sure, under certain social conditions (for instance, twentieth-century consumer capitalism) feelings of solidarity with suffering and desire for happiness, which are the main motivation for transformatory praxis, may wane or even disappear. In such situations the religious idea of God cannot easily connect up with these feelings, and struggle to overcome suffering and oppression is unlikely to result. Even here, however, religion's usefulness remains linked to the idea of transformatory struggle, for the religious idea of God is valuable only insofar as it keeps alive the insight that an alternative to the existing social order is a possibility for human action.[43] The second point is that the religious idea of God, although it expresses a genuine human longing for eternity and perfection, is an *illusion*. Unlike the content of religion's moral message, the religious idea of God has an *inherently* idealistic element that makes it ideological. This is the cause of its ambivalence. It is because it is so ambivalent that Horkheimer advises materialists to recognize that their longing for the absolute cannot be satisfied. They should relinquish the illusion, retaining only its fruitful impulse: the need for a dynamic transcending of the existing order through transformatory praxis.

I have suggested that, for Horkheimer the ideological character of the religious idea of God threatens to obscure its moment of validity. In his view, in order to preserve its valid insight, the idea of God has to be released from its positive religious framework. Only as a negatively construed, non-religious idea of the absolute does it play a central role in Horkheimer's dialectical materialism. To grasp this role we must take a brief look at his theory of truth.

Horkheimer's theory of truth

According to this theory, truth can never be defined in abstraction from the historically articulated interests and desires of human beings: truth is always historically conditioned, it is never abstract or timeless; furthermore, the process of cognition includes actual historical action just as much as experience and understanding.[44] Horkheimer's theory of truth is guided by this emphasis on historically based interests, desires and actions and has two important components. The first of these is the notion of 'corroboration' (*Bewährung*), the second is the method of determinate negation.

The pragmatist idea of *Bewährung* – the view that something is true only insofar as it can be corroborated, in the sense of 'proves its worth', 'turns out to be true'[45] – plays a central role in Horkheimer's materialist theory.[46] With its emphasis on concrete historical action and its reference to human interests and desires, it is easy to see why this idea is congenial to materialism. Horkheimer refers to the American pragmatist philosophers, John Dewey and William James, while acknowledging that the idea of *Bewährung* goes back much further. In the recent German tradition he cites Goethe and Nietzsche as proponents of it: both regard something as true only insofar as it proves to be fruitful, connects up with other true beliefs and is life-enhancing.[47] Horkheimer, too, insists that the verification and truth of ideas pertaining to human beings and social orders does not simply consist in laboratory experiments or in research activity but in historical struggles in which convictions play an essential role.[48] He maintains that 'so long as experiences gained through perception and inference, methodical research and historical events, everyday work and political struggles, withstand the cognitive tests available at any given time, they are true.'[49] He sees the notion of *Bewährung* as particularly important for materialist theory in that it acts as a weapon against all forms of mysticism: it attacks the thesis of a transcendent, superhuman truth that, instead of being accessible in principle to experience and praxis, remains the preserve of the revealed knowledge of a chosen few.[50] Despite the clear affinities between this aspect of materialist theory and the American pragmatists, however, Horkheimer underscores a fundamental distinction. As he sees it, contemporary pragmatists such as Dewey and James hold a view of social reality that is too harmonious. He attributes to them a boundless confidence in the world as it actually exists.[51] Far from constituting the theory's organizing principle, the need for change, if it is perceived at all, is seen as a subjective preference.[52] From the point of view of materialism, the crucial deficiency of contemporary pragmatism is its lack of reference to a general (normative) theory of society.[53] Such a theory is necessary if the notion of *Bewährung* is to avoid the twin dangers of subjectivism and uncritical affirmation of the status quo. For this reason, Horkheimer joins the idea of *Bewährung* to the dialectical method.

As we have seen, this operates by way of determinate negation. The dialectical materialist starts with the conceptual principles and standards of an object, unfolding their implications and consequences. It then re-examines and reassesses the object in light of these implications and consequences. The result is a new understanding of the object in which the original image of the object is transcended and the object itself is brought into flux. As Horkheimer (with Adorno) formulates it: determinate negation rejects defective ideas of the absolute by 'interpreting every image as writing' – by showing how the admission of its falsity is to be read in the lines of its features.[54] This process of critical examination and reinterpretation of concepts is guided by a general theory. In Horkheimer's case, the normative component of the theory is derived from an account of human interests and desires, as these have been articulated historically.[55] As we have also seen, this theory is progressive but open-ended: absolute knowledge – and, in consequence, an endpoint of history – is inconceivable. However, although Horkheimer, at least in his early writings, rejects the idea of absolute knowledge as an achievable – or even meaningful – goal of human action, the idea of the absolute does play a role in his negative dialectics.

Absolute knowledge is inconceivable for human beings and unattainable through human action. As such it is not a meaningful goal for materialists. Nonetheless, despite its illusory (and, as we have seen, potentially ideological) character, it plays a role in materialist theory. Its significance is that it marks the impossibility of closure. The essential open-endedness of the progress of history means that human beings' desire to overcome the limitations of their given historical condition through transformatory praxis can never be satisfied. In contrast to religious thinking, in which the idea of the absolute signifies the possibility of eternal, perfect truth, justice, or meaning, it has a negative, critical, function in materialist thinking. In illustration Horkheimer gives the example of the Jewish prohibition against naming the absolute with names: the 'prohibition against calling on what is false as God, against invoking the finite as the infinite, lies as truth'.[56] Thus, the idea of God as it functions within Horkheimer's version of dialectical materialism is a negative image that can be described as religious only in a derivative sense. More precisely, despite its religious origins, it can be described as a negatively construed, non-religious idea of God insofar as it lacks the framework of positive belief and concrete rituals and practices in which it has always been embedded in the main religious traditions.

Summary

Summarizing, it can be seen that religion either makes no distinctive contribution to a critical theory of society as conceived by Horkheimer or else one that is highly ambivalent. Although under certain conditions it may assume the role of a progressive social force, its value and significance is contingent on a number of factors. In addition, it is replaceable by non-religious kinds of beliefs as a vehicle for progressive social action. Finally, it can just as easily inhibit the struggle for more rational forms of social life as promote it. By contrast, an idea of God plays a crucial role in his critical social theory insofar as it marks the impossibility of closure, thereby testifying to the need for never-ending struggle to achieve a better order of things. Due to the inherently ideological character of religious interpretations of the idea of the absolute, however, this idea is most useful when it is released from its religious framework and understood in a purely negative, critical way.

Habermas's critique of Horkheimer's idea of God

It has been argued, however, that the idea of God fulfils *positive* functions in Horkheimer's later writings. The later Horkheimer, it is claimed, asserts a connection between absolute validity and unconditional meaning and the idea of God as arbiter of validity and bestower of such meaning. Habermas, for example, reads the later Horkheimer in this way. As a result, he accuses him of bad utopianism.

Habermas criticizes the role played by religion in Horkheimer's later work. He attributes to him the position that truth and meaning have a necessary connection with the idea of God. He takes this idea to comprise at least two positive components.[57]

The first of these is the idea of God as arbiter of truth (understood as validity in general). As Habermas reads the later Horkheimer, when critical theory loses its basis in the philosophy of history and when reason in its context-transcendent sense has been eclipsed completely by instrumental reason, religion remains as the sole authority that, if only it were recognized as such, would permit distinction between what is true and what is false, between what is moral and what is immoral.[58] Thus, on Habermas's reading, the later Horkheimer anchors truth (including moral truth) *ontologically* in a divine power.[59] The second component is the idea of God as bestower of comfort or consolation:[60] the idea of God, when construed in a positive way as salvation, draws together the disparate elements of human life to form a meaningful totality; its integrating power serves to reassure human beings that life is ultimately meaningful.[61] Again, when critical theory can no longer find potentials for transformatory social struggles in the philosophy of history, and rationality is reduced to instrumental reason, religion remains as the sole authority that *might* be able to give a meaning to life beyond that of mere self-preservation.[62]

On Habermas's reading, Horkheimer is guilty of bad utopianism.[63] He regards his recourse to a positive idea of God as an escape from history to messianic visions, comparing it to Adorno's messianic interpretation of the truth of art. For Adorno the utopian content of the truth of art preserves a form of knowledge that, because it is dependent for its transformatory power on interpretation by philosophical reason, constitutes a genuine yet *impotent* alternative to the instrumental rationality pervading all aspects of social life in the contemporary world.[64] Such utopianism is bad utopianism to the extent that it explodes the continuum of history: religion or art are assigned a purely messianic power for redemption that has no roots in the concrete social practices of real historical human beings. Such a notion of redemptive reason is aporetic insofar as it fails to link up with reason as embodied in the historical world of speech and action. The difficulties arising from this view of reason constitute the main reason for Habermas's endeavour to lead critical theory out of what he sees as a theoretical impasse – an impasse into which it was led by Horkheimer and Adorno with their jointly written *Dialectic of Enlightenment*.[65] Once Horkheimer and Adorno:

> 'lost their historico-philosophical faith in the rational potential of bourgeois culture which was to be set free in social movements under the pressure of developed forces of production ... the principal 'lever' of the theory was also lost ... instrumental reason, having become total, embodies itself in totalitarian society. With this the classical form of critical theory fell apart.'[66]

In response to this collapse, Habermas attempts to show that a potential for non-instrumental rationality is inherent in the real historical world of human speech and action; his strategy initially takes the form of a theory of knowledge and human interests,[67] and subsequently that of a linguistic theory: the programme of formal pragmatics.[68]

By contrast with what he sees as Horkheimer's anchoring of reason in the divine, Habermas defends the possibility of a notion of reason anchored in everyday communication, whose context-transcending power derives from the necessary presuppositions of discursive practices that have their basis in the everyday linguistic behaviour of historically situated agents. In his view, such a conception of communicative rationality preserves the meaning of the absolute without recourse to metaphysics.[69] Its transcendent character is a transcendence not from and into the Beyond, but a transcendence from within and into the lifeworld.[70]

Insofar as his reading of him is correct, Habermas's rejection of the later Horkheimer's position is understandable. From the point of view of a materialist social theory concerned with bringing about more rational forms of human life, the connection of truth and meaning with a positively construed idea of God is potentially risky. One possible danger is that the truth of the theory, having lost its empirical anchor in historically articulated human desires, needs and feelings, might become accessible only to religious believers. Another is that appeal to a positively construed idea of the absolute might encourage belief that the progress of history is divinely guaranteed, thus inducing passivity and impeding transformatory social praxis. Much depends, however, on the precise interpretation that normative social theory gives to a positively construed idea of God. For example, it makes an important difference whether *knowledge* of the divine will or being is conceived as subject to the constraints of history and context. For the assumption that the hand of God guides the progress of history is readily compatible with the view that human beings gain knowledge of God's guiding hand only by way of essentially fallible processes of interpretation. It also makes a difference whether or not free will is attributed to human beings. For the above assumption is equally compatible with the view that human beings have the freedom to disregard the divine guidance offered.[71] For this reason, it is relatively unimportant whether Habermas's reading of Horkheimer is the most plausible one.[72] The point is that even a positively construed idea of the absolute does not imply that human beings can have absolute knowledge of it; nor does it imply that the progress of history is guaranteed independent of human agency.

2

Habermas's critical social theory shares with Horkheimer the practical aim of bringing about more rational forms of human life. It also shares one central element of what Habermas refers to as the *postmetaphysical* impulse. This is its concern to examine the possibilities for a better life for human beings without relying primarily on philosophical insight for justification of the enterprise: for both, philosophy has lost its traditional status as a mode of knowledge with special insight into the nature of the human.[73] Despite their common aim and overlapping strategy, however, the two projects differ in a number of crucial ways. For example, despite a shared emphasis on the need for cooperation with the social sciences,[74] Horkheimer and Habermas pursue different strategies when it comes to finding an alternative mode of grounding for their theory. Whereas Horkheimer, as we have seen, derives the normative basis for his critical theory from human interests and desires as articulated over the course of history in social struggles, Habermas hopes that the rational reconstruction of everyday linguistic behaviour will provide a normative underpinning for his theory.[75] Since a full exploration of the various points of divergence is beyond the scope of the present chapter, my discussion focuses primarily on some points of convergence and divergence between Horkheimer and Habermas with respect to religion and the idea of the absolute. I first show how Habermas, like Horkheimer, maintains a connection between the idea of truth and a negatively construed idea of absolute. Unlike Horkheimer, however, Habermas insists that it is also possible and desirable to connect truth with a *positively construed yet postmetaphysical* idea of the absolute. I argue that Habermas's attempt to salvage a postmetaphysical conception of the positive aspect of truth is not successful. I then draw attention to some points of agreement between Horkheimer and Habermas concerning the question of the validity of religious ideas. However, here too there is an important disagreement. Unlike Horkheimer, Habermas concedes the possibility of religious truth. I argue, however, that accommodating such a notion would entail substantial revision of his formal pragmatic theory of validity claims.

Habermas's theory of truth

Discussion of Habermas's theory of truth is hampered by the fact that he has substantially amended the theory of truth which he presented in his 1973 essay, 'Wahrheitstheorien', without having fully developed a new, revised version.[76] However, some of his recent essays can be seen as part of an endeavour to make good this deficiency.[77] For our present purposes, it is especially important that Habermas continues to emphasize the difference between justification and truth.[78] For example, in a recent critique of Richard Rorty, Habermas associates himself with Rorty's pragmatist understanding of truth, while accusing him of a problematic naturalization of it.[79] Rorty is criticized for reducing truth to justification, thus losing sight of the potential power of validity claims to explode actual contexts of justification. Habermas, by contrast, wants to hold onto the moment of 'unconditionality' (*Unbedingtheit*) that he regards as inherent in the idea of truth, while retaining an internal relation between truth and justifiability. Habermas's aim, in other words, is to work out a theory of truth that is inherently pragmatic yet retains the notion of truth as a claim to 'unconditionality' that reaches beyond all the evidence available to us at any given time.

Although his emphasis on the unconditional nature of truth has remained unaltered, Habermas has recently moved away from his well-known account of truth as idealized rational acceptability.[80] He now proposes a view of truth as a concept that has a 'Janus-face'. On this understanding, the concept of truth has two aspects: a discursive one and a pragmatic, lifeworld one. On the one hand, truth is the concern of participants in certain kinds of rational discourse who are guided by the idea that a proposition, if true, would withstand any attempts to refute it under ideal justificatory conditions. On the other hand, truth is a pragmatic presupposition of participants in everyday communicative practices in the lifeworld who are guided by the need for behavioural certainty. Truth's 'Janus-face' refers to the dynamic interplay between everyday behavioural certainties and the process of critical rational discussion of these certainties once they fail to prove reliable as a basis for action in the lifeworld; the fallible results of such processes of rational discussion ('discourses') are fed back as 'truths' into the everyday communicative practices of the lifeworld. They then provide a reliable basis for action until, for contingent empirical reasons, they no longer 'work' – that is, no longer prove their truth (*sich bewähren*) by being proof against disappointment – and have to be reassessed discursively in the light of the new evidence and insight.

The idea of truth as a Janus-faced concept is supposed to show why truth is distinct from justification. It is helpful here to distinguish between two aspects of Habermas's idea of truth as justification-transcendent.[81] The first aspect is its *cautionary* function: the concept of truth warns us that even propositions that are justified under the best possible argumentative conditions may turn out to be false. Here, the context-transcendent power of truth is interpreted *negatively* as a warning about the fallibility of knowledge. The second aspect is the sense of *unconditionality* we attach to truth: truth is a property that cannot be lost.[82] Here, the context-transcendent power of truth is interpreted *positively* as the idea of perfection. One advantage of this distinction between a positive and negative aspect of Habermas's idea of the justification-transcendent character of truth is that it enables us to see clearly how his concept converges with, and diverges from, the negative and positive interpretations of the idea of the absolute offered by Horkheimer.

There are evident links between Horkheimer's defence of the idea of God in its negative, non-religious interpretation and Habermas's defence of the 'cautionary' function of the truth predicate. This is one of the main *agreements* between Horkheimer and Habermas as regards the function of the concept of truth. On my reading, both theorists uphold a negative interpretation of the idea of the absolute. For

Horkheimer, a negatively construed idea of God reminds us of the essential open-endedness of the dialectical process and marks the impossibility of closure. For Habermas, the 'cautionary' use of the truth predicate warns us that even rationally justified propositions may turn out to be false, signifying the fallibility of human knowledge. Both agree, therefore, that the concept of truth reminds us of human imperfection. But there is also an important point of *dis*agreement. This concerns truth in its positive aspect.

I have attributed to Horkheimer the view that, in its positive interpretation, the idea of the absolute promises perfection. I then argued that – at least in his early writings – he ultimately rejects a positive interpretation of the idea of the absolute on the grounds that it is illusory and potentially ideological. There are evident links between Horkheimer's idea of the absolute as perfection and Habermas's idea of 'unconditionality'. However, whereas Horkheimer thinks the dangers of the idea of perfection outweigh its acknowledged attractions and merits, Habermas proposes a postmetaphysical interpretation of this idea. But even Horkheimer's rejection of a positively construed conception of truth is not straightforward. As we have seen, he is deeply ambivalent about the idea of the absolute as perfection. Although, at least in his early writings, he ultimately recommends that materialists relinquish a positively construed idea of the absolute on grounds of its illusory, potentially ideological character, he fully acknowledges the *attraction* of the idea: even materialists, he writes, long for eternal, perfect justice for all human beings. This longing expresses an impulse towards transcending the given that is part of what it means to be human and can have positive, transformatory, social effects. Horkheimer's ambivalence here suggests that he would welcome the possibility of a non-illusory – and, for him, this means materialist – conception of the absolute in its positive aspect. Habermas's postmetaphysical interpretation of the idea of 'unconditionality' can be regarded as an attempt to provide such a conception.

As we know, Habermas claims that the idea of the absolute must be conceived as 'transcendence *from within and into the lifeworld*'. Our specific concern in the present instance is with the idea of the absolute in its positive interpretation, as expressed by his idea of 'unconditionality'. As we also know, Habermas now conceives of truth as a Janus-faced concept that faces in the direction both of rational discourses and of the lifeworld. Whereas discourses remind us of the *fallibility* of knowledge (the negative aspect of the idea of the absolute), the lifeworld reassures us of the *unconditionality* of truth (which I have referred to as its positive aspect). We could also say: it reassures us of the *objectivity* – of the necessity and universality – of the true propositions that are the pragmatic basis for the behavioural certainties that guide us in our everyday practices in the lifeworld.[83] Habermas stresses that action requires us to assume the unconditional truth of what we take to be true. 'We would step on no bridge, use no car, undergo no operation, not even eat an exquisitely prepared meal if we did not consider the knowledge used to be safeguarded, if we did not hold the assumptions employed in the production and execution of our actions to be true.'[84] There is thus 'a *practical* necessity to rely intuitively on what is unconditionally held-to-be-true'.[85] He also expresses this as the need for participants in lifeworld action-contexts to be realists:

> Because acting subjects have to cope with 'the world' [that is, with a world presumed to be objective in the sense of identical for everyone and not at anyone's disposal – MC], they cannot avoid being realists in the context of their lifeworld. Moreover, they are allowed to be realists because their language games and practices, so long as they function in a way that is proof against disappointment, 'prove their truth' (*sich bewähren*) in being carried on.[86]

Critique of Habermas's postmetaphysical 'idea of God'

However, Habermas's attempt to salvage a positively construed idea of the absolute without recourse to metaphysics is not successful.[87] His idea of 'unconditionality' appeals to a normative notion of 'coping with reality' that relies in turn on what he calls a 'weak' naturalist – and ultimately metaphysical – assumption about the progress of history. In order to see this we must look more closely at his pragmatically rooted notion of 'unconditionality'.

Habermas argues correctly that everyday action in the lifeworld requires us to behave *as though* we are realists, in the sense of *pragmatically supposing* the existence of an objective world, that is, of a single world, essentially identical for all of us and with some independence of our observations. At the same time, as he himself acknowledges, the fallibilist consciousness that guides participants in discourse also reacts back upon everyday practices without thereby destroying the dogmatism of the lifeworld: 'For actors, who as participants in argumentation have learned that no conviction is proof against criticism, develop in the lifeworld, too, rather less dogmatic attitudes toward their problematized convictions.'[88] Here, too, Habermas is correct. Human agents, when they act as participants in everyday practices in the lifeworld, have to presuppose unconditional truth for pragmatic reasons; however, they can also be aware reflexively of the pragmatic reasons motivating their assumption. In other words, it is not just behavioural certainties that have to 'work' in the sense of enabling agents to cope with reality; the idea of 'unconditionality' itself has to 'work' in the same sense. If it no longer enabled human agents to cope with reality, they would be justified in abandoning it. Put in this way the problem is clear: in Habermas's account, the positive aspect of the concept of truth has its basis in a pragmatic notion of coping with reality. This notion is, however, neither self-evident nor normatively neutral but rather an evaluative standard that itself requires justification. 'Coping with reality' implies that there are better and worse ways of relating to reality. Our conceptions of what counts as better and worse ways depend in turn on evaluative interpretations of human flourishing, which themselves depend on some kind of normative – and ultimately metaphysically based – theory of the progress of history. The normative theory on which Habermas relies is a 'weak' naturalist one.

The theory is *naturalist* insofar as it relies on the basic assumption 'that the organic equipment and cultural way of life of *homo sapiens* have a 'natural' origin and are accessible in principle to explanation by evolutionary theory'.[89] Its naturalism is '*weak*' insofar as it is nonreductionist. It does not *replace* conceptual analysis with natural scientific explanation; nor does it *reduce* the communicative practices of the lifeworld to, for example, neurologically or biogenetically explicable operations of the human brain.[90] Habermas claims that his 'weak' naturalism makes just one fundamental metatheoretical assumption. It assumes that 'our' learning processes – those possible within the framework of socio-cultural forms of life – in a certain way merely continue antecedent 'evolutionary learning processes' that have in turn given rise to the structures of our forms of life.[91]

However, even this 'weak' naturalist account of the progress of history relies on a metaphysical assumption. We can see this if we look more closely at Habermas's argument, which appears to have the following logic. On Habermas's account, natural evolutionary processes are 'coping' processes – processes of solving problems and dealing with disappointed expectations – that lead to ever more complex levels of development. Whereas these processes may in fact be purely contingent, we impute to them a cognitive context. This supposition is necessary if we are to be able to conceive of socio-cultural processes as learning processes. In other words, the attribution of a cognitive content to the practices that make possible 'our' socio-cultural forms of life requires us to impute a cognitive content to natural evolutionary processes.

However, as is evident from the above reconstruction, Habermas's argument does not explain why we are entitled to speak of 'learning' in either case. Rather, it relies on the metaphysical assumption that human beings unavoidably conceive of the progress of history as *learning* – as a process of acquiring knowledge – and not as a cognitively irrelevant, purely contingent shift from one perspective to another. It is this 'metaphysical' assumption that underlies Habermas's 'metatheoretical' assumption of the continuity between socio-cultural and evolutionary learning processes as a first principle that cannot be disproved.

In the end, therefore, Habermas is unable to salvage the positive aspect of the idea of absolute – the idea of 'unconditionality' or perfection – without recourse to metaphysics. However, as I have suggested in the first section, this need not be cause for concern. It is not the fact that normative social theory ultimately relies on metaphysics that is problematic but the tendency to deny the effects of history and context and the importance of human free will. It is not metaphysics that normative social theory has to guard against but rather the view that *access* to perfect knowledge is available and the view that the progress of history towards perfect knowledge and perfect justice is *guaranteed*.

For our present purposes, this rehabilitation of metaphysics has an important consequence. It opens the possibility of debate as to the respective merits of the various kinds of metaphysical assumptions that unavoidably underlie the idea of the progress of history. For there is, of course, no need to accept the particular metaphysical assumption on which Habermas's theory relies. What is required, rather, are processes of unconstrained, hermeneutically oriented dialogue with those who hold competing views of the progress of history. Such dialogues would permit discussion of the advantages and limitations of Habermas's 'weak' naturalist position *vis à vis* other normative accounts of the progress of history – including ones that assume the benign guidance of a divine will or being.

Habermas and the validity of the semantic contents of religion

There are also points of convergence and divergence between Horkheimer and Habermas with regard to the validity of religious ideas. Both agree that the validity of the semantic contents of religion is independent of the religious context in which they originated. However, only Habermas concedes the possibility of religious truth.

Habermas and Horkheimer agree that the value or importance of the semantic contents of religion is independent of the origins of these contents. For example, the validity of moral ideas of human dignity and universal solidarity can be assessed quite independently of the religious framework in which they were initially formulated. More comprehensively than Horkheimer, who tends to focus on religiously based *moral* ideas, Habermas recognizes the religious origins of the key normative conceptions guiding the project of a critical theory of society. Habermas acknowledges that normative ideas of fundamental importance to modern Western self-understanding (and to a critical theory concerned to explore the emancipatory potentials of this) such as ethics and morality, person and individuality, freedom and emancipation, cannot be grasped without 'appropriating the substance of the Judaeo-Christian understanding of history in terms of salvation'.[92] He refers to this as a 'semantic reservoir (of potential meanings)' (*semantisches Potential*) that has to be mastered anew by every generation.[93] At the same time, however, Habermas, like Horkheimer, distinguishes between the *origins* of ideas – their genealogy – and their *importance*. Moreover, like Horkheimer – although for different reasons[94] – he holds that religious *justifications* of moral ideas are not possible: the disenchantment of the world that follows in the wake of the European Enlightenment means that morality can no longer look to religion for support for the truth of its claims. According to the post-Enlightenment picture, reason is differentiated, split up into various moments of rationality: for Habermas, the Kantian trio of truth, morality and taste is paradigmatic for this differentiation. As a result of the disintegration of reason into its various moments, claims to moral validity – like truth and aesthetic validity – now constitute a distinct mode of rationality with its own internal standards of justification. For this reason, under conditions of modernity, moral (and other) insights originally articulated in a religious framework must be subjected to a process of critical appropriation and transformation if they are to be recuperated within the universe of justificatory modes of speech.[95] This holds not just for moral ideas but for semantic contents in general. Habermas refers to the need for *methodological atheism* in dealing with the semantic contents of religion: under conditions of modernity, neither philosophy nor critical theology[96] can simply appeal to divine revelation for justification of religious ideas but must rather subject them to argumentative testing in the appropriate types of discourse.[97]

At times Habermas has suggested that the philosophical task of critical appropriation and transformation of the semantic contents of religion is now concluded – that the valuable content of religion has been translated without remainder into the basic principles of a universalist ethics of the type he proposes.[98] More recently, there is evidence of willingness to acknowledge that the task is still ongoing: 'The process of critical appropriation of the essential contents of the religious tradition is still in process, its results hard to foresee.'[99] He allows that postmetaphysical philosophy will be able neither to replace nor displace religion so long as the language of religion carries with it inspirational or, possibly, even indispensable semantic contents that cannot – perhaps – be fully captured by philosophical language and still await translation into justificatory discourses.[100]

Habermas's formal pragmatics and religious truth

If we consider more closely what is at issue here, we can see that it is the question of religious truth. From the point of view of Habermas's theory, semantic contents may be of different types: they can, for example, be moral, aesthetic, or religious. We may presume that the predicate 'religious' applies when the experience from which they derive is a religious one; let us further presume that religious experiences can be described in positive terms, for example, as the feeling that there is an ultimate purpose to human life that makes it meaningful. Such experiences cannot as a rule be replaced by arguments: no-one who is unconvinced of the existence of God, for instance, is likely to be convinced of it solely through participation in discourse. Religious conviction seems to rely on an indispensable dimension of *personal* experience that is a necessary precondition for participation in discussion on matters of religious validity, and that provides the motivating force for argument. It is for this reason that religious truth is deemed to lay claim to a kind of validity that is only partially discursive. Thus, when Habermas concedes the possibility of specifically religious semantic contents that will always in part resist attempts to translate them into the language of justificatory discourse, he appears to be conceding the possibility of religious truth. If this is the case, it would constitute a further important difference between Horkheimer and Habermas. Although Horkheimer, as we have seen, asserts a connection between truth and a *negatively* construed idea of the absolute, at least in his early writings he argues against a theory of truth that relies on a *positively* construed idea. His theory thus rules out any positive conception of religious truth.[101]

In conclusion, I would like to make two points. The first – shorter – point is that there is an unmistakable note of caution in Habermas's writings as regards the possibility of non-discursively recuperable semantic contents, and particularly so when he refers to religious ones. At most, Habermas concedes the *possibility* of specifically religious semantic contents that would always resist translation into the language of justification: he by no means agrees that such contents exist.[102] At best, his position with regard to the question of religious truth seems to be that the jury is still out on whether it should be taken seriously. The second – longer – point is that it is far from clear how the notion of religious truth can be accommodated within the framework of Habermas's critical theory.

The challenge posed by religious truth

Habermas proposes a schema of validity claims that arguably fails to do justice to the multiplicity of modes of potentially rational everyday language use.[103] The question of religious truth highlights some of the difficulties of his schema.

For our present purposes, the main difficulty with Habermas's theory of validity claims is that the claims to religious truth raised by religious believers do not fit easily into either of the two broad categories identified by Habermas. Habermas distinguishes broadly between validity claims that can be vindicated in discourse and those that cannot. This distinction corresponds to his distinction between universal and non-universal validity claims. Discursively redeemable validity claims are universal in that they rest on the assumption that, if valid, everyone who participated in a discourse satisfying certain demanding conditions would have to agree with this judgement.[104] It is important to note here that, on Habermas's conception, agreement reached between participants in discourse is always agreement in a strong sense: participants agree to accept a validity claim *for the same reasons*.[105] Non-discursively redeemable validity claims are non-universal in the sense that they do not rest on this assumption of universal agreement. Habermas sees empirical and theoretical truth claims, on the one hand, and claims to moral validity, on the other, as examples of discursively redeemable – universal – validity claims. We will recall that, for Habermas, one aspect of the Janus-faced concept of truth is that we deem a proposition true if it withstands all attempts to refute it under the demanding conditions of rational argumentation. The connection between moral truth and argumentation is even more intimate as Habermas asserts an *internal* link between the two. On his account, the moral validity of a norm or principle is conceptually tied to a discursively achieved consensus to the effect that it is equally in the interests of all affected. In the case of questions of moral validity, universal agreement achieved under ideal justificatory conditions does not simply *authorize* validity, it *guarantees* the rightness of moral judgements. In short, whereas Habermas insists on the disjunction between truth and justification, he defends a purely epistemic conception of moral truth. Idealized rational acceptability *exhausts* the meaning of moral validity.[106]

By contrast, claims to aesthetic and to ethical validity fall into the category of non-discursively redeemable claims. For Habermas, ethical (as opposed to moral) validity claims cannot be vindicated discursively because they are always bound to the subjective perspective of a particular individual (or collectivity).[107] Ethical deliberation involves the hermeneutic clarification of an individual's (or collectivity's) self-understanding and raises clinical questions of a happy or not-failed life.[108] Ethical validity claims are thus always context-specific. They are not capable of commanding argumentatively achieved universal agreement but only, at most, the agreement of a particular group that shares a horizon of contingent cultural values.[109]

Habermas also characterizes aesthetic validity claims as context-specific. Like ethical claims they are held to depend on particularist cultural values and thus not to transcend local boundaries. For this reason they do not constitute universal validity claims that can be vindicated in discourse.[110] In addition, Habermas now emphasizes the world-disclosing function of works of art and literature. If I understand him correctly, this world-disclosing function suggests a further reason why aesthetic validity claims cannot be vindicated in discourse (we shall see that the argument here is also relevant in the case of religious validity claims).

In recent years Habermas has repeatedly drawn attention to the power of works of art (and literature) to disclose the world in a new way. Aesthetic claims refer to semantic contents that cast a new light on all aspects of reality and that have to be experienced personally as world-disclosure before they can be understood. The validity of aesthetic claims thus refers to the work of art's 'singularly illuminating power to open our eyes to what is seemingly familiar, to disclose anew an apparently familiar reality. This validity claim ... stands for a *potential* for "truth" that can be released only in the whole complexity of life-experience.'[111] Although Habermas has not worked out the details of this conception of aesthetic validity, the logic of the argument seems clear. I take his argument to run as follows.

If aesthetic validity claims refer primarily to an experience that shows us the world in a new way, potentially changing every aspect of our everyday life, the conditions for achieving agreement in discourse become even more demanding. In addition to satisfying presuppositions governing the conduct of argumentation (such as the requirement that only the force of the better argument obtains), participants would have to have undergone a similar world-disclosing experience that resulted in their seeing the world in a similar (new) way. Furthermore, this similar experience would have to be translatable for all affected by it into a mutually intelligible discursive language. Otherwise, discursively achieved universal agreement on the 'truth' of the work of art would be impossible. The difficulties involved in meeting these additional conditions make aesthetic claims unsuitable candidates for inclusion in the category of claims that can be vindicated in discourse. Whereas discursively reached universal agreement as to the validity of aesthetic claims is not *in principle* impossible, it would be so difficult to achieve that the idea of an idealized rational consensus would be robbed of its purpose: it could no longer serve as a criterion – or even guideline – for adjudicating aesthetic validity.

Their unsuitability as objects of a discursively achieved consensus means that aesthetic validity claims cannot, for Habermas, count as universal.[112] However, he does not appear to see this as cause for concern. Indeed, Habermas reinforces the thesis of their non-universality insofar as he seems to confine the world-disclosing power of works of art and literature to a culture of experts, maintaining that it requires translation by such experts before it can be made accessible for lay persons. More precisely, in the modern world, aesthetic experience is held to be the object of the specialized discourses of experts (in this case, literary or art critics) and thus split off from everyday life-experience.[113] It requires *mediation* by literary or art criticism before it can have an impact on everyday language and behaviour.[114] Such criticism 'accomplishes a process of translation of a unique kind. It draws the experiential content of the work of art into normal language ... This innovative potential then finds expression in the changed composition of an evaluative vocabulary – in the renovation of value-orientations and need interpretations – which alters the tincture of modes of life through altering modes of perception.'[115]

I do not want to pursue the question of whether Habermas's characterization of aesthetic validity claims is convincing. My main point in the present context is that Habermas explicitly compares and contrasts religious validity claims with aesthetic ones.[116] On his – admittedly sketchy – account, religious claims, like aesthetic ones, refer to an experience of world-disclosure that, as I have shown, creates problems so far as their possible vindication in discourse is concerned. Because claims to religious validity, like aesthetic claims, presuppose a personal world-disclosing experience as a necessary condition for participation in argumentation, the likelihood (under conditions of modernity) of achieving universal agreement in discourse is so remote as to make nonsense of universal consensus as a criterion of religious truth – or even as a guideline for ascertaining it. However, although a common reference to world-disclosing experience connects religious claims with aesthetic ones, there are also two important points of difference.

First of all, by contrast with aesthetic claims (as conceived by Habermas), religious claims are not the prerogative of experts in a particular field of specialization but are raised by ordinary participants in everyday practices of speech and action. Habermas acknowledges that the claims to religious truth raised by religious believers take place within the lifeworld, that is, on the level of everyday communication and action. To confine world-disclosing religious experience to the specialized discourses of experts (in this case, theologians) would amount to a complete neutralization of its experiential content: if its experiential content is not to be neutralized, therefore, religion has to assert its *holistic* position in the lifeworld.[117]

Secondly, religious claims, unlike aesthetic ones, are not bound to the contingent subjective values of individuals or groups but are rather universal in aspiration. Habermas explicitly acknowledges the universal orientation of theological claims.[118] Admittedly, as a discourse among experts, (critical) theology fulfils the Habermasian requirement that truth claims be formulated in the specialized language of discursive justification. But, as Habermas clearly recognizes, theological discourses, if they are to be distinguishable from philosophical discourses, have to take seriously the claims to truth raised by religious believers. If theology were to adopt the 'methodological atheism' appropriate for philosophy in dealing with religious semantic contents, it would undermine the entire theological enterprise. For this reason, at least some of the truth claims raised by theology merely articulate at a higher level the claims to truth raised by religious believers in their everyday lives. In other words, the theological claims that articulate religious validity claims are structurally similar to them. Therefore, what holds for theological validity claims must also hold for religious claims: their claim to validity is not *restricted* a priori to the experiential basis of a particular culture or context but transcends all purely local boundaries. This creates problems for Habermas's theory, however, for truth on his view must be capable of being vindicated in discourse.[119] Religious experiences would thus have to be translatable into the language of scientific discourse – and, as we have seen, there are serious difficulties here. From the point of view of Habermas's theory of validity claims, the main problem is the following: The claims of religious believers (which form the basis for many theological claims) cannot be vindicated in discourse and are thus non-universal. For this reason they cannot be compared with claims to theoretical or empirical truth, or with claims to moral validity. At the same time, as he acknowledges, they are neither the prerogative of a specialized culture nor are they bound to particularist and contingent cultural values. For this reason they cannot be compared with claims to ethical and to aesthetic validity. Habermas is thus left in the position of apparently recognizing the holistic and universal thrust of religious validity claims while denying them their entitlement to the predicate 'truth'.

As I see it, there are two paths open to Habermas here. One possibility is to leave his schema of validity claims as it is and find some way – however awkward – of subsuming religious validity into one or other of his two broad categories. The second possibility, which I favour, is a fundamental reconsideration of his theory of validity. Although I have not been able to show this in the present context, I think there are serious problems, in particular, with his accounts of ethical and of aesthetic validity. One problem here is his tendency to reduce the notion of 'experience' to empirical experience based on observation or controlled scientific experiment. Only experience of this kind is admitted by Habermas as evidence for argument in specialized discourses concerned with truth claims. In his recent writings, however, he seems to hold a broader view of the kind of evidence that may count as a reason in discursive processes of justification. In the case of moral discourse, for example, he now acknowledges that moral feelings count as relevant reasons.[120] This suggests that ethical, aesthetic, and religious feelings and experiences might also count as evidence when participants in discourses argue on disputed matters of validity. Admittedly, the question of how such evidence can be processed is a difficult one. For, against Horkheimer, it can be argued that the mere *presence* of a feeling or assertion of an experience is not sufficient: we need to find a vantage point that would permit a critical perspective on subjective feelings and experiences.[121] Nonetheless, if Habermas's theory is to do justice to ethical, aesthetic, and religious truth it must penetrate deeper into the relationship between argument and the varieties of human experience.

Notes

1. Mathias Lutz-Bachmann offers a good overview of the development of Horkheimer's thinking with respect to religion, drawing attention both to the line of continuity between the early and later Horkheimer and the pessimistic turn that characterizes his philosophy in the later period. *See* M. Lutz-Bachmann, 'Humanität und Religion. Zu Max Horkheimers Deutung des Christentums', in A. Schmidt und N. Altwicker (eds), *Max Horkheimer heute: Werk und Wirkung*, Frankfurt am Main, 1986 and M. Lutz-Bachmann, 'Erkenntniskritik und Gottesidee im Späwerk Max Horkheimers', in M. Lutz-Bachmann (ed.), *Kritische Theorie und Religion*, Würzburg, 1997. *See also* J. Habermas, 'Max Horkheimer: Zur Entwicklungsgeschichte seines Werks' in his *Texte und Kontexte*, Frankfurt am Main: Suhrkamp, 1991.
2. As far as I can see, this general theory, as conceived by Horkheimer, has a diagnostic component and a normative one. Its diagnostic component requires of it interdisciplinary research methods: in order to ascertain correctly the causes of social evils it must enter into a relationship of cooperation with the social sciences (cf. M. Horkheimer, 'Critical Theory and Traditional Theory', in his *Critical Theory*, trans. by M. O'Connell, New York: Continuum, 1972, p. 233). Its normative component requires of it an account of human interests and desires, as these have been articulated historically in social struggles (*see* note 51 below), and an account of the social structures most appropriate for satisfying these. Particularly in the case of the latter, critical theory draws on the methods and findings of various social sciences, for example, on those of political economy (*see*, for example, M. Horkheimer, 'Materialism and Metaphysics', in *Critical Theory*, pp. 42–6).
3. Horkheimer insists that materialist theory is primarily a theory of transformatory praxis. He criticizes the frequent misinterpretation of it as a response to metaphysical questions (for example, as an attempt to explain the 'enigma of being'). It is then reduced to the simple claim that only matter and its movements are real. Against this, Horkheimer stresses that materialism is defined principally in terms of the *tasks* it sets itself, specifically the overcoming of human suffering and oppression. (See his 'Materialism and Metaphysics', pp. 10–21.)
4. Horkheimer accuses Hegel of maintaining the possibility of a perfect reconciliation between concept and object, and hence of concluding the dialectical process of thought or history (*see*, for example, M. Horkheimer, 'Problem der Wahrheit', in his *Kritische Theorie*, vol. 1, edited by A. Schmidt, Frankfurt am Main: Fischer (1968); M. Horkheimer and T. W. Adorno, *Dialectic of Enlightenment*, trans. by John Cumming, New York: Continuum, 1972, p. 24. I leave open the question of whether his interpretation of Hegel is correct.
5. Horkheimer, 'Problem der Wahrheit', pp. 242–3.

6. Horkheimer is critical of Kantian formalism, claiming that the emptiness of its conception of morality is one reason why people seek to escape from it to more substantial religious views (cf. 'Problem der Wahrheit', pp. 236f.).
7. Horkheimer, 'Materialism and Metaphysics', pp. 45–6; M. Horkheimer, 'Materialismus und Moral', in *Kritische Theorie*, vol. 1, pp. 108–9.
8. Horkheimer, 'Materialismus und Moral', p. 97ff.
9. Ibid., p. 100.
10. M. Horkheimer, 'Bemerkungen zur philosophischen Anthropologie', in *Kritische Theorie*, vol. 1, p. 210 (cf. also 'Materialism and Metaphysics', p. 44).
11. Horkheimer, 'Bemerkungen zur philosophischen Anthropologie', p. 208.
12. Horkheimer does suggest that this incentive is felt particularly strongly by the social class that suffers most from the capitalist system – which in the 1930s he held to be the proletariat (cf. 'Materialismus und Moral', p. 104); nonetheless, he does not restrict the desire for a better order of things to this social class.
13. Horkheimer, 'Materialismus und Moral', p. 94ff.
14. Horkheimer offers such an explanation in 'Bemerkungen zur philosophischen Anthropologie', p. 213.
15. Horkheimer suggests that the principle of free and equal economic exchange leads to an idea of human beings as beings without a name or a place or a specific destiny, an idea that is essential to the modern conception of God: see his 'Zu Theodor Haeckers "Der Christ und die Geschichte"', in *Kritische Theorie*, vol. 1, p. 371.
16. Horkheimer, 'Problem der Wahrheit', p. 234.
17. Horkheimer, 'Problem der Wahrheit', p. 245; 'Materialism and Metaphysics', p. 11ff.
18. Cf. Horkheimer, 'Problem der Wahrheit', pp. 258–9; 'Materialismus und Moral', pp. 108–9.
19. Horkheimer, 'Materialism and Metaphysics', p. 26.
20. Horkheimer, 'Zu Theodor Haeckers "Der Christ und die Geschichte"', pp. 370–1.
21. M. Horkheimer, 'Egoismus und Freiheitsbewegung', in *Kritische Theorie*, vol. 2, edited by A. Schmidt, Frankfurt am Main: Fischer, 1968, p. 80.
22. Horkheimer, 'Egoismus und Freiheitsbewegung', p. 47. The phrase used by Horkheimer here is 'Atheist aus intellektueller Bedürfnislosigkeit'.
23. Horkheimer, 'Zu Theodor Haeckers "Der Christ und die Geschichte"', pp. 365–6.
24. Horkheimer, 'Bemerkungen zur philosophischen Anthropologie', p. 207.
25. Horkheimer, 'Materialism and Metaphysics', p. 27; 'Bemerkungen zur philosophischen Anthropologie', p. 211.
26. Horkheimer, 'Materialism and Metaphysics', p. 44.
27. Horkheimer, 'Materialism and Metaphysics', p. 45; 'Bemerkungen zur philosophischen Anthropologie', p. 211; 'Materialismus und Moral', p. 106.
28. Horkheimer, 'Materialismus und Moral', p. 93.
29. Horkheimer and Adorno, *Dialectic of Enlightenment*, p. 94.
30. Horkheimer, 'Materialismus und Moral', p. 93.
31. Horkheimer, 'Problem der Wahrheit', pp. 275–6; cf. also 'Zu Theodor Haeckers "Der Christ und die Geschichte"', p. 366.
32. Horkheimer, 'Zu Theodor Haeckers "Der Christ und die Geschichte"', p. 366.

33. M. Horkheimer, 'Gedanke zur Religion', in *Kritische Theorie*, vol. 1, p. 375.
34. M. Horkheimer, 'Theism and Atheism', in his *Critique of Instrumental Reason*, trans. by M. O'Connell and others, New York: Continuum, 1974, p. 47.
35. Cf. Horkheimer, 'Materialismus und Moral', p. 93.
36. Horkheimer, 'Gedanke zur Religion', p. 374.
37. Horkheimer, 'Zu Theodor Haeckers "Der Christ und die Geschichte"', p. 372.
38. Horkheimer, 'Gedanke zur Religion', p. 375.
39. Ibid.
40. Ibid. For a brief discussion of Benjamin's notion of anamnetic solidarity, *see* J. Habermas, 'A Reply to my Critics', in J.B. Thompson and D. Held (eds), *Habermas: Critical Debates*, Cambridge, MA: MIT Press, 1981, pp. 246–7.
41. Horkheimer, 'Zu Theodor Haeckers "Der Christ und die Geschichte"', p. 372.
42. Horkheimer, 'Gedanke zur Religion', pp. 375–6.
43. Horkheimer, 'Theism and Atheism', pp. 47ff.
44. Horkheimer, 'Problem der Wahrheit', p. 247.
45. The German term *'sich bewähren'* may be translated as 'corroboration' or 'proving to be true', in the sense of turning out to be true, standing the test, withstanding critical scrutiny (note its connection with *wahr*, true). Where confusion is likely I use the German term.
46. Horkheimer, 'Problem der Wahrheit', pp. 249ff.
47. Ibid., pp. 249–50.
48. Ibid., p. 245.
49. Ibid., p. 246.
50. Ibid., p. 254.
51. Ibid., pp. 251ff. It could be argued that in taking its orientation from historically articulated interests and desires Horkheimer's own theory is open to the charge he levels against pragmatism (that is, of boundless confidence in the world as it actually exists). In my view Horkheimer avoids this accusation insofar as he insists on a discrepancy between human interests and desires and their satisfaction under given social conditions. Social struggles are practical testimony to the gap between aspiration and actualization; the method of determinate negation is the theoretical tool designed to expose it. To be sure, the possibility of this gap rests on certain – possibly contentious – normative, naturalist presuppositions about the moral validity of desires and feelings.
52. Horkheimer, 'Problem der Wahrheit', p. 252.
53. Ibid., p. 253.
54. Horkheimer and Adorno, *Dialectic of Enlightenment*, p. 24.
55. *See* notes 2 and 51 above.
56. Horkheimer and Adorno, *Dialectic of Enlightenment*, pp. 23ff.
57. Habermas, *Texte und Kontexte*, pp. 110ff.
58. Ibid., pp. 105–6.
59. Ibid., p. 119.
60. Ibid., p. 125.
61. Habermas emphasizes the influence on Horkheimer of Schopenhauer's thesis of the unity of all forms of life (*see Texte und Kontexte*, p. 120). Although he does not draw this conclusion explicitly, one could say that in the modern world the function of the idea of God as *consolation* is connected not just with its ability to project a reconciliation between the individual and the

collectivity but also with its ability to effect a unity between the disparate aspects of an individual human life.

62. Habermas, *Texte und Kontexte*, pp. 105–6.
63. Ibid., p. 97.
64. Ibid., p. 103.
65. *See* J. Habermas, *The Theory of Communicative Action*, vol. 1, trans. by T. McCarthy, Cambridge, MA: MIT Press, 1984, pp. 377ff.
66. Habermas, 'A Reply to my Critics', p. 232.
67. J. Habermas, *Knowledge and Human Interests*, trans. by J. Shapiro, London: Heinemann, 1972.
68. J. Habermas, 'What is Universal Pragmatics?' in M. Cooke (ed.), *Habermas: On the Pragmatics of Communication*, Cambridge, MA: MIT Press, 1998, pp. 21–104.
69. Habermas, *Texte und Kontexte*, pp. 119–20.
70. The title of Habermas's essay in his *Texte und Kontexte* is: 'Transzendenz von innen, Transzendenz ins diesseits'. An approximate translation is: 'Transcendence from within, transcendence into this world'.
71. It also makes a difference at which *level* the idea of God enters the theory. Elsewhere I have argued that normative social theory requires a two-step justificatory strategy. In addition to a mode of justification that appeals to normative standards immanent to a given cultural and social context, it must also justify these fundamental normative standards through reference to a normative account of the progress of history. I contend, furthermore, that a normative account of the progress of history ultimately cannot avoid relying on a metaphysical assumption, be this a naturalist, rationalist or religious one. At this level, the metaphysical assumption of a divine will or a divine being competes, for example, with a metaphysical assumption of the necessary evolution of the species. *See* M. Cooke, 'Between "Contextualism" and "Objectivism": the Normative Foundations of Social Philosophy', *Critical Horizons*, 1, 2 (2000).
72. In my view, there is a line of continuity running through Horkheimer's writings that enables us to interpret even the later Horkheimer's notion of absolute meaning in a purely negative way: as signifying the impossibility of closure. However, since this issue is likely to be of interest mainly to scholars of Horkheimer, I do not wish to pursue it further here.
73. Habermas stresses this affinity between his theory and Horkheimer's when he writes: 'For Horkheimer "materialism" always also had the connotation of being *critical* of philosophy: it stood for *postmetaphysical* thinking.' (*Texte und Kontexte*, p. 92).
74. Both Horkheimer and Habermas share an emphasis on the need for an interdisciplinary approach to a critical theory of society (*see*, for example, Horkheimer, 'Traditional and Critical Theory', p. 233; J. Habermas, 'Philosophy as Stand-In and Interpreter' in his *Moral Consciousness and Communicative Action*, trans. by C. Lenhardt and S. Weber Nicholsen, Cambridge, MA: MIT Press, 1990, pp. 1–20).
75. See Habermas, 'What is Universal Pragmatics?' For a discussion of Habermas's linguistic grounding of critical theory, *see* my *Language and Reason: a Study of Habermas's Formal Pragmatics*, Cambridge, MA: MIT Press, 1994.
76. J. Habermas, 'Wahrheitstheorien', reprinted in his *Vorstudien und Ergänzungen zur 'Theorie des kommunikativen Handelns'*, Frankfurt: Suhrkamp, 1984.

77. The relevant essays can be found in J. Habermas, *Wahrheit und Rechtfertigung*, Frankfurt am Main: Suhrkamp, 1999. One of these, 'Richard Rorty's Pragmatic Turn', is translated in Cooke (ed.), *Habermas: on the Pragmatics of Communication*, pp. 343–82.
78. This is not a new departure. Although Habermas in his earlier writings defended a basically *epistemic* view of truth as idealized rational acceptability, he was usually also concerned to emphasize the difference between truth and justification by drawing attention to the unconditional character we attribute to truth. However, up to recently it was quite unclear what kind of postmetaphysical basis could be found for our understanding of truth as a property that cannot be lost.
79. *See* note 77 above.
80. From the early 1980s onwards, Habermas appeared to hold a view of truth as idealized rational acceptability. According to this position, a proposition is true if it could be justified under the conditions of the ideal speech situation. Truth is a regulative idea, the anticipation of an infinite rational consensus. In his more recent writings (*see* note 77 above), however, Habermas acknowledges convincing objections to this conception.
81. There is no evidence that Habermas himself distinguishes between these two aspects. It should be noted, therefore, that both the distinction between, and description of the two aspects as a 'negative' and a 'positive one', respectively, is based on *my* reading of his work.
82. Habermas, *Wahrheit und Rechtfertigung*, pp. 51, 247; Habermas, 'Rorty's Pragmatic Turn', p. 358.
83. Cf. Habermas, *Wahrheit und Rechtfertigung*, p. 293.
84. Habermas, 'Rorty's Pragmatic Turn', p. 364; cf. Habermas, *Wahrheit und Rechtfertigung*, p. 255.
85. Habermas, 'Rorty's Pragmatic Turn', p. 372.
86. Ibid., p. 370; *see also* Habermas, *Wahrheit und Rechtfertigung* pp. 52–5, 291–5.
87. The same can be said of his proposed postmetaphysical interpretation of the *negative* aspect of the idea of the absolute, as expressed by the notion of fallibility. However, I cannot pursue this matter here.
88. Habermas, 'Rorty's Pragmatic Turn', p. 371.
89. Habermas, *Wahrheit und Rechtfertigung*, p. 38.
90. Ibid.
91. Ibid., p. 37.
92. J. Habermas, *Postmetaphysical Thinking*, trans. by W.M. Hohengarten, Cambridge, MA: MIT Press, 1992, p. 15.
93. Ibid., p. 15.
94. We have seen that Horkheimer holds that justification of moral beliefs is neither necessary nor possible. Instead he appeals to historically articulated feelings, for example, of solidarity or of desire for happiness. Such feelings are 'natural facts' requiring no justification.
95. Habermas, *Texte und Kontexte*, pp. 135–6.
96. Ibid., p. 133. This is theology's dilemma; *see* esp. pp. 137ff.
97. Ibid., pp. 129 and 136.
98. J. Habermas, *Die neue Unübersichtlichkeit*, Frankfurt: Suhrkamp, 1985, p. 52.
99. Habermas, *Texte und Kontexte*, p. 141.

100. Ibid., pp. 141f. Originally in *Postmetaphysical Thinking*, p. 51.
101. Arguably, Horkheimer's theory has no room *conceptually* for a notion of specifically religious truth insofar as it fails to recognize modernity's differentiation of substantive reason into various, formally conceived, dimensions of validity. If we accept the basic premise of Habermas's view, which is that religious truth lays claim to validity that is of a different kind from, for example, the validity claims raised by physics, history, the law or literature, it is easy to agree that Horkheimer's conception of truth is too undifferentiated to allow for significant differences in modes of justification. Admittedly, acceptance of Habermas's thesis regarding the modern differentiation of reason raises complex issues about the relationship between the moments of rationality; in particular, it raises the question of whether these moments can be reintegrated without recourse to metaphysics.
102. When conceding the possibility of religious semantic contents that cannot be retrieved discursively, Habermas tends to suggest that the existence of such semantic contents is doubtful (*see*, for example, *Postmetaphysical Thinking*, p. 51, where he refers to a religious semantic content that 'eludes (*for the time being?*) the explanatory force of philosophical language and continues to resist translation into reasoning discourses'. Emphasis added.) A rare example of engagement with the question of religious truth can be found in his reply to some critics at a theological conference held in 1988 at the University of Chicago (*see Texte und Kontexte*, pp. 127–56). Here, Habermas argues that theology has to take seriously the validity claims of religion – and criticizes some theologians for failing to do so. At the same time, he acknowledges the difficulties connected with any such attempt – without, however, indicating any solution.
103. See my *Language and Reason*, ch. 3. My discussion in the following draws on the argument in this chapter.
104. Such conditions include, for example, the necessary presuppositions that only the force of the better argument prevails, or that everyone concerned is entitled to participate on an equal basis.
105. Cooke (ed.), *Habermas: on the Pragmatics of Communication*, pp. 320–1.
106. Habermas, *Wahrheit und Rechtfertigung*, p. 297.
107. Habermas, *Texte und Kontexte*, p. 149.
108. J. Habermas, *Justification and Application*, trans. by C. Cronin, Cambridge, MA: MIT Press, 1993, pp. 1–17.
109. In 'Realizing the Post-Conventional Self' (*Philosophy and Social Criticism*, vol. 20, no. 1/2 (1994), pp. 87–101). I argue that Habermas's account of ethical validity claims is unsatisfactory in that it fails to distinguish adequately between two senses in which validity claims can be context-specific. Cf. also my 'Are Ethical Conflicts Irreconcilable?' in *Philosophy and Social Criticism*, vol. 23, no. 2 (1997), pp. 1–19).
110. Habermas, *Theory of Communicative Action*, vol. 1, p. 42.
111. Cooke (ed.), *Habermas: on the Pragmatics of Communication*, p. 415. Habermas here cites Albrecht Wellmer's essay, 'Truth, Semblance, Reconciliation', in his *The Persistence of Modernity*, trans. by D. Midgely, Cambridge, MA: MIT Press, 1991.
112. Clearly, this contrasts with Kant's position on the universality of aesthetic judgements in his *Critique of Judgment*, trans. by W.S. Pluhar, Indianapolis: Hackett Publishing Co., 1987.

113. Habermas, *Texte und Kontexte*, pp. 146ff.
114. Cooke (ed.), *Habermas: on the Pragmatics of Communication*, pp. 396ff.
115. Ibid., p. 397.
116. Habermas, *Texte und Kontexte*, pp. 146–7.
117. Ibid., p. 147. Of course the same can be said of aesthetic experience. Indeed, Wellmer – whom Habermas cites approvingly in this regard – seems to be emphasizing precisely the holistic aspect of aesthetic experience (*see* Wellmer, 'Truth, Semblance, Reconciliation').
118. Habermas (*Texte und Kontexte*, p. 140) acknowledges that this must be true for theological claims *qua* validity claims. It must therefore also hold for religious claims *qua* validity claims.
119. Ibid., p. 137.
120. Habermas, *Wahrheit und Rechtfertigung*, pp. 277–8.
121. *See* Cooke, 'Between "Contextualism" and "Objectivism": the Normative Foundations of Social Philosophy'.

15
Voices in Discussion
D.Z. Phillips

H: I have endeavoured to expound critical theory through the developments in the work of Horkheimer. He gave this title to his theory to distinguish it from orthodox Marxism. His work went through three phases. His work during the first phase can be compared to that of Feuerbach and Marx. Once we have thrown off its religious guise, the essence of religion can be seen as the struggle for a better world. He did not agree with the Leninist view that religion was an oppressive institution. Instead, he emphasized the finitude of life, and thought that religion saves us from a thoughtless optimism. In this he was influenced by the pessimism of Schopenhauer.

In his second phase, Horkheimer cooperated with Adorno in a critique of the Enlightenment, by emphasizing the negative aspects of Judaism. The negation of optimism is not based any longer on a conception of absolute reasoning.

In his third phase, influenced by Kant, Horkheimer is far more sceptical. He said that 'the thing in itself' is unknowable. He did not trust human language or cognition. His notion of 'the unconditioned' must be thought of in a regulative, Kantian sense. As in Kant's First Critique it is not an actual reality, but a necessary feature of human reasoning. For the late Horkheimer the religious and the philosophical concept of God is one, via the notion of justice. The hope is for a better world.

O: It is essential to recognize that critical theory is a practically oriented philosophy, rather than a speculative theory. On the one hand, Horkheimer thought that religion is a regressive force if people are dependent on it. The better order he longed for was to be shaped by people's actual interests. This is the only way to overcome oppression. On the other hand, religion can have real dignity if it comes out from the midst of this oppression and furthers progressive interests. But Horkheimer thought that this link was contingent, since, like all idealist philosophies, religious concepts can mean anything. So religion is replaceable. The better order does not need an appeal to the absolute. It may have an important role at a certain time in history, but, again, this is contingent. Furthermore, its promise of salvation is an illusion and turns us away from the practical problems that need to be addressed. We need to be released from the doctrinal and institutional aspects of religion. Idealists and materialists alike need to recognize that an appeal to the absolute cannot be maintained. At last, Horkheimer sees the value of religion as a call for never-ending change, but he is ambivalent towards it since its value will always depend on circumstances.

Habermas thought that Horkheimer was more positive towards religion. He accuses him of utopianism and of turning away from the important issues. Habermas does not think that social action needs philosophical justification. Despite a common aim their purposes differ, but I shall concentrate on what Habermas says about their convergence.

Habermas has an idea of truth which is pragmatic and yet absolute in that it calls one beyond the present situation. No closure is possible. But this role is not religious. He is also interested in the semantic content of religion, and argues that its moral ideas are independent of their religious form. Reason is differentiated in different modes of reasoning. Therefore, we need a methodological atheism to deal with religion. Habermas thought that this critique has been concluded and that the hope lies in a universal human ethics. Lately, however, Habermas has changed his mind and said that this critique has not been fulfilled and that it may not be possible to capture religious truths in some philosophical form equivalent to them.

Can Habermas accommodate religious truth? The difficulty lies in his theory of validated claims. He argued that while empirical and moral claims can be vindicated in discourse, this cannot be said of aesthetic and religious claims.

Habermas said that certain aesthetic and ethical claims are specific in content, being dependent on cultural values. But he also recognized that art and literature can open up new worlds, but must be experienced to be understood. The conditions for vindication here are impossibly high, since all people would have to see the world in the same way. So it is in religion – it offers a world-view. But there are important differences. There are no experts in religion as there are in aesthetics. It concerns the everyday world. The trouble with philosophical arguments is that they negate the existential import of religion. The value of religion is not confined to the individual, but is universal in its aspiration. Yet, there is a problem, since, obviously, theology cannot adopt methodological atheism. How is religious truth to be vindicated in discourse? As far as I can see there are only two possible ways ahead for Habermas in this respect. First, he can retain his criteria of vindication and try to subsume religion under them. Second, he should revise his criteria of vindication and make them more flexible to accommodate different modes of thought. I hope this second course will be adopted.

D: You have presented two ways of assessing religion. One is to ask whether religious claims are true. The second is to ask whether these claims can be translated without remainder into moral or political terms. Obviously, the latter alternative will commend itself more to those who are non-religious.

H: I do not think one begins with religious experience. One must have the requisite concepts to have the experience. All we mean by methodological atheism is a methodological approach to these concepts, so you could say that you find it in Aquinas. But, of course, Habermas is discussing it in the context of post-metaphysical philosophy.

C: I have a question and a puzzle which I want to address to *H* and *O*. My question is whether Habermas has now gone further and said that in the cultural conversation religious meanings have to be recognized as *sui generis* and cannot be analysed away in other terms.

My puzzle concerns the use of 'methodological atheism'. I can see that it meant to deliver the enquiry from the framework of religious idealism. But if the aim is to do justice to different modes of thought, why is atheism privileged in that way? It should be one mode of thought among others. The aim would be to do justice to the world in all its variety. Once again, I thought of Wittgenstein's 'I'll teach you differences.' Instead of 'methodological atheism,' why not speak of disinterested enquiry or neutral enquiry?

H: I accept entirely what you say about 'methodological atheism'. It is an unfortunate term for the reasons you give and should be dropped. As to your first question, again you are right. Habermas now recognizes that religious content is *sui generis*.

O: The only thing I'd add to Habermas's recognition of the distinctive character of religious meanings, is the qualification that he'd wish it was not true.

G: You spoke of the 'world-transforming' experiences of aesthetics and religion. You also said that religion does not depend on experts as aesthetics does, and that its claims are more universal. Now, what if that 'world-transforming' experience of a religious kind happened to a philosopher? Wouldn't that mean that he would see all things, including philosophy, religiously? But your method or, at least, that of Habermas, insists that philosophy must be pluralist. So what is being advocated is a philosophy for the non-religious.

O: The experience you talk of would have extensive implications which could not be contained in Habermas's system. One could not maintain methodological atheism. Of course, in the end, everything depends on one's philosophy.

B: But is it simply a free-for-all as far as which philosophies are or are not included?

H: For Horkheimer there was a criterion by which philosophy is to be assessed, namely, whether it furthered sympathy for the oppressed. Furthering the moral law gives the opportunity for political action. But there is a problem once you recognize, as Habermas did, that there are different conceptions of justice.

M: It is difficult to get people to aim for an ideal when they are victims of oppression. The issue is how the claims of the innocent are to be heard.

O: Horkheimer recognized that, hence his denial that there can be closure on the call for justice. He becomes worried that any consensus reached will, in fact, fail to recognize the sufferings of some minority. Habermas recognizes this criticism, but chooses to disregard it.

H: Horkheimer is, in some ways, more realistic than Habermas. The latter hopes that the universal embraces everyone. He has a transcendental notion of consensus. It is a formal idea that is a precondition for any moral dispute. It is not that we know the goal and are working towards it, but it denies closure to the moral quest.

J: You say that it is not a theory of justice, but that it is normative nevertheless. I do not think that will be 'cool' enough for *C*.

O: Habermas's view is based on his notion of the normativity of language. The precondition for community, he thinks, means that certain implicit standards are already in place. These don't specify how we must act. They don't wield power.

J: The matter seems rather schizophrenic. The method is supposed to be neutral with respect, say, to religion, and yet it is not a neutral guide.

O: Habermas would want to argue that his methods are neutral, but that their findings are not.

J: It also seems to me that if no instance of justice is sufficient, this is a version of perfectionism.

S: I think that part of the difficulty comes from thinking that 'absolute' entails universality.

O: If it is true, he argued, it must be true for everyone and affect every aspect of life.

S: I do not see why the fact that there are views other than my own is sufficient in itself to make me doubt my own.

O: I agree that is the *de facto* situation, but I do find it difficult. If we want to speak of absolute truth what does 'true' mean?

H: We must remember that Horkheimer and Habermas were influenced by Hegel. For them, art is not subjective preference. Art is one stage at which truth appears. This emphasis is still in Adorno. Art and music are a kind of knowledge of the world. They are not private spheres.

O: Habermas seems to depart from this.

H: Yes and that is problematic, since you can give no account of moral judgement if you say that the way forward is to be determined simply by people's interests.

Q: I read Habermas as a kind of Kantian. He argues for universality as a regulative ideal, but what he actually looks for is different, namely, an approximation to the good. Anyone should in principle be able to see that and criticize it. So the aim shouldn't be identified with anything like the highest good.

H: I think that is correct.

Part VI
Process Thought

16
Process Thought
John B. Cobb, Jr

'Process thought' can include a wide range of philosophies and theologies. Hegel, for example, is clearly a process thinker. But the term has been used in recent times to refer especially to the ideas of Alfred North Whitehead and those who have been influenced by him. In the philosophy of religion, the key figure beyond Whitehead has been Charles Hartshorne. In this essay I will limit myself to those who associate themselves chiefly with the thought of Whitehead and Hartshorne. This is the branch of process thought committed to cosmology or metaphysics.

I thereby omit from consideration major schools of philosophy of religion closely related to process thought and sometimes included under the term. In the generation of Hartshorne, there were also Henry Nelson Wieman, Bernard Meland and Bernard Loomer, all of whom found much of value in Whitehead, but drew equally on other sources. They, too, continue to be influential in the American scene. Some of their followers are among the most articulate critics of the metaphysical and cosmological forms of process thought that I will represent.

The accent in this group is on the empirical, the cultural and the historical. If they are theistic at all, this feature of their thought tends to be marginal. Criticisms of these branches of process thought are likely to be quite different from criticisms of the school on which I will focus. Nevertheless, there is a continuum between the two groups and also a strong sense of relatedness in a wider context that rejects or ignores the radical empiricism and neo-naturalism that both groups have in common.

In order to develop a focused paper, I narrow the topic still more. Among followers of Whitehead, some have little interest in religion. Among those who do, some have rejected his doctrine of God. Some of those who find much of value in his cosmology and metaphysics do not want to be encumbered by any form of theism. Others want to connect his cosmology and metaphysics to a different form of theism. They play an important role in process thought, but to include them here would be confusing.

There is a further difficulty in identifying the topic of this paper. Like myself, many of the followers of Whitehead and Hartshorne are theologians rather than philosophers. Of course, we face both ways. Among theologians we are regarded as far too concerned with philosophical issues. They correctly judge that for us somewhat autonomous philosophical questions are of crucial importance for the formulations of faith. Among philosophers, of course, we are viewed with suspicion because of our theological commitments. They are correct that our philosophical reflection is ultimately in the service of faith, although, in our view, to be properly in the service of faith, such reflection should be as open and rigorous as possible.

1

Whitehead's latest works are those most influential among his current theological and philosophical followers. By the time he wrote these, he was out of step with the intellectual community. Both philosophers and theologians had rejected cosmological interests in favour of more narrowly defined disciplinary ones. Dominant streams of philosophy had become analytic or positivistic. Theology stressed its starting point in faith and its independence from all secular disciplines including philosophy. Hence both philosophers and theologians criticized the efforts of process thought to attain a coherent view of the whole that did justice both to science and to religion.

In the effort to attain such a view, dominant formulations both in science and theology had to be challenged. In other words, instead of accepting the autonomy of the several disciplines, process thought engages in criticizing their assumptions and seeking to formulate better ones. From its point of view, most of the disciplines operate with substantialist assumptions which, obviously, appear inadequate or misleading to process thinkers. This means that the metaphysical judgement of the primacy of event and relationship over substance and attribute is central to the project. These metaphysical claims have been pursued in a context in which, in general, both philosophers and theologians have been anti-metaphysical.

The most serious objections to process thought should be apparent from this account of its programme. It pursues a project, metaphysics, which is supposed to have been shown to be invalidated by David Hume and Immanuel Kant and many others in the past two centuries. It seeks a coherent, inclusive vision in a time when this has been shown to be impossible and, perhaps, oppressive as well. It ignores and confuses the boundaries between the sciences, philosophy and theology in such a way as to deny the integrity of each. In short, it continues an effort that has been outdated since the late eighteenth century.

Have these objections been met? Obviously, one who did not think so would not continue a project so out of tune with one's intellectual surroundings. Whitehead agreed with Hume and Kant that early modern philosophy was fundamentally flawed, but he understood himself to be providing an alternative solution to the problem, an alternative that has been little pursued during the past two centuries.

This is not the place to develop the argument in any detail. But it may be well to say that Whitehead's doctrine of physical prehensions introduces a way of thinking about causality that was not considered by either Hume or Kant. Those of us who are convinced of the superiority of the resulting understanding of causality are not persuaded by the arguments of Humeans and Kantians that cosmological and metaphysical thinking should be abandoned. These arguments in general seem to be based on understandings of causality we do not share.

On the other hand, Whiteheadians have also been convinced that the cosmology and metaphysics that are now needed are quite different from those that were dominant in the past. Hence they have been critical of Thomists and others who continued to defend more traditional views. The metaphysics that seems to us viable today on the basis of the evidence of both science and religious experience, as well as intrinsic intelligibility, is a process metaphysics. This requires quite radical changes in the understanding of the human self and God as well as of the natural world. Obviously, proposing major revisions evokes criticism from those who stay closer to the tradition.

This criticism is at two levels. First, there is criticism of the whole revisionist project. Some critics believe that the meanings of such words as 'God' are clearly established in the tradition, especially, perhaps, by St Thomas. The proper philosophical task is to debate the intelligility of the idea and the justification for affirming that God, so understood, exists. Process thinkers reply that the traditional doctrine today shows internal incoherences and that it does not fit well with moral and religious experience. To insist on maintaining it unchanged invites the atheism that has, in fact, been evoked in response to it. But to leave the alternatives only as traditional philosophical theism, on the one hand, and atheism, on the other, has appalling consequences. Far more useful is the constructive task of thinking about what or whom we can trust and worship today.

At this level, the process response to the criticism continues to commend itself to me. But there is another level of criticism which I take more seriously. Especially in an earlier generation, criticisms of traditional theism by process thinkers were often harsh and lacking in nuance. Traditional theism was depicted as inflexible and monolithic. We now know that its capacity for internal self-transformation is far greater than we had supposed. We have learned that it contains greater depths of insight and is subject to more fresh interpretations than we had imagined. The substance thinking to which it is attached does not entail all the consequences we projected upon it. There may have been some justification for the process polemic at one time, in order to open up the discussion of neglected issues, but today simplistic formulations of our differences from some of the revised forms of traditional theism are anachronistic. Differences remain, but process thought may not have provided adequate answers to all the subtler challenges that characterize the current discussion.

The other level of criticism is around particular doctrines of God. These are probably the best known debates in philosophy of religion involving process thinkers. One of these is the process doctrine of divine mutability. Metaphysically this follows in process thought from the principle that to be actual is both to act and to be acted upon. Every actual entity is internally related to its entire past. If God is actual, then God, too, prehends, and thereby incorporates, the past. As new events occur, the past incorporated by God grows. By incorporating that growing past, the divine experience grows, too. Growth is a form of change; so, for God to grow in this way presupposes some kind of divine mutability.

Process thought emphasizes that this form of mutability is compatible with, indeed requires, another form of immutability. God is always including whatever happens in the world. Perfect receptivity is immutably characteristic of God. It is not God's character that changes, but God's character is such that God is responsive to what happens in the world.

Although this is a metaphysical point implicit in the primacy of process, both Whitehead and Hartshorne understood it to have extensive religious and existential importance. Hence process thinkers have often polemicized against the doctrine of divine immutability for reasons that are not purely metaphysical. Because most of us are Christian, we have also appealed to the Bible for support and have argued that if Jesus reveals God, then God suffers with us in our suffering. Critics have objected that this makes God over after our image. It reduces God to finitude. The infinite cannot change. Those for whom God is conceived as Being Itself reject the idea of God changing because it makes no metaphysical sense. They join in the charge against process thinkers of anthropomorphism. The object of worship must be radically different from us, not the human writ large. Also, they believe that a personalistic doctrine of God cannot be defended against critical questioning.

During the period in which process theologians have been fighting this battle primarily at the philosophical level, others have done so on primarily Biblical and existential grounds. Dietrich Bonhoeffer and Juergen Moltmann are two of the most influential. The notion that God suffers with us has become almost a commonplace in many Christian circles. Hence, at that level, the critical objections have lessened, and process theology, in this one instance, seems to be on the winning side.

The philosophical challenge, however, remains. For many philosophers of religion the only locus in which they can affirm God is that of a metaphysical principle that is beyond all the distinctions that characterize creaturely things. In their eyes, process theism treats God too much like a creature. Indeed, in Whitehead we read that God is a 'creature of creativity'. Of course, that phrase is balanced by others that show how very different God is from the other 'creatures' of creativity, but it is significant nevertheless. For process thinkers God is *an* actuality or *a* being, not creativity or Being Itself. Although Hartshorne does not make this distinction, for him, too, metaphysical principles apply alike to God and creatures. God's transcendence does not have the radical metaphysical character that many philosophical theologians have affirmed of it. These thinkers object that such a being is not characterized by the mystery, and does not inspire the awe and wonder that are essential to the divine.

This objection is furthered by a certain form of religious experience as well. As personalistic, Biblical images of God have become less and less credible with the changing worldview, many who remain believers have accented the radical otherness and formlessness of God. The attractiveness of apophatic mysticism has increased. This is the way of negation. Precisely because of its negation of all images and concepts, it is free from many of the charges of incredibility that follow any positive affirmations about God. It also builds bridges to the Vedantic tradition in India and to Buddhist practice. Those who have been socialized in this way find the affirmations of process thinkers, at best, a distraction. This is a serious objection.

My own response has been to build on the distinction made by Whitehead between creativity and God. Creativity is the metaphysical ultimate, and plays, philosophically, an analogous role in Whitehead to Brahman in Vedanta and Emptiness in Zen. So far as I can tell, Whitehead did not make these connections or affirm any religious importance to the realization that we are Brahman or Empty or instances of creativity. But it is evident from the history of religion, that there is great importance in this realization. It is a quite different form of religious life from the trust and worship that are more characteristic of the Biblical tradition and that are directed toward One with whom creatures have some interaction. Thus far I have found this response to a very significant challenge satisfying.

The positing of two 'ultimates', in its turn, raises a whole new set of objections. For many people 'God' is virtually synonymous with 'The Ultimate' or 'The Absolute' in a way that makes the notion of two 'ultimates' inconceivable. My response is that by 'ultimate' I mean only the end of the line in some order of questioning. If we ask after material causes, the ultimate in that line is different from the ultimate in the line of efficient, formal or final causes. I take it that creativity is the ultimate material cause of all that is, including God. That is, God's 'matter' is creativity. But God is ultimate in all the other lines of questioning. In the Bible God is not the void or the chaos from which all things are created. This does lead to two Gods.

A second feature of process thought is the denial that God knows everything about the future. From the point of view of process thought, this is not a denial of omniscience, since God knows all that is and the probabilities of the future as well. There is nothing else to know. God cannot know exactly what will happen in the future, since the future is now genuinely open.

For those who defend the traditional doctrine, however, this is a denial of omniscience, another rejection of divine perfection on the basis of process anthropomorphism. For God not to know the future, it is argued, cuts against prophecy and the assurance that divine promises will be fulfilled. For some, faith is primarily the confidence that all will come out right in the end, and for these the denial that God knows that this will occur in the course of history is a flat rejection of faith. For some, omniscience is an essential attribute of God, and this necessarily includes knowledge of the future. For them, the God of process thought is not truly God at all.

Those who hold to a fully deterministic reading of history have no difficulty in believing in God's knowledge of the future. But many who hold to omniscience in this sense, also affirm the reality and importance of human freedom in shaping the future. In order to work out the tension between these beliefs, some assert that from the transcendent, divine perspective, all time already exists. Our human experience of the radical difference between past and future applies only to our creaturely perspective.

Clearly, this solution is not open to process thinkers. Neither is the deterministic view of events. The uncertainty of the future, and therefore the impossibility of God's knowing exactly what will occur, are built into process metaphysics. For the most part, this is satisfying to us religiously and existentially as well as intellectually. It unequivocally accents the importance of human decisions in the shaping of history.

On the other hand, a real objection lies in the strength many gain from the assurance that, despite all odds and apparent improbabilities, in the end truth will prevail and right will be done. Process thinkers join in singing 'We Shall Overcome' as an expression of hope and determination, but we know that for others it is an expression of confidence that God's promises will be fulfilled regardless of what creatures do. The inability to support that assurance can be painful. Those of us who are Christian theologians recognize that there are Biblical passages supporting an apocalyptic fulfilment of history which we must demythologize.

The challenge is to find other ways of providing assurance. Process thought offers several. First, there is the assurance that whatever happens God is with us, God loves us, God accepts us, and all that we are lives on in the divine life. Second, there is the assurance that in the course of history all our efforts count for something, even if the particular goals for which we strive are not attained. Third, there is the assurance that God works with us and through us in every situation to bring about what good there is possible, and that this introduces surprising new hope and promise. Fourth, some process thinkers hold out the hope for continued personal life beyond the grave.

These responses to the objection suffice for many of us. We can also argue that maturity requires that we accept responsibility for our world and not expect divine intervention to set things right or rescue us from our destructive practices. But whether any of this is an adequate response to the objection is hard to say. It is adequate for my own religious needs, but I cannot speak for those who find themselves in intolerable positions of oppression.

Closely related to the revision of divine omniscience is the rejection by process thinkers of the notion of divine omnipotence. We believe that the doctrine of omnipotence rests on a philosophically outdated understanding of causality, precisely the one that Hume and Kant found indefensible. The Whiteheadian doctrine of causality as physical prehensions cannot result in a single entity being capable of totally controlling everything.

Causality is here understood as influence, as one entity flowing into another and thus participating in its constitution. But every event results from the joint inflowing of many past events. No one can displace all the others.

Furthermore, although to a large extent an event is the product of the joint influences of the past, it is never entirely so. There is always an element of self-constitution as well. That self-constitution is a response to the physical prehensions that causally inform the event, but this response adds something, it supplements.

Finally, God's role in each event is unique. To understand it, consider as the event in question a momentary human experience. God is not so much one physical influence alongside the personal past, the fresh impulses through the sense organs, and the remainder of the body, although God's presence may play a role of that kind. God's distinctive role is that of making a creative response possible. God provides alternative possibilities for response to the physically given situation and calls the occasion of experience to realize that possibility which, in that situation, is best. It is God's role to give freedom to that experience and responsibility as to how that freedom is used. Thus, whereas past events compel us to incorporate aspects of themselves, God's primary role is persuasive.

The power of persuasion is very different from the power of coercion. If it were possible to speak of the ideal limit of the power of persuasion as 'omnipotence', process thinkers would be glad to appropriate this traditional word. But we have found that the notion of omnipotence is bound up with that of coercive power. We believe, on the other hand, that persuasive power is the greater power. It is true that coercive power can destroy and kill, but only persuasive power can give life, make free, and evoke love.

Again, those of us who are Christian theologians also believe that the revelation of God in Jesus is not of a monopoly of coercive power but of an ideal instance of persuasive power, liberating power, empowering power. God's activity in human life sets us free and calls us to responsibility. We find that this revision of traditional theism brings us closer to the Bible.

Critics object that in the Bible God is depicted as 'almighty'. Most of this widespread assumption follows from the translation of a proper name for God, 'Shaddai' as almighty. There is no justification for this translation in the Hebrew texts. But it would be going too far to say that the whole of the Bible is on our side. We must admit that some of the actions attributed to God, especially in the earlier books of the Old Testament, as well as the last book in the New Testament, imply a controlling power that does not fit well into process thought.

There is still much work to be done on these questions. Controlling and persuasive power cannot be wholly separated. The diverse understandings of divine power in the Bible have not been fully sorted out. But much has been done, and some advantages of process thought have been extensively displayed with regard, for example, to the problem of evil.

The most serious objection here, as in the case of the revised doctrine of omniscience, relates to the openness of the future. For some Christians the assurance that God has the power needed to transform all things in the end is what is chiefly at stake in the claim that God is omnipotent. Process thought cannot support that assurance.

The understanding of the self is another area in which process thought profoundly revises the tradition. Even persons who are attracted to other aspects of process thought often find themselves unable to follow here. From the process point of view, this shows how powerfully our language has caused us to adopt substance thinking even when we are not conscious of doing so.

Process metaphysics requires us to recognize that the human person *is* the flow of human experiences. Alternately, we may define the person as the flow of human experiences in conjunction with all those other events that make up the human body. In neither case is there any underlying self or 'I' distinct from the experiences. The self or 'I' lies within the flow of experience.

The vast majority of Westerners habitually think of themselves, implicitly, as the subjects of their experiences rather than as elements within those experiences. If one spells out what is implicit, the experiences are attributes of a substantial self that remains self-identical despite changes in the experience. The self that experiences pain in one moment is the same as the self that experiences joy in another. A major objection to process thought is that it dissolves this substantial, underlying self into the flux of experience.

Have process thinkers responded adequately to this objection? If we do not suppose that we have, then we must recognize that the basic claim of process thought is incorrect. That has in fact led some to turn away. Others of us find that the process view is phenomenologically more accurate and that there are others who, independently of commitment to process metaphysics, are finding this to be the case. We take comfort in the fact that Buddhists have supported this view, lived with it, and gained spiritually from it, for thousands of years.

This affinity of process thought with Buddhism provides another ground of objection, this time from Christians. Is not a major difference between Buddhism and Christianity, they ask, the depreciation of personal existence in the former and its affirmation in the latter? Does not acceptance of the Buddhist denial of an underlying self lead to the depreciation of personal existence? Can that be reconciled with Christianity?

My response to this has been to agree that Christians prize personal continuity through time, along with the responsibilities that continuity engenders, in ways that Buddhists ultimately do not. But Christians need not understand this personal continuity as based on a self-identical self underlying the process. Instead, we can view each momentary experience as maintaining continuity with a particular sequence of predecessors, embodying them with some peculiar completeness, and aiming at the continuation of this sequence into the future.

Phenomenologically, Buddhists do not deny that this occurs. Far from it. They know how very difficult it is to break these connections. But they see the spiritual gains that occur when the lack of identity through time is fully appreciated and the present cuts off its ties to past and future. They develop disciplines that help this to happen. Christians, on the other hand, can accent the positive values of identifying our personal being with a particular past, taking responsibility for it, and committing the future of this personal being. Christianity and Buddhism then appear as complementary responses to the same metaphysical situation rather than as metaphysically opposed traditions.

2

Perhaps the most serious objection to process thought is that it has engaged too little with other philosophies. It has functioned too much as a ghetto within the wider community. For example, it has engaged too little with the other philosophies of religion represented in this conference. This is a valid objection, but our failure in this respect has more justification than may initially be recognized.

First, process thought in the form of process theology has engaged quite extensively with other forms of theology. By itself this has been an absorbing task, and it has involved us secondarily in interaction with philosophers of religion who enter the theological discussion. Of course, even here, we have by no means engaged all forms of theology, and certainly we have not been remarkably successful in shaping the mind of the church!

Second, process thought is inherently transdisciplinary and interested in interaction with thinkers in many different fields. We are interested in the implications of our basic stance for physics and biology as well as the social sciences. We need also to see whether developments in these fields cut for or against our assumption of the primacy of events and relationships over substances and attributes. What revisions in our cosmology do new developments require? This too is an absorbing and never completed task.

Third, process thought points toward the importance of practice. We believe that it has contributions to make not only to theology, but also to the practical life of the church. We have written on Christian education, pastoral counselling, church administration and preaching. Articulating these contributions and trying to implement them also take a great deal of time. Furthermore, this work in the church is only a tiny part of the work we wish we could do in the wider society in education, in therapy, and in political and economic life. I personally have become particularly absorbed in the critique of economic theory and practice and have been privileged to work with a Whiteheadian economist in this field.

Fourth, much philosophy, including philosophy of religion, seems to operate within rather narrow disciplinary boundaries. Our belief that the most important tasks confronting humanity are not well dealt with in that way tends to make the discussion with philosophers less urgent than some other conversations. Of course, there are many exceptions.

Fifth, the discussion with philosophers that would be most helpful to us would be about the points at which our branch of thought breaks away from the Euro-American mainstream. In this paper I have touched on that briefly with regard to the issue of causality. If other philosophers are willing critically to evaluate the Whiteheadian idea of physical feelings, we will certainly benefit from their help. But our experience has been that when we point out the Humean or Kantian assumptions underlying the way problems are formulated in much of recent philosophy and propose that there are better assumptions, our contribution is rarely appreciated. On the whole, process thinkers have dealt more seriously with philosophers of other schools than they have dealt with us.

The criticism that is most valuable to us is criticism of basic assumtions. For this reason the most challenging criticism that has developed in recent decades has been directed to our social location as process thinkers. This social location has been chiefly in the North American university and oldline (read middle-class) church. Most process thinkers have been males of European descent. In other words, most process thought has taken place within the establishment. Furthermore, the effects of this location can be seen in the issues that we have taken up and the way we have dealt with them.

This kind of criticism can be simply relativizing and disempowering. But it need not be that. White, male process thinkers can ask, and to some extent have asked, whether process thought as such contributed to their preoccupation with issues posed by the dominant society or whether this was the consequence of our general socialization into university and church. The answer seems to be mixed. On the one hand, abstract philosophical questioning and even theological doubts are much more likely to take place among the privileged than among those they oppress. That means that raising cosmological and metaphysical questions at all does express the privileged social location of most process thinkers. But that social location is not responsible for the way those questions are answered. Indeed, process thinking has more tendency to destabilize the establishment than simply to supply justification for it.

Furthermore, some of the earliest stirrings of contemporary feminism made use of process categories. Although most process thinkers are still male, the ideas tend to cut against stereotypically masculine habits of mind and to be much more supportive of feminism. The social location of process thought no doubt blinded most of its advocates to this tendency, but as we became aware of these issues, most of us have been supportive of the feminist movement if not participants therein.

The initial encounter with Black and liberation theologians was less friendly. The suspicions based on our social location were justified, but the content of our affirmations was more supportive of their positions than they realized. As we became clearer about the implications of our own ideas and as liberationists realized that we were supportive, alliances have to some extent replaced opposition. Fortunately for us, from an early date a few Blacks and liberationists saw the potential of process thinking to contribute to their ends.

Although interactions with feminist and liberationist movements and examination of social location are not identical with what would be entailed in engagement with critical theory, I describe it because it is the closest we have come on any large scale to such engagement. This interaction has accounted, I think, for more significant changes in process thought than any other, with the possible exception of environmentalism. Together these have contributed both to emphasizing engagement with real issues in the world and to the approach to that engagement. Many of us feel that in these moves we are realizing more fully what is practically involved in our theoretical commitments.

Our engagement with deconstructive postmodernism has been much less. The pervasive importance of that movement in religious studies programmes and in the American Academy of Religion have made it impossible to ignore. The use of deconstrucive methods by feminists and liberationists has also drawn attention to it. So most process thinkers with religious interests have paid some attention to it.

Furthermore, there are many features of deconstruction that are congenial. Much of what is deconstructed in the tradition is what process thinkers also have been trying to deconstruct with less success. This applies, for example, to the idea of an underlying or substantial self discussed above.

Nevertheless, there are deep differences. Deconstructive postmodernism carries forward the Kantian trajectory against every form of objectivity or realism. The natural world seems to exist only as it is constructed by various humans. The process view that consciousness in general and human experience as a whole arise out of natural processes seems virtually unformulable in deconstructive terms. Furthermore, the process project of coherent and unifying thinking is systematically rejected both as illusory and oppressive, and Whitehead's deconstruction of ordinary sensory experience into its two modes is ignored.

David Griffin has been the process thinker who has engaged this form of postmodernism most vigorously. He has argued that by carrying forward to its consistent conclusions the late modern project of limiting reason and denying the intelligibility of the world, it deserves the name most-modern rather than truly postmodern. He has proposed an alternative constructive postmodernism which deconstructs the basic metaphysics of both early and late modernity and proposes a processive alternative. The most sustained engagement of process thinkers with the issues of postmodernism is in *Varieties of Postmodern Theology*, by David Ray Griffin, William A. Beardslee and Joe Holland (Albany: SUNY Press, 1989).

Wittgenstein's influence in the Anglo-American philosophical scene in the past half-century has been so extensive that it would be impossible not to engage it in some measure. Some process philosophers, such as George Lucas, have tried to present process ideas in such a way that they could be understood and even appreciated inside the dominant discussion. Others have complained about the linguistic turn which tends to erect the implicit metaphysics of the English language into the ultimate arbiter. Still others have complained that the notion of language games can be so interpreted as to provide a space for fideism. But I am not aware of an extended study of Wittgenstein himself by a process thinker, with the possible exception of Nicholas Gier.

The most promising development in the dialogue with Wittgensteinians is the serious and friendly work of Nicholas Rescher, *Process Metaphysics*. This recent effort by a participant in the philosophical mainstream to understand and assess process thought opens the door to a kind of interaction that has been difficult in the past. The 'Special Focus on Analytic Philosophy' in a recent issue of *Process Studies* (Vol. XXV) is also promising. Whether these developments can open doors to worthwhile interaction with Wittgensteinian philosophers of religion remains to be seen.

A good portion of the discussion of objections to process philosophy of religion in Part I dealt with classical philosophical theism. Charles Hartshorne devoted extensive attention to the critique of that theism, and over the years there has been considerable response. I noted that process thinkers such as he may be faulted for treating this tradition as monolithic and failing to consider adequately the nuances and changes that take place through time. This failure applies to some extent to response to more recent philosophers of religion who continue the classical tradition of philosophical theism but often with different accents and arguments. Nevertheless, from the perspective of process thought, as long as they affirm such key doctrines as divine immutability and omnipotence, the arguments that have long been trademarks of the process tradition are relevant.

Reformed Epistemology, at least in the person of Alvin Plantinga, is a contemporary exponent of classical theism. David Griffin gave considerable attention to Plantinga's formulations in his work on the problem of evil. Griffin is currently dealing sympathetically with Plantinga's claims that science should free itself from its bondage to a materialistic worldview and open itself to the hypothesis of God's activity in the world. As a process thinker, however, he objects to viewing this activity as external disruption, and he proposes viewing it as involvement in each of the events that make up the history of the world.

Process theology shares with Reformed Epistemology the desire for a coherent worldview that can be affirmed by Christians. It shares in the denial that the now dominant worldview in science is required for the advancement of science and in arguing for its reform. It shares in belief that the Christian perspective can play a role in proposing ways in which that reform can and should take place. But from the process perspective, Reformed Epistemology's claim that its revelatory starting point suffices for justifying its proposals, as long as they cannot be disproved, is not justified by the fact that all thinking begins with some presuppositions. For process thought, all proposals arise from presuppositions, but each must be justified on its merits in the arena of public discourse.

17

Process Thought – a Response to John B. Cobb, Jr

Schubert M. Ogden

1

One of the merits of John Cobb's chapter is his deft and fair-minded delimitation of what, for his purposes, is to be understood by 'process thought'. Accepting his delimitation, which I have no trouble doing, I would have to say that, if I am a 'process thinker' at all, I belong to the same group of such thinkers to which he identifies himself as belonging, that is, those who associate themselves with the thought of Alfred North Whitehead and Charles Hartshorne in their concern with cosmology and metaphysics; who have a particular interest in religion, and thus in philosophy of religion and philosophical theology; and who pursue this interest, not as professional philosophers, but because of their calling as Christian theologians. It will hardly seem strange, then, if I also confess to sharing, to a considerable extent, the same point of view that Cobb represents in his chapter.

Specifically, I view the place of process thought on the twentieth-century intellectual scene in very much the same way; and I, too, would say that the usual objections to it are explained by its clear-cut differences, formal or material, from other modes of thought in both philosophy and theology that continue to be or have become more widely influential. Formally, its theory and praxis of philosophy in a more classical sense as comprehensive critical reflection on human existence as such, and thus as perforce having a critico-constructive function centrally involving metaphysics and ethics, put it decidedly at odds with all understandings of philosophy as having only the one function of analysis, as well as with other philosophies that are anti-, non-, or only semi-metaphysical. Materially, its insistence that process is the inclusive category and that God is to be treated, not as an exception to metaphysical principles, but as their 'chief exemplification' sets it no less sharply over against the classical and, in many ways, still dominant traditions in both metaphysics and theology.

But if I agree with Cobb's account of the place of process thought and of the usual objections to it, I also accept his distinction between the two levels at which it is usually criticized and his differentiated assessment of the extent to which process thinkers have adequately responded to the criticisms. I, too, would say that the defence we have made of what he calls 'the whole revisionist project' more or less effectively meets the usual objections to it, while our responses to criticisms of our neoclassical metaphysics and philosophical theology can very definitely be improved upon. One of the reasons for this, certainly, is just the reason he gives – that we can and should be more attentive than we have sometimes been to other revisions of classical metaphysics and philosophical theology that, while scarcely neoclassical, are not obviously open to the same objections that have become the stock in trade of our polemic against more traditional kinds of thought. And I can say this without changing my judgement that some of the most deliberate attempts, by philosophers as well as theologians, to commend something like a mediating position between classical and neoclassical types of theism do not stand up well to careful criticism (Ogden, 1991).

As for Cobb's discussion of particular doctrines of process thought that are commonly criticized and his responses to the criticisms, here, again, there is much with which I agree. In fact, I feel very close to him in his frank admissions that there are assurances associated with traditional doctrines of God's omniscience and omnipotence that process thought simply cannot offer. But, then, I also find, as he does, that process thought is by no means without its own assurances and that, with the possibility it opens up for at last dealing with the problem of evil, it is as satisfying religiously or existentially as it is philosophically.

Beyond all this, I can also accept most of what Cobb says in the second part of his paper, including his specific responses to the third question about the extent to which process thought has engaged with the other points of view represented in the conference. Although I am not bothered, as he is, by philosophies that operate within 'rather narrow disciplinary boundaries', I do share his judgement that process thinkers, on the whole, 'have dealt more seriously with philosophers of other schools than they have dealt with us'. Not only are critics of process thought who have first taken the trouble to understand it exceedingly hard to come by, but some of the philosophers who have responded to it have stooped to outright parody and ridicule. In my own work, certainly, the critical factor determining the nature and extent of my engagement with other philosophical points of view has been my vocation and tasks as a Christian theologian. While this has in no way precluded entering into extensive discussion with philosophers as well as theologians, it has definitely limited such discussion to philosophers whose work has been significant for the theologians who have been my primary *Gesprächs-partner* – not all of which work, incidentally, is represented in the conference. In any case, my own engagement with some of the points of view that are represented – notably, critical theory and Wittgenstein – has been rather more extensive than Cobb indicates to have been true of process thinkers generally.

2

For all my agreements with Cobb's chapter, however, there are a number of ways in which my own point of view is different; and my guess is that we would both judge that at least some of the differences are not only real but important. Thus, if he can admit to sharing 'radical empiricism and neo-naturalism' with the other main group of process thinkers whose accent he describes as falling on 'the empirical, the cultural, and the historical', I would have to speak more cautiously. What most impresses me about this group is less their radical empiricism than their *pan*empiricism, their evident assumption that the only meaningful assertions, apart from those of logic and mathematics, are empirical or merely factual assertions. And what I understand by the reality of God so radically transcends everything in nature, taken either in its individual parts or as the collection thereof, that any characterization of my understanding as 'neo-naturalism' could only lead to confusion.

It is also clear to me that, at certain points, Cobb and I have really different understandings of philosophy, including metaphysics and cosmology. As much as I share the general Whiteheadian view of philosophy as the criticism of abstractions, I do not understand such criticism, as he does, to be an alternative to accepting 'the autonomy of the several disciplines'. To be sure, philosophy in my view does have a proper critico-constructive function with respect to all answers to the existential question, religious and theological as well as philosophical; and, to this extent, philosophy may be said to cover some of the same ground as theology. But if this means that philosophy does indeed act as a control on the answers of theology as well as of religion, it in no way denies their proper autonomy; for the converse statement is equally true: theology and religion also act as a control on philosophy's answers to the same existential question. As for the autonomy of science or the sciences, I see no reason at all why philosophy should be thought to challenge it. Even if philosophy may quite properly criticize presuppositions of the sciences that are philosophical rather than scientific, it is logically different from the sciences and so may neither control nor be controlled by them.

This means, of course, that I discern a view very different from my own when Cobb talks about process metaphysics seeming 'viable today on the basis of the evidence of both science and religious experience, as well as intrinsic intelligibility'. I do indeed think with Whitehead that 'the best rendering' of 'that ultimate, integral experience...whose elucidation is the final aim of philosophy' is 'often to be found in the utterances of religious aspiration' (Whitehead, 1978: 208). And so I, too, would say that religious experience as expressed through religious utterances is very definitely primary evidence for philosophical, and, specifically, metaphysical and ethical reflection. But I cannot say the same for science, even though I quite agree that the conclusions of process metaphysics, like any metaphysics, cannot be viable in the long run unless they are compatible with the results of scientific research.

The experience of which I understand science to be the best rendering, at the secondary level of critical reflection and proper theory, is not the 'ultimate, integral experience' of ourselves and others as parts of the encompassing whole, which I distinguish as our *existential* experience, but rather our *empirical* experience, by which I mean our derived, external perception of ourselves and the world by means of our senses. There is also the difference that, whereas the assertions of science, being properly empirical, must be at some point empirically falsifiable, the assertions of metaphysics, and therefore of process metaphysics, cannot be empirically falsified. In fact, strictly metaphysical assertions cannot be factually falsified at all, because they formulate the necessary conditions of the possibility not only of human existence, but of anything whatever. On my understanding, then, to suppose that process metaphysics even could be viable on the basis of the evidence of science as well as of religious experience is to imply another, very different view of metaphysics as, after all, an empirical, or quasi-empirical, undertaking that differs from science only or primarily in the scope of its generalizations.

I shall say more about this difference presently. But I first want to point to a couple of others that I take to be important.

The first pertains to what Cobb speaks of as 'the rejection by most process thinkers of the notion of divine omnipotence'. Like other such thinkers – including, in some of his more recent statements, I regret to say, even Hartshorne (Hartshorne, 1984) – Cobb so discusses this matter as to leave the impression that the very notion of God's omnipotence is mistaken. There are indications, of course, that what he really objects to is not the notion of divine omnipotence, but rather the most common way of construing this notion, or, if you will, the most common way of talking about God's transcendent power. According to this way, the notion of omnipotence is bound up with talk of power as coercive, and God is said to be capable of totally controlling everything. But for all Cobb clearly says to the contrary, he can be fairly taken to reject not only this particular way of talking about divine omnipotence, but any other way of saying that God's power over all things is *the* power, the power than which none greater can be conceived. The contrast at this point with his earlier discussion of omniscience is striking. Whereas in that discussion he clearly explains why, from the point of view of process thought, 'the denial that God knows everything about the future … is not a denial of omniscience', there is no comparable explanation in what he has to say about God's power – to the effect that the denial that God can totally control everything is just as little a denial of omnipotence. My view, however, is that there can and should be just such an explanation and that process thought at its best provides it. Instead of making it easy for critics who allege that the God of process theism is little more than the well-known 'finite God' of certain modern philosophers and theologians, process thinkers have again and again made clear that and why, in their understanding, the power of God, like everything else about God, can only be spoken of in such terms as 'ideal', 'maximal', 'unfailing', 'infallible', 'irresistible' – in a word, 'unsurpassable'. Thus Hartshorne, for one, having argued that 'no teleology can exclude unfortunate accidents and frustrations, for goals have to be reached through mutiple acts of freedom, none of which can be entirely controlled, even by God,' goes on to add, 'The point is not that [God] cannot control them, but that they cannot be controlled. It is not [God's] influence which has limits, but their capacity to receive influence. Absolute control of a free being, and there can be no others, is self-contradictory' (Hartshorne, 1962: 81). But, then, omnipotence is not a mistake; the mistake is a merely verbal construal of omnipotence that we have the best of reasons for rejecting even while holding that God's power as the all-worshipful cannot be surpassed.

The other difference is closely related in that it has to do with Cobb's endorsement of Whitehead's view that 'God is *an* actuality or *a* being, not creativity or Being Itself.' He refers in this connection to Whitehead's

well-known distinction between creativity and God and to his characterizations of God as a 'creature', albeit a unique creature, of creativity.
But, surely, if there is anything unchallengeably problematic in Whitehead's metaphysics, it is just these characterizations – along with his
closely parallel statements that 'God is the ultimate limitation', and
God's existence, 'the ultimate irrationality' (Whitehead, 1925: 257).

Aside from the evident self-contradiction of saying that God is 'the
primordial creature', or the 'primordial, non-temporal accident' of creativity, there is the deeper difficulty that neither God nor anything else
may be properly said to be a creature of creativity, given Whitehead's
own use of terms. He expressly states that 'creativity' is his term for the
ultimate spoken of somehow in all philosophical theory, and he defines
it as referring to 'the universal of universals characterizing ultimate matter of fact'. He is also careful to explain that the creativity thus referred
to is 'actual in virtue of its accidents…. and apart from these accidents
is devoid of actuality'. But, then, according to 'the general Aristotelian
principle', or his own 'ontological principle', if there is no actual
entity, there is no reason, because 'agency belongs exclusively to actual
occasions', and 'apart from things that are actual, there is nothing –
nothing either in fact or in efficacy' (1978: 31, 7, 21, 40, 18). In other
words, because 'creativity' refers to nothing actual, but only to the
utmost of abstractions, it may not be properly said to create anything,
nor may anything, God included, be properly said to be *its* creature.
Thus, even given the distinction between creativity and God, the only
creators allowed for in a consistently Whiteheadian metaphysics are
God and those who, in a unique sense, may be said to be *God's* creatures, but not the creatures of creativity.

But quite apart from this clear implication of Whitehead's own metaphysical principles, Hartshorne has long since given good reasons for
saying that God is and must be not only *a* being, but also Being Itself, or,
as he usually puts it, 'Process Itself', or even 'Creativity Itself'. On this
point, I fear, Cobb is simply wrong; for Hartshorne not only accepts the
distinction in question – repeatedly, in his many exchanges with Paul
Tillich – but also insists on it as necessary to his own understanding of
God as 'the universal individual'. 'God must, in spite of all difficulties',
he says, 'be a case under rules, he must be an individual being. However,
he must not be a mere, even the greatest, individual being; rather, he
must also in some fashion coincide with being or reality as such or in
general…. [God's] uniqueness must consist precisely in being both
reality as such *and* an individual reality, insofar comparable to other
individuals' (Hartshorne, 1967: 34 f.).

Of course, Hartshorne's admission that God *qua* an individual is insofar comparable to other individuals confirms Cobb's claim that, for him, too, metaphysical principles apply to God as well as to creatures. But it is misleading to say, as Cobb does, that Hartshorne takes them to apply '*alike*' to God and to creatures; for nothing is more important to his neoclasical theism – or, I may add, my own – than to insist that the difference between God and any creature is itself a categorial, or, as I say, a transcendental, difference. This means that God cannot be just *an* exemplification, but can only be – in the most exact sense of the words – the *chief* exemplification, of metaphysical principles, the difference between their meaning in this application and in every other being not merely a finite, but an infinite difference.

How effective insisting on this is likely to be in meeting the objection that 'process theism treats God too much like a creature' may obviously be questioned. But I see no reason to question either the difference or the importance of the difference between this way of responding to the objection and Cobb's.

3

Another more fundamental difference I, at least, judge to be more important. In this case, however, it is a difference not only from Cobb's point of view, but also from that of most, although not all, process thinkers, in the delimited sense in which I, too, am using the term. It is because of this difference, indeed, that I signalled at the outset that whether I am a process thinker even in this sense is not a closed question. But be this as it may, the difference to which I refer pertains to yet another respect in which Cobb's view of metaphysics clearly seems to be other than my own.

For all he says to indicate otherwise, he fully shares the same panpsychist, or, as Hartshorne prefers to say, psychicalist, metaphysics that certainly appears to be implied by Whitehead's doctrine of prehensions. I put it this way because some of Whitehead's formulations may be thought free of this implication – as when he says, for example, 'The way in which one actual entity is qualified by other actual entities is the "experience" of the actual world enjoyed by that actual entity, as subject' (1978: 166). On the other hand, Whitehead asserts unequivocally that 'the key notion' from which construction of a metaphysical cosmology should start is that 'the energetic activity considered in physics is the emotional intensity entertained in life' (1938: 231 f.); and most of his other formulations as well take 'experience' to be the *explicans*, not the *explicandum*, and may therefore be reasonably taken to assert or imply the same psychicalism. In any case, Hartshorne's espousal of this kind of categorial metaphysics is notorious, and, so far as I can see, Cobb is like most other process thinkers in following him in this. This means that, as I understand it, Cobb's view, also, is that not only God, but anything else that is actual and comparably singular, as distinct from a mere aggregate, is, in its own content or quality in itself, some form or other of experience.

Of course, what is meant by 'experience' here is not specifically human experience, or even animal experience more generally, but experience in the completely generalized sense that Hartshorne calls 'experience as such'. In other words, the category 'experience' so used is supposed to function neither literally nor merely symbolically or metaphorically, but *analogically*, in that it is held to apply to all the different things to which it is applicable even within the same logical or ontological type, not in the same sense, but in different senses. This is why there can be said to be many different forms of experience, ranging all the way from that of the least actuality that can be conceived to that of the greatest – to the experience of God.

But it is just this supposedly analogical use of 'experience', which is required by the psychicalist metaphysics of most process thought, including Cobb's, that I find unacceptable. For reasons that I have developed at length elsewhere, it is impossible to distinguish other than verbally between a so-called analogical use of 'experience' and other psychical terms, on the one hand, and their use merely as symbols or metaphors, on the other (Ogden, 1984). At the same time, the meaning of these terms when supposedly used as metaphysical 'analogies' can be really distinguished from the other purely formal, literal concepts that they necessarily presuppose only by tacitly committing the pathetic fallacy of treating a merely local variable as cosmic or universal.

Thus, to take Whitehead's point in the sentence quoted, one actual entity may be said to experience another if, and only if, it is somehow qualified by, and therefore internally related to, the other actual entity. In this way, the purely formal, literal concept of one actual entity's being internally related to another is necessarily presupposed by the meaning of one actual entity's experiencing another on any use of 'experience', including its supposed analogical use. The difficulty with any analogical use, however, is that saying, as psychicalists do, that all actual entities 'experience' others then either becomes empty, saying no more than that all actual entities are internally related to others, or else can be taken to say more than this only by tacitly taking 'experience' in some other, less fully generalized sense, thereby committing the fallacy in question.

My conclusion from this reasoning is that the assumption of most process thinkers that there is a third, 'analogical' use of psychicalist terms that is just as proper as their literal and symbolic uses is mistaken. But, then, since just such an analogical use of *some* categorial terms, physicalist if not psychicalist, is evidently essential to any categorial metaphysics, I also conclude that no acceptable metaphysics can be categorial, but must be strictly transcendental.

This is not the place, obviously, to explain adequately all that is involved in this distinction. Suffice it to say that, whereas a categorial metaphysics such as psychicalism or physicalism proceeds speculatively, by generalizing the meaning of certain terms until they supposedly become metaphysical analogies, a transcendental metaphysics dispenses with such analogies and proceeds strictly analytically, by analyzing the meaning of all terms with a view to explicating their necessary presuppositions, the unconditionally necessary among which it distinguishes as properly 'transcendentals'. Thus if the method of a categorial metaphysics is said to be, in Whitehead's phrase, 'imaginative generalization', the method of a transcendental metaphysics can be said to be 'presuppositional analysis', or, taking such transcendentals into account, 'transcendental deduction' (cf. Nygren).

In any case, the concepts and principles that a strictly transcendental metaphysics seeks to explicate are purely formal, and so the terms formulating them are used literally rather than symbolically. This means that, within any of the different logical or ontological types in which they are applicable, they are always applied in the same sense, not in different senses. Thus, when I say, in the terms of my neoclassical transcendental metaphysics, that God is the universal individual, this is to be understood quite literally, as meaning both that God is literally *an* individual, and thus a centre of interaction with itself and other individuals and events, *and* that God is literally universal, and so *the* individual, the one centre whose field of interaction with self and others is unrestricted and which, therefore, is just as literally reality as such.

That I say God is literally an individual, however, does not imply that I would call God literally 'a person'. A person must indeed be literally an individual because being a centre of interaction with self and others is a necessary condition of the possibility of being a person, not only literally but even symbolically. But the converse does not hold – not even, consistently, for psychicalists, who concede when pressed that 'person', being by its very meaning a local variable, cannot be predicated of God either literally or analogically, but only symbolically or metaphorically. Unfortunately, this concession does not keep psychicalists from reverting to their usual habits and continuing to use 'person' and what Cobb calls 'personalistic, Biblical images of God' generally as though they could be something more than symbols or metaphors.

Their justification for this, presumably, is that thought and speech about persons, being based primarily in our original, existential experience of ourselves, others, and the whole, may indeed be held to provide more fundamental concepts and terms for thinking and talking about the whole than language based in our derived, empirical experience of ourselves and the world around us. Nevertheless, once a distinctively analogical use of personalistic language is ruled out as groundless and improper, the only other possibility is to say candidly that God is not literally, but only symbolically or metaphorically a person.

The virtue of a *neoclassical* transcendental metaphysics, however, is that it does not undercut, but rather fully supports saying this, so that '*only* symbolically or metaphorically' need not have the disparaging implication that Paul Tillich, for one, so vigorously resisted. Because in the terms of such a metaphysics God can be literally said to be the universal individual that not only unsurpassably acts on all others as well as itself, but is also unsurpassably acted on by them, any talk of God as a person who loves and knows self and others, and so on is symbolically or metaphorically apt – as it cannot be given other metaphysical terms in which God may be literally said to act on all others, but is just as literally said or implied *not* to be acted on by them.

But if symbolic or metaphorical talk about God as personal is fully supported by my transcendental neoclassical theism, it is in no way required by it. Consequently, if using 'God' in a proper theistic sense is deemed to require such personalistic talk, then my designation of the universal individual integral to an adequate transcendental metaphysics as 'God' is not properly theistic. In any event, taking all talk about God as personal to be only symbolic or metaphorical obviates Cobb's recourse to distinguishing 'two "ultimates"' as the way to take full account of nontheistic as well as theistic religious ways of thinking and speaking about strictly ultimate reality. What I understand Mahayana Buddhists to refer to in distinguishing '*dharmakaya-as-suchness*' or, for that matter, Meister Eckhart, in distinguishing '*deitas*', is not the mere abstraction that 'creativity' can alone properly refer to, but something eminently concrete and actual – the one strictly universal individual that is at once the fathomless mystery and the ground of all rationality and that, as such, is the primal source and the final end of all things.

I should add, to obviate a possible misunderstanding that, on my analysis, the main function of religious symbols or metaphors is in any case not metaphysical but existential. Although religious utterances perforce have metaphysical presuppositions and implications, but for the truth of which they could not themselves be true, they are properly concerned with communicating the meaning of ultimate reality for us, as distinct from describing even symbolically or metaphorically the structure of ultimate reality in itself. Accordingly, beyond claiming to be authorized, finally, by ultimate reality itself, they mainly function to express and commend a certain way of understanding ourselves and leading our lives as parts of that reality.

As for the most serious objections to my view, I see two. The first is the objection also made to Hartshorne's metaphysics that to assume, as I do, that among the necessary presuppositions of our self-understanding and life-praxis generally are certain unconditionally necessary ones that, as such, imply existence is to confuse necessity *de dicto* with necessity *de re*. But so far as I am able to judge, Hartshorne's theory of 'objective modality', according to which modal distinctions on the logical level correlate with temporal distinctions on the ontological level, effectively meets this objection. After all, confusion is one thing, correlation, something else. And what metaphysics in my sense as well as his assumes is not that logical necessity simply *is* ontological, but only that the two are correlative – necessary existence being what is common to all possibilities even as necessary propositions asserting such existence are implied by any proposition.

The other objection is the one Hartshorne himself makes to my rejection of psychicalism and the theism that is of a piece with it. To his mind, this rejection forces one either to accept some other much less tenable metaphysics, that is, physicalism or dualism, or else to acquiesce in metaphysical agnosticism. But what I reject, of course, is not simply psychicalism, but physicalism and dualism as well, as equally unacceptable insofar as they, too, are categorial rather than strictly transcendental. And so far as having to settle for agnosticism is concerned, my response is twofold. To know only that x must be internally related to y is indeed not to know that x must somehow experience y. But it is certainly not to know nothing about x, and so 'agnosticism' it clearly is not. On the contrary, if I am right that any so-called analogical knowing is not really knowing at all, then Hartshorne's metaphysics, for all its claims to know more than mine, must be equally 'agnostic'. Moreover, if the proper concern of metaphysics, like science, is with the structure of things, and in the case of metaphysics, their *necessary* structure, then it has every reason to abstract from, and in that sense to be agnostic about, not only their meaning for us, but also their own content or quality in themselves.

4

There is one other important difference between Cobb's point of view and mine that has to do with the philosophy of philosophy of religion, or, if you will, prolegomena to it. It is as clear from what he does not say as from what he says that philosophy of religion, in his view, consists primarily, if not entirely, in the critico-constructive task of formulating some kind of a religious, not to say theistic, cosmology or metaphysics. In my view, by contrast, philosophy of religion, properly so-called, either also has or entirely consists in another purely analytic task – the task, namely, of critically interpreting the meaning of religion, or of self-understanding and life-praxis as explicitly mediated by religion, in the distinctive way in which philosophy generally critically interprets the different forms of culture and life-praxis.

That way, as I understand it, is not simply to interpret the 'surface meaning' of particular expressions, as the other humanities, in their various ways, may be said to do, but to analyze the 'deep structure', or the 'depth grammar', of all the different *kinds* of meaning, so as thereby to disclose their 'tacit presuppositions' and to map their 'logical frontiers'. That the impulse behind such analysis, as John Passmore insists, is '*metaphysical*, not linguistic' I take to be perfectly clear (Passmore: 78). But metaphysics is one thing, philosophy something else. And as certain as I am that philosophy does indeed have the critico-constructive task that Cobb assigns to philosophy of religion, and that carrying out this task centrally involves doing metaphysics as well as ethics, I would rather distinguish this by speaking of 'philosophical theology'. I use 'philosophy of religion', then, to refer to what either includes or, in the strict sense in which I prefer to use the term, simply consists in philosophy's other essential task of analyzing the religious kind of meaning.

The issue here, obviously, is not how we are to use certain terms. The issue is whether we are somehow to recognize the importance, if not, indeed, the primacy of this other analytic task in our discussion of 'philosophy of religion 2000'. As soon as we do recognize it, however, we realize that there are some other and rather different things to be said from the point of view of process thought from anything Cobb has to say in his chapter.

Of course, there can hardly be such a thing as a distinctively 'process' way of analyzing the kind of meaning expressed by religious life and language. In direct proportion to its adequacy, any such analysis by a process thinker would need to agree in all essentials with any other adequate analyses by philosophers' working out of more or less different points of view. Even so, process thinkers have devoted considerable time and energy directly to the philosophical analysis of religious meaning, and some of their contributions are, in my judgement, very much worth taking into account.

Thus, for example, the South African thinker, Martin Prozesky, although a philosopher rather than a Christian theologian, has interests in process cosmology and metaphysics as well as in religion comparable to Cobb's or my own. But most of his work, as represented by his book, *Religion and Ultimate Well-Being: an Explanatory Theory*, is concerned with analyzing the meaning of religion and, as the subtitle indicates, is particularly directed toward identifying the factors, cosmological as well as anthropological, necessary to explaining religion as a form of life and culture (Prozesky, 1984; 1986).

Or, again, I think especially of the work of William A. Christian, who is also, in his way, something of a process thinker, as is clear already from his early book on Whitehead's metaphysics (Christian, 1959). Most of his thinking and writing, however, are concerned precisely with what he calls, in the title of probably his best known book, 'meaning and truth in religion' (1964). In this book and in the two others that followed it, *Oppositions of Religious Doctrines* (1972) and *Doctrines of Religious Communities* (1987), Christian contributes significantly to the purely analytic task of the philosophy of religion. Indeed, in my own experience and reading, his clarification of the structure of religious inquiry and of the logic of religious argument remains unsurpassed.

But still more impressive, in my judgment, is the contribution that Hartshorne has made to this other, purely analytic task. At the heart of his account of religious utterances is the recognition that they are, in my sense of the term, 'existential', and so at once clearly different from strictly metaphysical assertions and closely related to them. They are different from such assertions because, arising out of personal encounter with '*my* God', as he likes to say, as distinct from God as such, they either are or imply broadly factual assertions that are factually, even if not empirically, falsifiable. At the same time, they are related to strictly metaphysical assertions because they also imply assertions about God as such that cannot be falsified either factually or empirically. By then elucidating the logical connections between these strictly metaphysical assertions about God and other intuitively less problematic ones, such as 'Something exists', Hartshorne directly challenges the most fundamental assumption made by all parties to the debate on 'theology and falsification' – that, apart from the tautologies of logic and mathematics, the only meaningful assertions are factual assertions that can be factually, if not empirically, falsified. But more than that, he also defines a clear alternative to other so-called functional analyses that purport to show the meaningfulness of religious utterances without clarifying how, if at all, their claim to truth is to be critically validated (Ogden, 1977).

These few examples will have to do to make my final point. If I am right, they show clearly enough that process thinkers as a group, far from having only one string to their bow, have, in their ways, contributed to both of the tasks of the philosophical study of religion 2000.

Bibliography

Christian, W.A. (1959) *An Interpretation of Whitehead's Metaphysics*, New Haven: Yale University Press.
——(1964) *Meaning and Truth in Religion*, Princeton: Princeton University Press.
——(1972) *Oppositions of Religious Doctrines: a Study in the Logic of Dialogue among Religions*, New York: Herder and Herder.
——(1987) *Doctrines of Religious Communities: a Philosophical Study*, New Haven: Yale University Press.
Hartshorne, C. (1962) 'The Modern World and a Modern View of God', *The Crane Review*, 4, 2: 73–85.
——(1967) *A Natural Theology for Our Time*, LaSalle, IL: Open Court.
——(1984) *Omnipotence and Other Theological Mistakes*, Albany: State University of New York Press.
Nygren, A. (1972) *Meaning and Method: Prolegomena to a Scientific Philosophy of Religion and a Scientific Theology*, trans. Philip S. Watson, Philadelphia: Fortress Press.
Ogden, S.M. (1977) 'Linguistic Analysis and Theology', *Theologische Zeitschrift*, 33: 318–25.
——(1984) 'The Experience of God: Critical Reflections on Hartshorne's Theory of Analogy', in *Existence and Actuality: Conversations with Charles Hartshorne*, eds J.B. Cobb, Jr. and F.I. Gamwell, Chicago: University of Chicago Press: 16–42.
——(1991) 'Must God Be Really Related to Creatures?', *Process Studies*, 20, 1: 54–6.
Passmore, John (1961) *Philosophical Reasoning*, London: Gerald Duckworth & Co.
Prozesky, Martin (1984) *Religion and Ultimate Well-Being: an Explanatory Theory*, New York: St. Martin's Press.

Prozesky, Martin (1986) 'Philosophical Cosmology and Anthropology in the Explanation of Religion', *Theoria*, 66: 29–39.

Whitehead, Alfred North (1925) *Science and the Modern World*, New York: Macmillan Co.

—— (1938) *Modes of Thought*, New York: Macmillan Co.

—— (1978) *Process in Reality: an Essay in Cosmology*, ed. D.R. Griffin and D.W. Sherburne, New York: Free Press.

18
Voices in Discussion
D.Z. Phillips

U: In the first three symposia we heard a lot about the relation between religious experience and reason. I doubt whether we can generalize about this. I was brought up in a pious Southern Methodist home in Japan. I was socialized into Christianity. My world was theocentric. While in the army I not only had ordinary religious experiences, but also some dramatic ones. One of the latter was a call to be a minister. I thought, however, that I ought to study objections to Christianity before answering it. Most of the people I had met in the army were Roman Catholics, as different from Southern Methodists as one could imagine.

In the university I studied models of analysis of ideas and methods. I was taught by Richard McKeon, who never accepted what any student said. I kept as quiet as I could. McKeon taught the history of philosophy. He put the patterns of thought of the different philosophers on the blackboard. What emerged was a pluralist history. There was no question of truth and falsity, but only of which pattern was most appropriate for our day. Each system was self-contained, as though this were a basic way of organizing thought.

I now think more in historical terms. I believe that the way the mind works is determined by the questions people ask. The mind cannot generate a universal, right philosophy. This reflects my attitude to what philosophy can and cannot do. Some claim to be arguing from a neutral position. I am not convinced. It is an Olympian height only within that system. Philosophy cannot tell theology what to think or vice versa.

I found objections to Christianity in modern thought. But it wasn't so much that I found good arguments and assessed evidence, but that I found that my former faith simply was not there. It wasn't a matter of choice. I could remember my former experiences, but they now made

281

belief impossible. So I experienced a shift of world-view, from a pious one to a secular one. I lost any idea that philosophy could provide me with a rational foundation for faith. Then I came into contact with Charles Hartshorne, as different a philosopher from McKeon as one could get. Understanding reality was his life. His classes were an introduction into his conversation with himself on these matters, one that was going on before the class started, and continued after it ended. I was attracted to this immediately, and, over the years, this attraction grew. I became aware that one didn't have to choose between different world-views. There was a third way, one that took advances in modernity seriously – a process way of studying reality, in which 'becoming' is more important than 'being', and 'events' are more important than 'substances'. God was now in everything, but not in a pietistic way. I didn't want to evaluate it too quickly like McKeon and say 'This is just another system.' On the other hand, I admit that what I go on to say is confessional. I speak as a Process thinker.

Hartshorne emphasized arguments, but in a context where the data seemed to support them. It depends on seeing the world in a certain way. What attracted me was not the arguments so much as the world-view. Is that reasonable? I won't pursue the larger tale which would have to be told to answer that question.

I then became aware of differences between Hartshorne and White-head. I was learning about the latter through the former, and my teachers were neo-naturalists. These teachers said that changes in the twentieth century opened up the world in a new way. The process thus revealed included human beings. They called this process 'God'. I was helped more by Hartshorne than by Wieman and wrote my master's thesis criticizing the latter in a way I would modify today. So I was exposed to disputes within the Process family.

I find Whitehead's speculative philosophy congenial. It is a philosophy which advances hypotheses. You study a particular field as rigorously as you can (although you have your presuppositions). You appreciate some factors and then see that a full appreciation of them takes you into another field of study. This is an endless task. It is a cosmological task. For Whitehead, science gives us the most reliable basis for judgement concerning what we are given. The subjective side of things is explained more fully in religion.

Religion is a global phenomenon. We cannot confine ourselves in our studies to traditional Christianity. If you look at physics, the current theories are already loaded with presuppositions. Many of them owe their form to substance-thinking. Paradoxes arise from that conceptuality. So we don't settle for present hypotheses, but check to see whether you can arrive at better ones. This is true of religion, too, so the task is essentially revisionist.

For Whitehead and Harthsorne, to be is to be constituted by all that has happened in the past, and one must form oneself creatively out of that. I find an analogy in Buddhism, with its non-substantial view of religion. We are Johnny-come-latelys in this respect. God is the supremely inclusive real. All that happens in the world happens in God. This is radical interactive thinking. It could be argued that so far from being revisionist, this is a more faithful reflection of Biblical thought than classical theism.

E: I want to make four points on matters not said in my paper.

First, what is philosophy of religion? This involves asking, What is philosophy? As I understand it, it is motivated by an existential question which asks whether existence has a meaning as part of an encompassing whole. How should we conduct ourselves given that this is our lot? Philosophy attempts to clarify these questions.

But although philosophy is motivated by these questions, it is not constituted by them. It is constituted by theoretical questions about the meaning of our various practices. Reflection sees whether these are valid. Here I am indebted to Habermas's conception of philosophy as critically motivated self-understanding. This is love of wisdom or authentic self-understanding.

Philosophy has two related tasks. First, it has a purely analytic task, that of elucidating the conditions for the possibility of self-understanding. This task results in a transcendental metaphysics, because it is an attempt to elucidate the necessary conditions of human discourse as such. Second, it has the task of critically evaluating the various answers which have been given to the existential question I mentioned at the outset. I want to formulate an answer to that question. Here, philosophy and theology have a mutual contact.

My second point arises out of my preoccupation as a Christian theologian. Theology or philosophical theology is reflection on a religious tradition. So the data here are already religious. My particular concern is with the distinctive claims claimed to be valid by Christian witness. Here we have to do with the claim which is specific in its content involving a reference to Jesus Christ. This witness is possible for any person by our common experience. So this claim necessarily involves philosophical reflection. Christian witness is historically determined and must be dealt with historically, but it also involves asking what kind of meaning this witness involves. This task is not only theological, but eminently philosophical. Are Christian claims as valid as they claim to be? These claims are validated in the same way as we validate other claims.

Third, given that I am a Process theologian, let me say a few things about that. Process philosophy seems to me to be the right philosophy – right, not because I am a Christian, but because it articulates better than any other philosophy, the understanding of existence, and the necessary conditions of that existence. Here I think of it as my primary source. It continues to prove itself in my task as a Christian theologian.

Fourth, let me indicate where I find myself at odds with most of my fellow Process philosophers and theologians. Process thought has a transcendental metaphysics. Because it is an answer to an existential question it implies both a metaphysics and an ethics. Metaphysics is an explanation of ultimate reality. But, then, it is essential not to confuse the metaphysical conditions with factual states of affairs. This is a lesson to be learned from Wittgenstein.

Take the example of myth. A myth is the condition of certain facts being the case, but it is not itself a further fact. We see the trouble that comes from treating metaphysics as a fact in the work of Thales and other pre-Socratics. This is precisely the confusion we find in White-head, but it persists even more in Hartshorne in his notion of a psychicalist ontology. My own way has been to concentrate on those questions which are of concern to everyone. We see this not only in Kant, but also in Duns Scotus.

V: Wouldn't you say that a general ontology and metaphysics is necessary for the Christian faith, but not the categorical metaphysics we are offered?

E: The consequence of the metaphysics we are offered so often is that it does not recognize that God is not a fact, but the condition of the possibility of any fact. So 'God exists' is not a statement of fact.

A: U says that 'becoming' is more important than 'being', and that 'events' are more important than substances. You also say that every event is internally related to its past. I find that wildly implausible. The world may have started in a different way, but I can't see that that affects who I am. You say that this reasoning has its ancestry in Hegel, but that doesn't make it less criticizable.

We have to distinguish between things. Is a table an event? It is an instantiation of various properties. But this is not true of other things. Am I just a bundle of feelings? If my brain is transplanted in another person, have I survived the operation?

U: As long as you think in terms of substances and attributes you can't see the problem. Take an example from physics. It was thought that the understanding of light as light waves required the postulation of ether – there must be a substance underlying the events. There is no ether, but people still talk of light waves. But the notion of 'waves' itself comes from substance-thinking. We must ask whether we can have events without postulating substances, and some are now retelling quantum theory from this point of view.

Now think of a moment in human experience. Antecedent moments are functioning in that moment. When we hear a word, there is the relation of the present to antecedent experiences. That is an internal relation which enters into memory, perception and causality, and which differs from postulating or thinking of an underlying 'I'.

B: I am puzzled by *E*'s distinction between necessary conditions and factuality. Are there necessary propositions that are facts? As long as a statement is not a fact it cannot have existential import. Can't we say that what is necessarily true exists, but is not a fact?

M: I criticize the metaphysics out of which your question arises. I want to re-emphasize the importance of internal relations as *U* did to *A*. For example, it throws light on the doctrine of the Trinity. We can be brought to see that each person of the Trinity has no identity apart from the others.

A: That notion is congenial to me, and I have argued as much. The Son is the Son by virtue of the Father, and the Holy Spirit is what it is by virtue of the Father and the Son. But this is not an example of a metaphysical truth which would hold in all cases.

D: *U* says in his paper, 'It is true that coercive power can destroy and kill, but only persuasive power can give life and evoke love.' I do not see this. Surely coercive or persuasive power may destroy and kill.

U: I agree the matter is more complex than the way I put it 'Persuasive power' is a shorthand way of referring to something I want to emphasize. Much of what we are at present has been determined by the past, but there is also the possibility of the novel in the occasion. This depends on creative responses to the possibilities which present themselves from the past.

C: I think that by persuasive power you mean a certain kind of power, not the one power which may be used persuasively or coercively. I am reminded of Kierkegaard's remark that love cannot conquer by force. That marks out the kind of power love has.

U: Agreed.

C: But now, correct me if I am wrong, I have heard Process theologians speak in a way which disturbs me about God being limited in what he can do, as though this were a limitation. But if God's only power is the power of love, and love cannot conquer by force (that is, that suggestion does not make sense), then it is highly misleading to call that a limitation, or to say, as some do, that God does the best he can, or that God has good days and bad days.

U: I think the theologians you refer to are anxious to rid us of a magical conception of power where God is concerned.

C: I understand that, and accept the negative point. It has always seemed to me a jarring aspect of the Passion story when Jesus says that if he wanted to he could call a legion of angels to get him off the cross. It seems like a religious version of those bad films which end with 'Here comes the cavalry'.

No, it is the positive account of Process theologians which worries me when they refer to limitations in God, and so forth. If love cannot conquer by force, it follows that it can be rejected. At the heart of Christianity is a radical rejection of love; a rejection so severe that it involves the one who reveals the love being deprived of an informed death, such as that of Socrates. Instead he cries out, 'My God, my God, why hast thou abandoned me?' To reveal how far love can go, Jesus becomes the transparent vehicle for it, the price of which is his sense of abandonment. I am unhappy at calling this a limitation since, rather, it is the paradigm of the expression of what divine compassion is. So far from being a limitation, it is said to be a full and final revelation.

I: In your autobiographical account *U*, you told us of how you moved beyond your early pietism, how you came to embrace a secular perspective, but, then, in time, moved beyond that. You gave up your old objectivism and practised theological praxis. Why, then, have you come to rest in Process thought? This seems to be a final resting place.

But, dialectically, a genuine pluralism would ask to continue struggling. Are you still struggling?

U: That's fine. You speak as one who is open to what is new. So you're a process thinker whether you like it or not. But, seriously, I'm certainly still struggling. I want things to change. In these latter days I have devoted more attention to economic factors than to technical issues in philosophy and theology. There are new movements I had to come to grips with. Feminism made me rethink many questions. But I suppose the biggest hurdle I had to face was Black Theology. I am a descendant of a slave-owning family who were leaders of the Confederacy. So these matters were painful for me. I was made to realize how many of our theological categories reflect certain assumptions about White supremacy. I could deal with Latin American economic issues far more easily than I could face up to Black Theology. So I am still struggling. There are movements represented in this conference, such as Postmodernism, which I recognize as having major implications for our times. If I were a younger man I would have attempted to address it thoroughly. So I am not complacent at all.

19
Voices in Discussion
D.Z. Phillips

In the last discussion session graduate students addressed six questions to some of the participants.

V: I have a question for *U*. When you are attracted to notions of emptiness in Buddhism you seem to see them as reflecting states of reality which are truer than other states of a more substantive kind. But isn't the reference to 'emptiness' part of the grammar of a Buddhist perspective which is one among many?

U: You may well be right, and you are certainly entitled to advance that view. All I can say by way of reply is that in my experience the teachings about 'emptiness' or the experience of it do not seem to be captured by your suggestion.

W: I spoke of a liberating totality in liberation theology. Who is to decide what is liberating? What one regards as liberating progress, another may regard as decline.

I: This reference owes much to the tradition of Hegel and Marx in which society is seen as a totality. But that totality may be oppressive and totalitarian. Now, to the extent that there is a society at all there will be a certain amount of agreement in language, law, customs, and so on. But there will also be the cry of the oppressed, since some laws may be oppressive. A philosopher reflecting on these social realities, on the importance of tradition and consensus, can also be a political activist who seeks to bring about changes in those laws.

X: I want to ask a related question of *F*. When Levinas speaks of understanding and responding to the other, the face of the other is the face of the widow and the orphan. This gives the response a concrete context.

But with Derrida, the matter seems open-ended, and so chaotic. The face of the other is any face. But what if it is the face of a killer?

F: Derrida does derive his views from Levinas. But he says that there is no set of rules which determines these matters. There is no hospitality without risk. It is not a formal notion. The homicidal rapist is not the other. The other is the one who requires help.

S: As *K* pointed out in his paper, there are many concepts of truth in religion. I want to ask *O* and *H*, therefore, why this point cannot be an answer to the difficulties of Habermas's criteria of vindication with respect to religious belief.

O: I think the reason why I don't want to embrace that response is that it privatizes truth. Public vindication seems to be surrendered.

S: But, surely, you don't think that makes it a free-for-all. There are criteria which are internal to perspectives. People may take an absolute stand on these, since, as I said before 'absolute' need not mean 'universal'.

O: I agree, but the evidence would still be extremely difficult to assess.

H: I think the question shows the need for a critique of Habermas. How do we look for a vindication of religious experience? It is not going to be a matter of straightforward inference. This is because it brings something which cannot be found in the world, but belongs to a notion of the limits of the world. Habermas's public criteria need to be supplemented by inner criteria which recognize the affective character of religious belief. These criteria will involve spiritual and ethical values. Habermas can never arrive at these as long as he bases future progress on whatever the interests of people happen to be.

Y: I want to ask *A* and *K* about their different notions of the relations between belief and practice.

A: I want to distinguish between belief and practice, because what I do about the beliefs I have is always a further question. Some beliefs are more relevant to my purposes than others. I may learn as part of my education that William the Conqueror invaded Britain in 1066, but that belief may have little to do with my immediate purposes. If I believe in God I must still decide what I am going to do about my belief. The most natural and rational response is worship, but that is only one response among a number to that belief.

K: I think there are important differences between beliefs. There are thousands of empirical beliefs that I have which I am indifferent to.

They have little, if any, effect on me. With others, like belief in gravity, I am certain and have no choice. With moral and religious beliefs it is different again. Here, there are internal relations between belief and practice. So I disagree with *A*. You can't distinguish between a belief in generosity and what you do about it. If I am never generous, then I can't be said to believe in generosity, since to believe in generosity is to be generous. Belief in God is like this too, since its primary form is 'trust in God'. This is what believing in God comes to.

Z: Throughout the conference we have had different views expressed about the relation of philosophy to religion. I want to ask *A*, *U*, *G* and *J* to say what they think philosophy can do in this context.

A: Philosophy can help religion in a number of contexts. First, it can clarify the credal elements in religion. Second, it can assess arguments for or against the truth of religion. Gregory of Nyssa is a model in this respect. Third, a lot will depend on the way philosophy is practised. If it is done with analytic rigour, philosophy can help by giving a clear presentation of the ideas involved in religion. So although religion does not need philosophy's help in all contexts, it certainly does in some.

U: The strong separation of philosophy from religion is a problem of modernity. If we look to India or China we see that philosophy is a way of life. I prefer the ancient view to the modern alternative. I believe philosophy can help us to say 'Christ is Lord of all', and that therefore there are good philosophical reasons for saying this.

G: Philosophy can certainly help religion in meeting *ad hoc* objections to it. But philosophers aren't omnicompetent in this respect. If, for example, someone tries to link a religious movement with economic decline, then what I need is not a philosopher, but an economist. Similarly, philosophers can't tackle the problems of delinquency.

More positively, the model I am attracted to is that of Clement of Alexandria, who saw the life of the mind, in our case philosophy, as itself a mode of worship and thanksgiving. So to do one's best to display what Christ's Lordship means for art, justice, and so forth, is, for me, at the heart of my calling as a philosopher. On the other hand, it is important to recognize that philosophy can't save you.

J: I just want to re-emphasize two things I have said before. First, in what philosophical attention asks of us in relation to the world, there is a spiritual dimension. Second, in giving this attention there is often a need to save religion from what philosophy has done to it. Here, we need philosophy to overcome philosophy.

Index

Abraham, 158, 163, 179
acquaintance
  belief, 54–5
  deductive arguments, 54
  entities, 53
  facts, 53–4
Adams, Marilyn, 22–3
Adams, Robert, 24
Adorno, Theodor W.,
  art, 221, 248
  Californian exile, 198
  determinate negation, 199, 219
  Enlightenment, 199, 244
  Frankfurt School, 193
  Habermas, 206–7, 221–2
  Hegel, 199–200
  identity, 205
  materialism, 205–6
  metaphysics, 205
  negative dialectics, 205
  positivism, 200–1
  reflection and knowledge, 200
aesthetics, 230, 233–5
al-Ghazali, Abu Hamid Mohammed,
  26
Alston, William P., 23, 40, 51–2, 65
American Academy of Religion, 263
analytical philosophy,
  Continental philosophy, 17
  non-theistic religion, 33
  ontological arguments, 5, 35
  Reformed Epistemology, 15
  theistic religion, 22, 65
  Wittgenstein, 16
Anselm (St),
  belief, 109
  contemplation, 26
  existence of God, 34, 104
  faith, 35
  inquiry, 26–7
  ontological arguments, 34–5, 110
  religious framework, 35
antecedent judgements, xii, xv, 32

anthropology,
  psychology, 197
  religion, 50, 56
anthropomorphism, 12, 255–6
apologetic arguments, 24–6, 33
apophatics, 168, 174, 255
Aquinas, Thomas (St),
  deductive arguments, 6, 31
  existence of God, 104, 109–10, 253
  faith, 25, 32
  first principles, 36
  methodology, 246
  philosophical theism, 4, 22
Aristotle,
  creativity, 271
  First Mover, 3
  inference, 77
  metaphysics, 186
  moral reasoning, 33
art, 200, 221, 233–4, 248
atheism,
  atrocities, 205
  intellectual passivity, 214
  Marxism, 198
  metaphysics, 254
  methodological atheism, 230, 235,
    246–7
  philosophical theism, 5, 36
  sophistication, 4, 26
  theism compared, 204
  Wittgensteinianism, 48, 88
Atonement, 23–4
Audi, Robert, 78
Augustine of Hippo (St),
  belief, 56
  Confessions, 159
  contemplation, 26
  Derrida, 159–60
  faith, 42, 49, 85
  love of God, 174
Austin, John Langsham, 164
Averroës, Ibn Rushd, 26
Avicenna (ibn Sina), 26